THE BLASPHEMOUS WAR

R.Rajanna As he is straight forward in writing and is one of the best journalists in India who writes exclusive stories and has left his competitors feel more jealous about his work and the style of his writing.

He is currently working as the Editor - in - Chief of Metrofax News International (MNI news agency) and continues to work on investigative related subjects.

In his long time restless schedule he has never felt tired and continues to work more and more actively and planning for more investigations, and has never compromised with whosoever.

THE BLASPHEMOUS WAR

R.Rajanna's best written on international politics and global issue continues to make the reading more interesting page after page till the last page is turned, and will echo in the mind for a long time.

".... his best narration thrilling political and true story"
MNI news agency

TO MY MOTHER

S.NANJAMMA

Director

MNI news agency

Who ultimately is the inspiration,
to me for writing this book

THE BLASPHEMOUS WAR

Self Published by

R.Rajanna
No. 1143, 18th main
'E' block, 2nd stage
J.P.Nagar, Mysore - 31
Karnataka, INDIA

Mobile : 9886523687
Landline : 0821 - 2372082
Fax : 0821 - 2372082
Email : rajannarchandra@hotmail.com
rajannaramachandra71@gmail.com
Whats App No : 8073220352

ISBN No: 978-93-6039-166-9

First Edition : 2023

Price : Rs.795-00

Printed in India by
Emerald Star Studio Pvt Ltd.,
Mysuru, Karnataka, INDIA.
Email : esspvtltd23@gmail.com

With Heartfelt Thanks

To

Kofi Annan

Former Secretary General of the United Nations

My deepest sympathy

To all those journalists who lost their lives while covering the war.

At least 136 journalist and 51 media supporter workers were killed during the war in 2003.

With Heartfelt Thanks

To All the
News agencies,
Television,
Radio,
Print media and
Electronic media,
around the world.

INTRODUCTION

After the Gulf War-1 and the liberation of Kuwait from the occupation of Iraq, the U.S. remained trapped in the Gulf without any clear ideas or planning and was totally separated from the international coalition which it had perfectly built to defeat the Iraqi leader Saddam Hussain.

The New world order that was proclaimed by the then U.S. President, Mr. George Bush Sr. The Dazzling Military Victory against Saddam Hussein's forces after it was droned out of Kuwait. This victory in February 1991 and the collapse of the Soviet Union at the end of 1991 was the biggest gain for the U.S. resulting in the U.S. was duly proclaimed the only Super Power in the world.

Immediately after the Gulf War-1 President Bush Sr, diverted focus on the Arab Israeli dispute. The defeat of Saddam Hussain and the collapse of the Soviet Union gave a timely opportunity for the U.S. to reshape the politics in the Middle East. Undoubtedly huge progress was made on all the attempts but the prospects for peace had been shattered by unending violence between Israelis and Palestinian. However the separation of Palestinian from Israel now is a big relief from conflict and violence in the region.

Despite the huge sanctions of United Nations, the restriction on Iraq's defence program's and the U.S. no-fly zones imposed on Iraq. The U.S. had lost the propaganda war with Iraq on sanctions because Saddam Hussain became stronger than ever. The expectation of U.S. failed when there was no internal revolt against Saddam Hussain.

In a Preemptive move the U.S. and Great Britain made a different move with the unpopular sanctions and the Bush Administration decided to offer a relaxation of sanction that affect civilian business on the condition that stronger limitation on Iraq's programs on developing weapons of mass distraction and its military freedom.

With the political limitations and the sanction imposed on Iraq the U.S. was fully exposed and then the idea of bringing a regime change in Iraq became a strong decision in the U.S. government, but before this decision was taken the U.S. Central Intelligence Agency had made efforts to promote internal dissent to bring down Saddam Hussain, but the effort of CIA had failed miserably.

The Bush Administration then decided to steep up disbursement of funds to Iraq National Congress and the opposition forces to resume its activities inside Iraq.

CONTENTS

CHAPTER - 1

BAGHDAD

Capital City of Iraq

The International Media was surprised and had serious doubts over the surprise nature of new arms inspections in Iraq.

As soon as the International Media team consisting of about 40 Journalists from print media holding their recorders and the electronic media men ready with their cameras on their shoulders arrived at the airport in Baghdad a U.N. spokesman admitted the need of a suspected weapons site had been given advanced-warning of the visit by the U.N. experts to his facility.

"He was informed the day before (Friday) that the team was coming to remove an air samples and install a new one".

" That is all to it" the spokes man said in an apparent bid to quash a possible controversy about whether U.N. inspections of suspected weapons sites which resumed on November 27, 2002, were really on no-notice basis.

Reporters started questioning Veki, earlier about remarks by an Iraqi official, Hussein Hammideh, who told Journalists he had prior notice of a visit to his facility by International Atomic Energy Agency (IAEA) experts.

"The Inspectors arrived unannounced and that the U.N. dose not notify Iraqis of planned visit"

But he said that it was not surprising if officials at specific sites expected visits since such sites had been marked for inspection by the former U.N. experts who pulled out of Iraq in 1998 ahead of U.S. and British air strike on Iraq.

Explaining his apparent flip flop, Veki issued a statement elaborating on what he told the Media.

He defended the advance notice given to Iraq as purely as matter of logistics, but added the U.N. had also given prior notice to a second inspection site.

A convey of disarmament experts head towards Khan Bani Saad some 25 KM south-east of Baghdad where Iraq once tested devices that can spray deadly microbes.

The current inspector's predecessors in the 1990's learned that the Iraqis apparently from this airfield at Khan Bani Saad successfully tested the so-called Zubaidy device, using it to disperse toxic bacteria's from a helicopter.

More than a dozen helicopters stripped of their motors, sat on the disused tarmac on Sunday as U.N. inspectors checked the grounds, Journalists observed from beyond a distant fence.

The Inspectors, who also wore hunting for signs of chemical and Biological agents, seemed interested in holding tanks that could have been used for aviation fuel.

As usual, the U.K. teams said nothing about the 'days' mission.

It was the fourth day of renewed inspection's, after a four year break, under a U.N. security council mandate for Iraq finally give up any remaining weapons of mass destruction or face "serious consequences".

The U.S. supported the U.N. Inspectors, but threatens war to disarm Iraq. The U.S. President in his weekly address to the nation on television announced "the U.S. will act alone if it believes that is necessary".

Immediately after the U.N. Inspectors completed their work a news in the television appeared, the western war planes attacked an oil instillation in Basra in Southern Iraq today, killing four people and wounding several others.

This was due to the U.S. and British war planes police two no-fly Zones in southern and Northern Iraq. "U.S. and British war planes raided the Southern oil company in Basra.

The Iraqi South Oil Company supervises Iraq's oil exports under oil-for -food deal with the United Nations via Mina-al-Bark terminal in southern Iraq. The Zones was set up after the 1991 Gulf War-1 to protect a Kurdish enclave in the north and Shia Muslims in the south from attack by President Saddam Hussein's Military.

Several countries in the world had to make up their mind about how to deal with the impending war in Gulf and the future of Iraq.

It was more or less clear that countries had to make decisions and come to a conclusion how to deal with Iraq with or without Saddam Hussain while the dead line for Iraq approached over the week end on the complete disclosure of its Weapons of Mass Destruction (WMD).

Even as the International arms inspectors comb through suspected sites in Iraq, war clouds wore beginning to gather.

The main political objective of the Bush administration in Iraq was neither the eliminations of its Weapons of Mass Destruction or the expected sources of international terrorism in the Gulf Nation.

The real American aim was to over through Mr. Saddam Hussein without the use of military offence on Iraq.

The U.S. war planners were so eager to get the orders from the White House and how quick the wars against Iraq happen.

The Final U.S. Military Confrontation with Mr. Saddam Hussein might have never taken place if the Iraqis leaders accepted for voluntary exile.

Despite all possibilities there was another view that if Mr. Saddam Hussein fully complies with the U.N. demands on WMD, there were no real reasons for a war.

The U.N. process of arms inspection is a means of providing legitimacy and broader international support to the US action against Iraq, but this was not an ultimate goal of the Bush Administration.

The U.S. had increased its bombarding activity in the no-fly zones that had been imposed sever Southern and Northern parts of Iraq, increased attack on oil instillations wore being to soften up the Iraqi military activity in the region. The north and southern parts of Iraq was on the verge of separation as the Shia's and the Kurdish from the military control of Saddam Hussein.

At the same time the U.S. wanted a logical conclusion that Saddam Hussein is in material breach of the U.N. resolution and exercise its proclaimed right to go for a war.

On the other side the U.S. Military was mobilized and the plan for a war on the territories of Iraq was on the board. The U.S. had also started Psychological Pressures on Iraqi military to demoralize them and gain support from the people.

The U.S. President had also appointed a special envoy to deal with the Iraqis dissident groups in London.

The projections was made as if the U.S. was planning to free and unite Iraq but the political frame work was to over through Saddam Hussein.

The U.S. Military were planning the war in such a way that the Gulf War-1 was a prolonged bombing of Iraqi cities and military targets before starting a full scale military invasion on Iraq. But the Gulf War-2 was decided to keep the war short and avoiding excessive bombardment of civilian population in Iraq.

There was more antiwar demonstration in western countries than in Arab countries. The U.S. persuaded all the key Iraqi opposition groups that wore in exile to join the war effort against Saddam Hussein.

The U.S. Deputy Defence Secretary Paul Wolfwitz, was in Turkey lobbying for Turkish support of an Iraq operation. With the Turkey, Foreign Minister, Yasar Yakis, and his government had given the support of Turkey of Military bases for a strike against Iraq, which was approved by the U.N.

Yakis had told the Journalists after a discussion with the U.S. Deputy Defence Secretary that "if there is a war against Iraq then of course, we will cooperate with the U.S., because it is a big ally and we have excellent relationship with the U.S.".

In what could be clinching evidence against Iraq's claims to there U.N. that it destroyed all its chemical weapons, the U.S. had received "credible reports" that Al-Qaeda militants received in Iraq the Nerve agent VX, used as a chemical weapon, which was smuggled through Turkey.

The Expert's had come to a conclusion that the transaction could have taken place on two significant milestones. It could be the first known acquisition of a non conventional weapon other than cyanide by Al-Qaeda or a member of its net work.

There was a high drama in the Arabian seas where Spanish authorities intercepted and boarded a North Korean vessel with the suspect cargo. Some of it was also Foggy Bottom and at the White House involving the Secretary of State Colin Powell and the U.S. Vice President, Dick Cheney. The U.S. Intelligence agencies had been tracking this particular ship: and had asked Yemen if it was expecting any kind of missile shipment from North Korea.

The Bush administration was specifically concerned that a shipment of weapons was heading to the Persian Gulf when the US was trying to "disarm" Iraq. On whether or not Yemen was "entitled" to the Seized send missiles in the Arabian Sea.

The State Department took the decision that since Yemen purchased these weapons prior to its pledge in 2001 not to obtain any more weapons from North Korea, the shipment had to proceed. The Pentagon apparently disagreed saying that the 2001 pledge applied to previous commitment as well.

The dream off the high seas off the Horn of Africa involved the Spanish military, forces from the amphibious assault ship the U.S.S. Nissan and Cambodia.

The North Korean Central News Agency reported the government's reaction the day after the U.S. Military took charge of the ship, but then allowed it to sail on after high level diplomacy between the U.S. and Yemen.

With the inter Korean reconciliation in jeopardy, North Korea demanded an apology from the U.S. for what it described as piracy in the seizure of a ship carrying missiles to Yemen.

North Korea declared that it would immediately revive frozen nuclear power facilities that the U.S. and its allies suspect wore being used to develop nuclear weapons before they were frozen in 1994.

The conflict threatened to disrupt cross border railway construction and other prominent projects aimed at reconciling North Korea and South Korea. Also at stake wore two modern nuclear reactors that a U.S. led consortium agreed to build in North Korea in exchange for the suspension of the nuclear program that it now plans to revive.

North Korea said U.S. actions forced it to revive its old nuclear program, despite an international outcry and rears of a nuclear crisis on the Korean peninsula Similar to one in 1994 that nearly led to war.

The Japanese government was worried over the new development it said "it is extremely regrettable". North Korea is abandoning its objections under the frame work agreed between the U.S. and North Korea.

The North Korea government said the missile components wore part of a "legal trade contract" and that the ship was "on a normal voyage along the publicly recognized sea route.

For U.S. Qatar's importance appeared to have grown substantially as it is one of the few countries in the Arab world that publicly announced that it would allow the U.S. to use its facilities and air space, in case there is an invasion of Iraq.

From a distance, the As Sayliyah camp, which had become a key U.S military facility in the Persian Gulf, could hardly be noticed its low buildings that wore painted light brown blend effortlessly with the surrounding landscape of the Arabian Desert.

It was only at closer look that the camp's concrete boundary was topped by the mandatory barbed wire and a mounted machine gun post was visible. From inside the camp resembles a well-planned town ship. Pre-fabricated buildings including sprawling ware houses had been raised in neat rows and special care had been taken to keep the area well lit.

The facility was a hub of activity. The U.S. Forces in their battle fatigues mingle with British troops that wore fewer in numbers. A few French aviators who wore involved in operations in Afghanistan could also be seen.

The camp became the new forward head quarters of General Tommy Frank's, Chief of the U.S. Central Command.

Essentially it was a portable high technology command post which in digitally linked to all the major military facilities in the region as well as the central commands permanent headquarters in Florida.

There were 25 nations that comes under the U.S. Central; Commands jurisdiction including countries in West Asia, Central Asia, and Afghanistan.

General Frank's was in contact with the Air Force Commander in Saudi Arabia, Navel Commanders in Bahrain and Army Commanders in Kuwait. U.S. officials wore of the opinion that the presence of a forward head quarter would help in spreading up and improving decision making, which in tern would result in managing a battle field better.

General franks was planning to frequently travel to the regions other locations for regular face-to-face meetings with his commanders. With the new command facility, Qatar had emerged as the key U.S. Ally in the Persian Gulf region.

Qatar was already hosting U.S forces at the Al Udeid air base, which is also not for from Doha. Al Udeid is a strategic air base and has the longest runway in West Asia. The Facility can be used for deploying heavy bombers, transport planes as well as the giant sized mid-air refueling planes.

The air base was already being used for operations associated with military activities in Afghanistan. Significantly, the U.S. Defence Secretary, Donald Rums field, had signed an agreement in Qatar claiming the way for improving the Al-Vdeid facility. At that time there wore about 3300 U.S. troops stationed at Qatar.

The U.S. was of the view that the Iraqi list that was presented to the U.N. on December 7, 2002 actually reinforced the Iraqi President, Saddam Hussein's conclusion that the country had no programs based on weapon's of mass destruction or any weapon of such kind but Washington's assertion according to Bush Administration was still only tentative but appeared to be very clearly leaning in a negative direction.

In clear terms the Bush Administration was of the conclusion that the Iraqi declaration of its programs in connection with the Chemical, Biological and Nuclear Weapons is fully of "holes" and dose not give the clear picture of the issue. In this regard Washington had taken the conclusion that the list fails to explain what the Pentagon and the CIA believes to be purchases related to nuclear program.

Other than U.S. and Britain no one in the Security Council was of the opinion on rushing to this conclusion. Even the Senior most officials of the Bush Administration had also suggested that they needed to spend a "few months" in scrutinising the Iraqi declaration and had clearly advised Mr. Bush that no one is in a hurry to rush to the war conclusion.

On passing the Security Council resolution 1441, the U.S. President, George.W.Bush, had warned the Iraqi leader to come clear this time with the list and that the U.S. had no patience for "Tom and Jerry" cartoon games.

Disputing the Iraqi declaration means the U.S. could challenge Iraq by providing U.S. intelligence data to weapon inspectors so that they could rapidly go over the "Weapon Inspection" in Iraq.

The U.S. officials had also com to the conclusion that Iraq had not clearly explained its purchases related to the nuclear program regarding the transaction on uranium in Africa and purchases of high technology equipment needed for uranium enrichment form Specialized Countries.

According to the CIA and Pentagon which was analyzing the Declaration very closely was not getting any clues or details in the declaration, the U.S. intelligence wanted to know what happened to those quantities of chemical and biological agents that wore missing when the U.N. inspectors wore thrown out in 1998. The U.S. Intelligence wanted to know what happened to hundreds of mustered gas shells which remained unaccounted, and on this basis the U.S. intelligence repeatedly said that the words of the Iraqi leaders cannot be trusted.

This leading question had arisen in the U.N. Security Council also and all the members had to be provided their initial assessment of the Declarations within a week, and in this regard Chief Weapon Inspector, Hans Blix was also asked to provide a report to the Security Council.

The Syrian President Assad who was the first leader of his country to visit Britain was greeted with protest by the pro Israel groups for his support for Palestinian militants. But the British, Prime Minister, Toni Blair, could not have asked for more than significant diplomatic initiative to win over Iraqis closest Arab ally ahead of a possible military intervention in Iraq.

As the only Arab member of the U.N. Security Council, role was crucial if the U.S. decided to go to war with Iraq, Blair's idea was to seek a fresh U.N. mandate and all efforts was made to "soften" up the Syrian President in order to avoid a confrontation in the U.N.

The differences remained after the two leaders met at Downing Street and neither leader's tried to hide them in their brief remarks to the press.

The Syrian President warned of the consequences of a war on Iraq reviving memories of their last encounter. The Syrian President had even publicly embarrassed Blair with some points remarks on the U.S. led "war on terror" and the Palestinian crisis. He had even warned that an attack on Iraq would create a "fertile soil" for terrorists in the region. Assad had even said that the consequence wore not going to be contained within Iraq. The entire region would enter in to the unknown. He also defended Palestinian suicide bombers saying they wore a "reaction" to Israeli terrorism against the civilian Palestinian population.

In return Blair criticized the Syrian President for supporting the Palestinian extremist group and had said "you cannot be any thing about 100 percent against terrorism".

While the U.N. and the world leaders wore trying to solve the Iraq problem the U.S. and British forces frequently targeted key locations in southern Iraq. The Fighter Jets wore attempting to weaken Iraq military forces in an area which was of vital strategic importance to both sides.

The U.S. Fighter Jets targeted at Iraqi air defense instillations at Al Amarah near the Tigris-Euphrates confluence as well as at Al Kut and Qatat Sukkar South East of Baghdad.

The U.S. and British struck locations at Al Basra, the state Al Arab port city which is Iraq's only out let to the Persian Gulf.

The Iraqi's wore aware of the repercussions of these air strikes which could lead to conflict in future. The Iraqi Foreign Minister, Naji Sabri, had complained to the U.N. about the air strike conducted by the U.S. and British forces on a self declared "No

Fly Zone" in South Iraq and demanded the U.N. to bring an end to such flights.

In return the U.N. Security Council announced that the council resolutions dose not authorise maintenance of the North and South No-Fly Zones in Iraq.

The U.S. and British Forces was planning further strikes similarly, other areas, which can come under military pressure in the early days of a possible preparation on the two cities of Kirkuk and Mosul in North Iraq.

These cities wore considered as the strong holds of ethnic Kurds. There wore reports about the moment of Turkish forces in the Iraqi Kurdish areas already.

The U.S. and British forces wore having a specific strategy to take control over the oil fields which could become the basis for mounting economic pressures on the Iraqi leader Saddam Hussein. Mean while the analysists pointed out that it would be logical to assume that this strategy would be supplemented by the narrowing of attention on key locations along the Tigris and Euphrates River.

The defence analysts repeatedly pointed out at the U.S. focus could become fixated to Halafiyah, north east of Al Amarah and Musallan further to the north. At Musallan, the T igris River Widens out before heading north after passing through the Iraqi capital.

Control over Musallan, there force, could give U.S. forces a possible access towards Baghdad. Another potential area, that could be subjected to military pressure in An Nasiryah. This was said to be the confluence of the Euphrates and Tigris River.

From here the Euphrates River heads west, passing through the Shia populated cities of Najaf and Karabla before heading in a direction not far from Baghdad. According to analysts, it was not surprising that the bombings carried out by the U.S. and British fighter jets that were maintaining the North and South No-Fly Zones wore close to these locations.

After the talks with the Syrian President failed to mobalise support against Iraq the British, Prime minister Tony Blair, planned to call a summit of Arab leaders in London in what is being called major new diplomatic initiative to push the Palestinian peace process, but the analysts dismissed it as a tactical move to divert Arab anger over the British-U.S. obsession with Iraq even as Palestine was burning.

The matter came up in the British Parliament immediately after the unsuccessful meeting with the Syrian President, Bashar al Assad, who had continuously accused Britain and U.S. of pursuing double standards over Iraq and Israel and had warned that an attack on Iraq without the Palestinian issue still remains unsolved would create a "fertile Soil" for terrorism across West Asia.

Blair first exposed his idea of a "peace conference" on Palestine at a Labour Party meeting sought to separate the Palestinian issue from what Blair described as the threat from Iraq's undisclosed weapons of destruction.

"The thing I would say passionately to the people in the Arab world today is you do not have to choose between dealing with the threat that Iraq poses with its weapons of mass destruction and dealing with the question of Palestinians and the Middle East peace process. We should actually be dealing with both issues, we should be strong against international terrorism and equally strong in making sure there in justice, based on the two-state solution for people in the Middle East" Blair explained to the delegates.

Leaders from Egypt, Jordan, Saudi Arabia and the Palestinian representatives would sit down with the representatives of the "Quartet group" comprising the U.N, W.U, U.S. and Russia at the London conference to be chaired by the then Foreign Secretary Jack Straw, but contrary to Blair's original promise of a full fledged peace conference would be by restricted to discussing "reforms" to the Palestinian Authority with America and Israel concern wore necessary before talks on creating an independent Palestinian state wore held.

Blair tried to convenience the House of Commons that it was in the interest of both the Palestinians and the Israelis that "these reforms succeeded so we can make a reality of the U.S. President Mr. George Bush's vision of two states-Israel and Palestine living side by side in peace and security"

Jack Straw said it was "medium level but it is a step in the right direction". The Palestinian chief virtual Israeli siege for months welcomed the initiative and said he would send senior representatives to the conference.

Though this attempt of peace process by Blair seamed to be independent attempt by the analysts could guess that Blair was moving the peace process between Israel and Palestine on the directions of the U.S. President, George Bush, but Blair pretended his move as independent British role on the issue.

Five days later the Bush administration claimed the 12,000 page declaration as woe fully short of facts "we know that Iraq has weapons of mass destruction and has programs to create more". The U.S. Secretary of State, Colin Powell, had said saying that using force to disarm Saddam Hussein remains an option because the declaration appears suspect.

Making his first public comments Colin Powell had said "We said at the very beginning when we approached at it with skepticism, and the information I have received so for is that skepticism is well-found.

Powell had warned Iraq saying that "The International community has an obligation to act and do what ever is necessary".

Russia accuses the U.S. of making politically motivated charges against Iraq and North Korea. Accusations that Iraq was holding weapons of mass destruction have no proof, a senior Russian diplomat revealed. "If anyone possesses factual information that Iraq has banned weapons or continues efforts to build them, it would be logical to make it available to UNMOVIC and IAEA inspectors," Russia's First Deputy Foreign Minister, Vyacheslav Trubnikov, told the Itar-Tas news agency on 4, January 2003.

Trubnikov said such information could then be verified by over a hundred international inspectors deployed in Iraq. Baseless charges wore "counterproductive and strengthen apprehensions that the issue of Iraqi weapons of mass destruction is nothing but a smokescreen for pursuing other goals"

Similarly Trubnikov described any Western charges against North Korea as politically-motivated.

'We of course pay attention to Western nation's concerns. But we also take note of the fact that many of them are dictated by political imperatives." While calling on North Korea to "strictly fulfill its obligations as a signatory to the Nuclear Non-Proliferation Treaty." Trubnikov described the row over Pyongyang's nuclear programme as a problem between North Korea and the U.S. and called on them to resolve it though constructive dialogue and mutual adherence to the 1994 framework accord" between the two countries. Russia is opposed not only to the policy of double standards, but also to the inclusion of many countries in the so called blacklists or white lists.

South Korea and Japan intensified their diplomatic pressure on North Korea after joining hands with the United States to urge Pyongyang to eliminate its nuclear weapons programme. No time table had been set at that stage for any such action by Pyongyang, South Korea indicated that the issue however, had to be sorted out in view of the worsening situation on this front.

The Japanese Prime Minister, Junichiro Koizumi, sought to widen the circle of pressure by indicating in Tokyo that he would discuss the North Korean issues, including the nuclear question, with the Russian President, Vladimir Puttin.

Koizumi was reported to have told the Japanese Journalists in Tokyo, on the eve of his departure to Moscow, that he would focus attention on the North Korean issue in addition to his country's ties with Russia. This pact of Koizumi's agenda intends to strive for the peaceful resolution of the North Korean nuclear issue by consulting closely with Washington and Seoul and also by seeking cooperation with other interested countries such as China and Russia and with the International Atomic Energy Agency (IAEA). At this stage Japan underscored its hope that the North would quickly take concrete action to abolish in a verifiable manner all of Pyongyang's plans for nuclear weapons development.

Britain while playing the peace tune had started to mobilize troops and in this regard Britain intensified it preparation for a war with Iraq by deploying up to 20,000 troops in the Gulf and mobilization of hundreds of reservists, but the Government played down the idea that a conflict was inevitable and insisted that search for a diplomatic solution was still going on.

A formal announcement about deployment of British troops was expected to be made by the British Prime Minister, Tony Blair, in Parliament the next week giving a new momentum to the British-U.S. show of force ahead of a possible attack on Iraq.

The British government was anxious to make the point that, till now, the military build up was intended simply to put pressure on Iraq to comply with the U.N. Security Council resolution which requires it to declare its weapons of mass destruction. According to the "The Times" magazine, Blair and his foreign secretary, Jack Straw, planned a "fresh initiative to keep upon the prospect of a diplomatic solution to resolve the crisis."

Downing Street maintained that a war was not inevitable. "We want a peaceful solution but Iraq will not comply with a credible threat of military action. Ultimately the choice is Saddam Hussein's." A spokesman said repeating the U.S. President, George W. Bush's remarks to American soldiers in Texas that it was for Hussein to decide whether he wanted to "seal his fate by refusing to disarm and also ignoring the opinion of the world."

There were attempts to scotch speculation that the countdowns for a war could begin on January 27th 2003 when the weapons inspectors wore due to give their first full report to the U.N. Security council. The speculation is based on the premise that the report would not satisfy Britain and American who would then seek a mandate to 'disarm' Saddam Hussein by force.

But one of the Cabinet Minister in Blair's government were quoted as saying that January 27 would not provide the trigger for a war and that Britain and America were ready to allow the U.N. process to continue for "many more months." "You should not be holding our breath for January 27. You should not run away with the idea that war has to start in February," the minister told leading American magazine "The Times" amid reports that Arab leaders wore trying to persuade Hussein to go into exile and avert a war which could prove catastrophic for his country. The idea appeared to have American baking commentators said citing a U.S. State Department spokesman's statement that the Iraqi leader must "change his ways or change his venue."

The general expectation with the Asian Pacific diplomatic circles was that the Democratic People's Republic of Korea (DPRK) might come up with a considered response to the latest U.S. offer. The U.S. had indicated its willingness to engage

Pyongyang in talks about how it will meet its obligations to the international community by renouncing the North Korean nuclear weapons programme itself.

However, the DPRK renewed its demand that the U.S. sign a bilateral non aggression pact as the best means to ensure a complete de nuclearisation of the Korean peninsula. Reacting to this statement the North Korean official news agency outlined the 'Kim Jong-il' regime's updated position in highly political terms. The U.S., it was said, was well advised not to forget the lesson drawn from the history of the DPRK-U.S., relations and the present reality. Demanding the U.S. to give up its "anachronistic hostile policy" towards the DPRK, it called upon the U.S. to immediately withdraw its aggression troops from South Korea.

China being the most influential player in North East Asia as regards the DPRK's nuclear weapons issue, did not rush to respond to the latest consensus among the U.S. as also South Korea and Japan in this connection. Japan on the other hand reaffirmed its status as a proactive member of the IAEA's Board of Governors, besides arguing that North Korea should abide by the latest resolution adopted by the this organization in Vienna.

U.S. war planners had reached Qatar for the next strategy to impose on Iraq. Though war was not at the doorstep of Iraq but American preparation was such that any body could understand there was a possibility of a war against Iraq.

Amid an accelerating flow of the U.S. troops and weapons to the Gulf region, the battle staff that would run a military campaign against Iraq was beginning to assemble at a command post in the central Gulf.

Battle planners from the Central Command wore heading from their permanent headquarters in Florida to Camp As Sayliyah in Qatar to be in position to carry out any attack order from the President, George W. Bush.

The U.S. military spokes persons wore regularly in touch with the media giving out information's about their move to Qatar does not mean war was imminent or inevitable. But it is an important step in the assembling of troops, weapons, supplies and technology needed to carry out an invasion.

The same Central Command planners wore at the command post in December 2002 for a weeklong exercise before returning to their headquarters in Florida, but this time it was not an exercise.

Some U.S. military officials who discussed the matter on condition of anonymity said the moment of central Command battle planners which began in January first week in 2003 was part of an accelerating buildup of forces in the Gulf region.

Several thousand's combat forces wore scheduled to flow in to the region over a short period of days. F-15E and F-15C fighters and B-1B bombers wore among forces scheduled to join the region. Also headed to the Gulf is the Army's mobile biological weapon testing laboratory.

The Maryland based lab, which helps tests samples to confirm whether a biological attack had taken place, the Army's top biological defence expert Col. Erik Henchal had said this to the media.

Amid the force buildup, U.S. war planners continued to strike an Iraqi air defences in the southern part of the country. On 8 January 2003 they targeted air defence communication sites between the cities of Al Kut and An Nasiriyah.

The Central Command had informed that the air strike wore executed after Iraq defence forces fired anti aircraft artillery at U.S. planes patrolling the southern "no fly" zone and Iraqi military aircraft entered the zone.

On 6th January 2003 the U.S. planes targeted two Iraqi military radars near the city of Al Amarah, south of Al Kut on the Tigris River. Iraqi officials had reported casualty of citizens in that attack.

In the first week of January 2003 the French President, Jacques Chirac, called on troops to be prepared for deployment for a possible war against Iraq in the clearest signal yet that France would participate in any military move against Baghdad.

"To be prepared is at the heart of the soldier's job" Chirac had said during annual New Year's wishes to the armed forces.

"Particularly we have to be attentive to the way in which United Nations Security Council Resolution 1441 is applied by Iraq".

The resolution authorizes U.N. weapons inspectors to visit any facility or property in Iraq at any time and warns Baghdad of serious consequences if it fails to comply with weapons inspections.

Paris had been opposed to unilateral American action in Iraq and had demanded that Washington get Security Council approved before sending in troops if Baghdad does not prove it has given up all its banned weapons.

Chirac said there wore several reasons to believe that French forces would continue to be needed in certain "operational theaters," a reference to Ivory Coast, where more than 2000 French troops wore currently engaged.

Chirac hinted out that there many other issues could open up with reference to Iraq.

Supporting to Chirac statement, the French Defence Minister, Michele Alliot-Marie, said that the army was not specific preparations for an eventual war in Iraq but that "the France army is ready to fulfill its obligations when necessary."

She reconfirmed France's stance on Iraq, saying any armed intervention must be used only as a last resort in forcing Saddam Hussein to comply with the U.N. resolution.

She also said that for the moment, U.N. inspectors had faced "no hindrances" in the course of their work.

CHAPTER - 2

At the same time the alliance partner Britain was also reportedly making war preparations.

The British Defence Secretary, Geoff Hoon, was expected to announce the call-up of between 5000 to 7000 troops as part of a military mobilization,

The British Government said that six navy vessels would leave Britain for a training exercise in Southeast Asia that includes a stop in the Gulf.

In Iraq thousands of armed men and women took part in a military parade near Baghdad, to defend their country against any U.S. attack.

The men and women, in military uniform and with AK-47 assault rifles in hand, marched in the city of Baquba, 40 km northeast of Baghdad, one day after Hussein said Iraq was prepared to confront any U.S. military action.

The armed units wore part of Jerusalem Army, which is a volunteer force that Iraq said and they numbered around seven million fighters.

The parade was so good that row after row of women in veils and men in military uniform paraded under the watchful observation of senior officials.

The Israel army under orders to crack down further in the hunt for Palestinian militants also killed three Palestinians during an incursion in to the Gaza Strip on 7, January 2003.

Israel, which reoccupied most of the West Bank more than six months ago and keeps close control on the Gaza Strip, said that it would further tighten restrictions on Palestinian moment after the Tel Aviv bombing, which killed 22 people as well as the bomber.

Israel prevented a top-level Palestinian delegation, including Erakat, from traveling to London for talks on international reforms with other regional and international players, at the invitation of the British Prime Minister, Tony Blair.

The British Prime Minister Tony Blair decided to conduct a mini-summit with the Arab leaders in London to revive the Palestinian peace process after the Israeli Government refused to allow Palestinian delegates to travel to Britain, provoking an angry reaction from the Foreign secretary, Jack Straw, who was to have chaired the conference.

The immediate provocation for the Israel decision was said to be suicide bombings in which 22 Israelis wore killed but even before that, Israel had made clear its unhappiness with Blair's initiative.

It was publicly criticized by Israel's hard line Foreign Minister, Binyamin Nitanyahu, who was bitterly opposed to any contacts with the present Palestinian leadership.

Israel was dissatisfied for not been invited to the meeting, and Netanyahu felt personally insulted when Blair declined to meet him when the Israeli leader was in London.

Blair compounded this by inviting the new Israeli opposition Labour Party leader, Amram Mitzna, who was to contest elections to unseat the Sharon Government.

Straw denounced the Israeli decision to ban Palestinian delegates, saying it would not advance the cause of peace in the region but when he telephoned Netanyahu to urge him to reconsider the decision, the latter accused Britain of giving respectability to Palestinian leaders compromised by terror.

Israelis further angered Britain by making public the transcript of the Straw-Netanyahu conversation which was regarded here as a breach of diplomatic etiquette. According to the transcript, Netanyahu told straw that Britain should follow the U.S. policy of no compromise with those who believed in terror. "You in Britain, are doing the exact opposite," Straw who in return said "No, it is Israel who is doing the opposite. Instead of concentrating on dealing with terrorism, it is striking at Palestinian delegates."

The conference was portrayed as a major Blair initiative to engage with the Palestinian crisis but critics dismissed it as an attempt ahead of an expected attack on Iraq to cool down Arab leaders who have been angry with doing nothing to address the Palestinian issue.

Leaders from Egypt, Jordan, Saudi Arabia and the Palestinian Authority had been invited to sit down with representatives from the U.S., the European Union, Russia and the U.N. to discuss reforms to the Palestinian Authority.

Both Britain and the U.S. insist that no progress is possible unless the Authority is radically restructured, though Britain does not share the American-Israeli view that Yasser Arafat must go before any meaning full negotiation can take place.

With renewed assurances by President, George W. Bush, that he will not order an attack on North Korea, worried Asian allies were resuming talks on how to defuse a nuclear crisis that is threatening their security.

Bush said the U.S. was open to dialogue with Pyongyang but he also told reporters at the White House that North Korea must permit international monitoring of its nuclear facilities.

"We have no intention of invading North Korea," Bush said renewing an assurance that so far has failed to deter North Korea from taking steps to build new nuclear weapons.

High level South Korean and Japanese delegations met for a second day at the State Department to share their concerns with the U.S. officials. The two allies could be vulnerable to North Korean missiles and wore seeking a diplomatic solution.

Bush had said that North Korea must keep the pledge it made to build new nuclear weapons.

We will have dialogue Bush said.

The Iraqi government was seeking guarantees to allow President, Saddam Hussein, and other Iraqi leaders to go into exile as a way to end current tension, some German magazine published this article some time in the middle of January 2014.

The European Union, foreign policy, coordinator, Javier Solana, however, said that he had no information about any such negotiations.

The German magazine Der Spiegel did not name the country that Saddam was seeking for exile. An African nation was being discussed.

The Iraqi conditions also include the withdrawal of American soldiers from the region, an insistence that weapon inspections and U.N. sanctions end and that measures wore taken against what Iraq was blamed as the production of weapons of mass destruction by Israel.

The diplomats, who decline to be named, have not revealed the source of their information; however the U.S. considered the conditions unacceptable, while Egypt was seeking to persuade Baghdad to compromise, the magazine coated.

The United States brought an end to all speculations that United States has declared Iraq in "material Breach of a U.N. disarmament resolution for omitting key details in a declaration of its weapons given to the United Nations in December 2002.

Mean while several Arab countries wore aiming for Saddam Hussein cooperates fully with U.N. demands on inspections or even to persuade him to step down and go in to exile.

As rumors spread about Saddam Hussein the crude oil prices fell 47 cents to $30.11 a barrel while the U.S. light crude lost 25 cents to $33.41 a barrel. This fall in crude oil was in the hope that the war would not take place.

Saddam Hussein remained defiant by saying Iraq had mobilized its forces to defeat U.S. troops at the gates of Baghdad if they invaded the country.

There was panic among oil traders that any attack on Iraq may disrupt crude supplies from the Middle East at a time when Venezuelan oil sales remain severely reduced due to an opposition-led strike against President Hugo Chavez.

A defiant Saddam Hussein called on his people to rise up and defend the nation against a new United States-led attack even as the chief weapon inspector of the U.N., Hans Blix, stated that he would seek an explanation from the Baghdad regime on the empty chemical warheads discovered two days earlier.

As Saddam made his statement on television and seeking the cooperation of the Iraqi people members of the ruling Baath party raised anti-U.S. slogans during a march in Baghdad marking the 12th anniversary of the Gulf War.

In a 40 minute televised address, delivered on the 12th anniversary of the Gulf War, Hussein, promised that Iraq's enemies would face "Suicide" at the gates of his capital.

Saddam's speech revealed no sign that he was prepared to neither bow to the demands of the U.N. nor step down as has been suggested by Arab leaders as a way to avoid war.

"The people of Baghdad, have resolved to compel the moguls of this age to commit suicide on its walls; every one who tried to climb over its walls will fail in their attempt." Hussein had said referring to the U.S.

Hussein said the Iraqi nation was fully mobilized against the threat of a new conflict and told the U.S. President, George W. Bush to "keep your evil away from the mother of civilization."

He said "the whole nation will rise in defence of its right to live, its role and sacred sites, and their arrows will go a stray or backfire, God willing."

In an appeal for Arab support, Hussein said "Western peoples and circles" had long interfered with the nations of West Asia, "in particular Zionist Jews and Zionists who are not of the Jewish people."

"Long live Palestine, free and Arab, from the Mediterranean Sea to the Jordan River," Hussein said. On January 17, 1991, the U.S. led coalition launched devastating air attacks against Baghdad and their Iraqi cities, opening Operation Storm which drove Iraqi forces out of Kuwait.

Meanwhile the Chief U.N. inspector, Hans Blix, said that he wanted "to have more explanations" from Baghdad about chemical warheads found two days ago.

Blix was speaking in Paris one day after his inspectors found 11 empty chemical warheads at an Iraqi munitions dump.

The Iraqis had claimed the find was not linked to any prohibited weapons, but the U.S. said it was not surprised, adding that chemical munitions were one of the areas of omission in Baghdad's declaration.

At a press conference along with the French President, Jacques Chirac, Blix said that he was not certain about whether the warheads were listed in the declaration. The newly found empty warheads would be destroyed Blix added.

Reacting to the development, Britain said it was not rushing to judgment on the discovery of the warheads.

Questions from the media persons came out that if the finding was a "material breach" of the U.N. resolution 1441, a phrase widely seen as a trigger for a possible U.S. led war against Iraq, the British junior Foreign Office Minister, Mike O'Brien, said, "Our response at this stage is cautious. We will look at the details of the evidence when Hans Blix provides it. There's no rush to judgment."

United States spokesman said the empty warheads appeared in "excellent condition" and were undergoing X-ray and chemical analyses.

South Korea's president-elect supported the United States to negotiate fully with North Korea to defuse the stand-off over its nuclear weapons development.

The South Korean call for talks was echoed by the Russian, Deputy Foreign Minister, Alexander Losyukov, who visited Beijing to discuss the impasse. Losyukov was expected to visit Pyongyang later for talks with North Korean officials.

The South Korean President-Elect, Roh Moo-Hyun speaking to American and European chambers of commerce, suggested the .S. should push for negotiations with Pyongang. Washington has said it is willing to talk, but ruled out bargaining with North Korea to get it to dismantle its nuclear programmes.

"I would like to persuade the U.S. to engage actively in dialogue with North Korea," said Roh, who was to assumes office in February 2013. He expressed optimism that a deepening of the confrontation could be averted through talks.

The U.S. has taken a more conciliatory one with North Koreans this week, offering the possibility of energy and agricultural aid for the impoverished country if it gives up its nuclear hopes. But Washington has refused to make any guarantees to Pyongyang.

Roh also said at this point of time he thought North Korea, one of the most closed nations in the world, was serious about reforming its decrepit economic system. "I think North Korea is sincere about opening up and reforming because they have no choice," he expressed.

Roah said he wanted South Korea to play a prominent role in resolving the crisis.

South Korea had said it would use its contact with the North to press for an end to its nuclear programmes, but the officials from the North Korea said Pyongyang would refuse to discuss the nuclear issue in Cabinet-level talks in Seoul.

"The Nuclear issue had to be resolved through talks between the Democratic Peoples Republic of Korea (North Korea) and the United States," Cho Chung-hun, deputy bureau chief of the Secretariat of the Committee for the peaceful Reunification of the Fatherland, was quoted as saying.

"It cannot be resolved by South Koreans."

Losyukov, the Russian envoy, said that Washington Pyongyang negotiations should be opened.

Russian Interfax News Agency later quoted the Foreign Ministry's public affairs office as saying Moscow did not intend to play mediator. China had offered to host such talks. Losyukov said it was a time for "quiet diplomacy" and added that it is important to refrain from loud statements and from further criticism by two sides.

The Chief United Nations, Weapons Inspector, Hans Blix arrives in Baghdad on 19 January 2003 and expectations of hard negotiations with the Iraqi leadership that could provide an opening for averting a possible United States Led war with Iraq. Blix was seeking a full disclosure of unconventional weapons from Iraq before submitting a key report to the U.N. Security Council on 27, January 2003.

As Blix findings wore likely to influence a decision on a war in Iraq. The U.S., which was playing a leading role in shaping the U.N. debate, wanted the Iraqi President, Saddam Hussein, to be unseated apart from seeking the removal of all mass destruction weapons from Iraq. There was considerable speculation in diplomatic circles that in case Hussein surrenders his conventional weapons by providing the inspectors a full list of those arms which Iraq possessed he could choose to go into exile in a country of his choice.

There were expectations that despite the enormous pressure that he is facing Hussein may not be in a hurry to strike a deal. It was the expectations of every one that he was likely to drive a hard bargain both with the U.N. and the forces that stood behind it. On the new developments in Iraq's neighborhood have given him fresh room for maneuver. Among them, the most significant are the developments in Turkey.

Turkey had shown great reluctance to funnel U.S. troops into northern Iraq. The U.S. had apparently, at one point of time, sought to stage 1,30,000 troops from Turkey in to northern Iraq. The Turkish military however was opposed to the presence of more than 1.00.000 U.S. forces on its soil. Subsequently, the U.S. sought to push 80,000 troops, but this demand was further scaled down to 15,000 troops. The final word on stationing of U.S. forces for the northern Iraqi campaign was expected to be out after the chairman of the U.S. Joint Chief of Staff, Gen. Richard B. Myers, concludes consultations with his Turkish interlocutors. Concerned about the weakening of the "northern front", the U.S. had plans to encourage the 50,000 strong Kurdish forces in the northern Iraq to make up for the shortfall of its own troops.

That however would also mean diverting forces from its elite 101st airborne division that had trained hand for a massive airborne assault in Baghdad. Analysts pointed out that the U.S. forces would have to occupy northern Iraqi oil cities of Kirkuk and Mosul, as both the ethnic Kurds and Turkey wore competing for exercising control over them, even if it means redrawing the plans to assault Baghdad. Apart from Turkey which is central to the northern campaign, Jordan which is the centerpiece for launching armed thrust in to Iraq from the west, was also demonstrating its reluctance to stage U.S. forces from its territory? Without Jordanian support, the U.S. campaign in Iraq along the western axis could become seriously compromised. U.S. forces was also need to establish a presence in western Iraq, in order to deny Iraq an opportunity to position improved Scud Missiles that can target Israel. Knowing about the difficulties that the U.S. forces along Iraq's Northern and Western fronts. Hussein knew that he had some time on his hand before they can be prosecuted.

Beside the shaky diplomacy among Iraq's neighbors to avert war was also feeding into this line of thinking.

Turkey was staging a summit, while Syria was willing to hold a Foreign Ministers meeting with the participations of Turkey, Syria, Saudi, Egyptian, Iranian and Jordanian leaders. Saudi Arabia was also trying to fix another summit. Consequently, Hussein was likely to exploit the emerging diplomatic space to demonstrate his defiance of the U.S. for at least some more time.

A top Russian envoy submitted a plan on resolving the North Korean nuclear standoff to leaders in Pyongyang on 18, January 2003, while the United States said it was willing to consider a wide range of aid to end the dispute.

Russian Deputy Foreign Minister, Alexander Losyukv, told Russia's Itar-Tass news agency that he expected a response on Monday to the so-called "package plan," which calls for security guarantees and resumption of economic aid to North Korea in return for a commitment to keep the Korean Peninsula nuclear-free zone.

Losyukov arrived in Pyongyang as part of the international bid to bring a diplomatic solution to the crisis over North Korea's decision to reactivate facilities that could be used to make nuclear bombs. The Russian diplomat said the dialogue was "very active and substantive, while the situation at the talks was very warm, friendly and constructive," Itar-Tass published this report.

Diplomatic efforts elsewhere were also stepping up with the U.S. Assistant Secretary of State, James A. Kelly, in Japan to coordinate policies on North Korea and U.S. Undersecretary of State, John Bolton, in Beijing for similar talks.

State welcoming reception for Losyukov in Pyongyang, North Korea's First Vice-Minister of Foreign Affairs, Kang Sok Ju, thanks Russia for sending the diplomat, saying it stemmed from Russia's "good will stand to settle the present situation on the Korean peninsula at any cost." According to, North Korean, state-run, 'Korean Central News Agency'. In Seoul, the U.S. Ambassador, Thomas Hubbard, said the United States intends to take the lead in defusing the crisis but wants other nations to play a large role.

His comments, made on a talk show, came amid mounting international pressure for Washington to engage North Korea in direct talks. In previous days South Korean President-elect, Roh Moo-Hyun,urged Washington to "actively" take part in dialogue, while Losyukov characterized the crisis as mainly a problem between North Korea and the United States.

"We don't see North Korea as exclusively a U.S. problem," Hubbard told South Korea's largest broad caster, KBS, "its nuclear threat is not just a threat to the United States, it's a challenge to the entire international system."

Ariel Sharon believes an international "road map" to Palestinian statehood was unrealistic and could not be implemented, a senior advisor to the Prime Minister said confirming Sharon's harshest public criticism yet of the plan.

The blueprint was formulated by the so called Quartet of West Asia mediators-the U.S., the U.N., the European Union and Russia- and a final version was to be adopted on February 22, 2003, a month after an Israeli general election Sharon was expected to win.

Speaking on the plan in a weekend interview with Newsweek, Sharon was quoted as saying, "Oh, the Quartet is nothing. Don't take it seriously; there is another plan that will work."

In the interview, Sharon said Palestinian reform, including the removal of Yasser Arafat from power and the appointment of a Prime Minister and decisive action against Palestinian militants are a precondition for renewing peace efforts, in such a case Israel was willing to recognize a provisional demilitarized Palestinian state with temporary borders. After prolong calm, Israel was willing to enter negotiations on a final peace deal, Sharon said.

Sharon advisor Raanan Gissin, denied what the Prime Minister told Newsweek that "the Quartet is nothing," he also said "what was published was not the original full answer the Prime Minister gave. The words are to tally taken out of context. He meant the plan cannot be implemented- not that the quartet is nothing."

Gissin added that Sharon's own plan was coordinated with the U.S. administration.

"Israel and the United States see eye to eye-on the way to fulfill President George W. Bush's speech, unlike other members." Of Quartet, the Prime Minister office said in a statement, referring to a vision for Palestinian statehood outlined in June 2002 by U.S. President Bush.

In that speech, Bush said a Palestinian state could be created alongside Israel within three years, but also called on Palestinians to change leaders.

However, the United States had not distanced itself from the Quartet's blueprint. The Quartet plan is based on the Bush vision, with mediators formulating a three stage timetable that leads to Palestinian statehood by 2005.

The Quartet plan includes elements Sharon mentioned, including Palestinian reform, decisive action against militants and a provisional state as an interim step, but it also insists that Israel freeze settlement construction and withdraw from Palestinian population canters it now occupies.

One of the Palestinian, Cabinet Minister, Saeb Erekat, accused Sharon of sabotaging efforts to revive peace talks. Sharon's plan has had no chance of success, Erekat said, and "his real intention was to make it impossible for any future negotiators to discuss peace."

In the United States, Deputy Defence Secretary, Paul Wolfowitz, said U.S. pressure to resolve the Israeli-Palestinian conflict would increase after a possible war on Iraq. "Our demand in pushing for a Palestinian state will grow." The Washington Post Quoted.

Reacting to the statements made by the U.S. diplomats on Iraq Britain warned that it was prepared to risk a confrontation with the U.N. Security Council if there is an attempt to block military action against Iraq to disarm Saddam Hussein if he refuses to do so on his own.

In his most defiant remarks yet on Iraq, the British Prime Minister, Tony Blair, had made it clear that if Iraq is found to be in material breach of the existing U.N. resolution "action will follow" even if others on the Security Council try to block it. The opponents of military action would not be allowed to put an "unreasonable or unilateral block," Blair said at his monthly press conference in Downing Street.

"In those circumstances we have said we can't be in a position where we are confined in that way. Don't be under any doubts whatever. If there is a breach of the U.N. resolution that we have passed then action will follow," he said prompting parallels with the NATO military intervention in Kosovo in 1999 despite Russian veto at the U.N.

Blair's statement came even as Chris Patten, the European Union Commissioner for External Relations, insisted on a specific U.N. mandate for a military action saying that otherwise E.U. might not be willing to pay for the reconstruction of a post war Iraq. "I would find it much more difficult to get the approval of member-states and the European Parliament for development aid if the military intervention did not have a U.N. mandate," he said drawing comparison with the conflict in Afghanistan which "everybody supported."

Although Blair had talked even before, of disarming Hussein at any cost, his latest remarks were seen as the most unequivocal and prompted speculation that a war now looked inevitable and the question was no longer of 'if but when.' Senior Labour MPs reacted with fury and demanded an 'emergency' debate in the commons. They warned that if he backed unilateral U.S. military action, he could be risking his political career. Alan Simpson said "If you choose to operate outside international law and you act in defiance of any democratic mandate, sooner rather than later the mandate the Prime Minister will be withdrawn by the British people."

The Liberal Democratic leader Charles Kennedy said it was "disingenuous to argue that we want to work through the U.N. but only if the U.N. does what we want." The country's most moderate Muslim body, the Muslim Council of Britain, urged the Prime Minister to avert a war with Iraq, saying that Muslims were not convinced of American motives.

Even as the United States began preparation to re-engage some of North Korea's close neighbors over its latest withdrawal from the Nuclear Non Proliferation Treaty (NPT), Japan sought to explore how for Pyongyang might be willing to go in its strategic 'brinkmanship' at this stage. The U.S. Assistant Secretary of State for East Asia and Pacific affairs, James Kelly, expected to hold talks with South Korea's President-elect, Roh Moo-hyun, and other leaders in Seoul the very next day.

Ahead of this American exercise of sizing up North Korea through the eyes of its neighbors, the South Korean President, Kim Dae-Jung, underlined the need to make an all-out diplomatic effort to try and resolve the issues arising out of Pyongyang's withdrawal from the NPT and declarations of intent about resuming ballistic missile testing. On an altogether different yet related plane, the Japanese Prime Minister, Juichiro Koizumi, held talks with Konstantin Pulikovskii, Russia's federal official in the country's far-eastern region and a friend of North Korean leader Kim Jong-il.

The meeting, which took place in Russia's eastern city of Khabarovsk, was seen in the regional diplomatic crisis as a clear signal that Japan is eager to explore all avenues to try and deflect the Democratic People's Republic of Korea (DPRK) back towards the NPT and the missile-test ban. In this context, Japan had categorically indicated its reluctance to normalize ties with a 'nuclearising' North Korea.

Elsewhere in the DPRK'S extended neighborhood, China and Russia did not make any fresh moves. While the Russian President, Vladimir Putin, had joined Koizumi two days ago to turn the diplomatic heat on the DPRK, an important task before Kelly fight out how far China would go in translating its 'concern' over North Korea's latest nuclear escalation into 'concerted action' in the company of other major powers, according to diplomatic observations. Moves were initiated, through, within the 10-member Association of South East Asian Nations (ASEAN) to formulate a unified stand on the DPRK's nuclear stakes.

With North Korea being a member of the ASEAN Regional Forum, which includes India and the U.S. too among others, considered it likely that the ARF itself might evince more than a mere academic interest in the DPRK's current game plan.

Russia proposed a package deal for North Korea to resolve the crisis triggered by Pyongyang's withdrawal from the Nuclear Non -Proliferation Treaty. A three-point plan calls for North

Korea to reverse its decision to pull out of the NPT in exchange for international security guarantees and a resumption of humanitarian and economic aid to Pyongyang.

Russia aired the plan a day after the North Korea crisis was discussed in Moscow between the Russian President, Vladimir Putin, and the visiting Japanese Prime Minister, Junichiro Koizumi. A spokesman for the Russian Foreign Ministry said that the Russian plan provides, first of all, for the Korean Peninsular to remain a nuclear-free zone and for all sides to honor their obligations under the NPT and other international accords, including the 1994 agreement between the U.S. and North Korea. Secondly, Russia proposes bilateral and multilateral dialogues that should result, among other things, insecurity guarantees to North Korea. Thirdly, the plan calls for a revival of humanitarian and economic assistance programmes to North Korea. Russia also opposed France's proposal to call an emergency meeting of the U.N. Security Council to discuss the North Korea standoff. The Russian Foreign Ministry spokesman, described the proposal as "premature" because bilateral and multilateral contacts with Pyongyang" are for from having exhausted their potential.

Russia's Foreign Minister, Igor Ivanov, discussed the Russian plan in telephonic conversations with his opposite numbers in the United States, China, France and South Korea. He was quoted as saying that the crisis could be only resolved through "a package solution taking in to account the interests of all parties involved."

Yasser Arafat must step up his efforts to make the Palestinian authority more democratic in order to get the Western Asia peace process back on track, the British Foreign Secretary; Jack Straw said this in London.

Straw's advice for the Palestinian leader came just before he opened a one-day, international conference on Palestinian issues at the Foreign Office. It was held despite an Israel government ban that prevented the in-person participation of a Palestinian delegation from the West Bank and Gaza Strip.

The meeting included delegates from the United States, the United Nations, the European Union, Russia, Jordan, Egypt, and Saudi Arabia to discuss the reform of the Palestinian authority. Egypt was represented by the country's intelligence chief, Omar Suleiman. Most Palestinian representatives were to address the meeting via a video hookup from the territories.

The U.S. Assistant Secretary of State, William Burns, who heads the State Department's Middle East Bureau, was representing United States.

The Israeli Prime Minister, Ariel Sharon, barred Palestinians from traveling in the conference in retaliation for a double Palestinian suicide bombing attack in Tel Aviv a few days ago that killed 22 civilians.

The U.S. had supported the British-sponsored conference and opposed Israel's decision to prevent a Palestinian delegation from attending, Israel controls Palestinian travel and decides who can and cannot leave.

In Washington, the U.S. State Department spokesman, Richard Boucher, said the conference is designed to advance the U.S. President, George W. Bush's "vision of two states, Israel and Palestine, living side-by-side in peace and stability."

In an interview with the British Broadcasting Corporation, Straw acknowledged that the ban on the Palestinian delegation was unhelpful, but insisted it would not distract attention from the principal issues.

He said they include the need for reforms of the authority's finances as well as constitutional issues, such its establishment of a Prime Minister's office, a Cabinet, a proper legislative council and an independent judiciary.

Straw said one goal of the conference is to "accelerate the momentum towards internal reform in the occupied territories, the West Bank and Gaza, for the Palestinian Authority.

Straw said "the Israeli travel ban cannot be used as an excuse to top the reform process in its tracks. Precisely because the security situation is so adverse, you need a higher quality of public administration, not a lower quality."

The Palestinian delegation included two officials Afif Safieh, the Palestinian representative in London, and Michael Tarazi, a Palestinian legal adviser.

In the context of the international crisis over a 'nuclearising' North Korea, an aspect that was not overshadowed by the Yasukuni episode, China said the U.S. Undersecretary of State for Arms Control and International Security Affairs, John Bolton, would arrive in Beijing on January 20th 2003 to hold the first round of a new strategic dialogue on the bilateral front.

The dialogue was agreed upon during the Crawford Sino-U.S. summit in October 2002, and the issues to be covered would include "strategic security, multilateral arms control and anti proliferation," according to a Chinese spokeswoman, Zhang Qiyue.

Another top U.S. official, James Kelly, was on the agenda to hold talks with the Chinese leaders on the North Korean issue, which acquired a international dimension as a United Nations official, Morris Strong, and an Australian delegation arrived in Pongyang for talks.

Faced with intense pressure from his party MP's and Cabinet colleagues not to plunge Britain into a U.S. led war with Iraq, the British, Prime Minister, Tony Blair, was to visit Washington later in January 2003 to persuade the U.S. President George W. Bush, not to rush in to a decision to attack Baghdad.

Significance is attached to the visit as there are fears that headliners in the Bush administration might push for a war if as seems almost certain the U.N. weapons inspectors in their first full report to the Security Council, on January 27th 2003, say that they have not been able to find any weapons of mass destruction in Iraq.

Blair who was expected to meet President Bush after the inspectors have given their report, is likely to stress that they should be given more time to complete their work. In a move believed to be aimed more at containing an anti-war rebellion within his party than a real change of heart, Blair has softened his thinking on Iraq in recent days and earlier that week he told a Cabinet meeting that the weapons inspectors needed more "time and space" to complete a process which had just begun.

He also played down the significance of January 27 which is widely seen as a "deadline" for a decision on military action against Baghdad, He said January 27 was an "important staging post" but should not be regarded "in any sense as a deadline."

Blair remarks came as opposition to a war grew after the chief weapons inspector, Hans Blix, told the U.N. Security Council that his team had not yet found a "smoking gun" that would point to Iraq's alleged arsenal of weapons of mass destruction. Unnamed Ministers were quoted as saying that Blair's statement was also intended to restrain the Bush administration.

"The Prime Minister's remarks was seen as a warning to Washington that he would not necessarily support a war in Iraq in all circumstances," ' The Independent' noted as more Labour MP's joined the growing anti-war sentiment in the party prompting fears of a revolt against Blair.

Anti-war Labour MP's whose number now exceeds 150, said that after Blix's latest report Blair would find it even more difficult to justify support to a U.S. led war against Iraq without a specific U.N. mandate. The Liberal Democrat leader, Charles Kennedy, warned that "if necessary, Blair will have to part ways with the U.S. administration, if it decides on an U.N. set of unilateral actions in Iraq.

As peace activists stepped up their campaign with a meeting in London ahead of a series of rallies planned by Stop the War Coalition, the Government was keen to stress that far from pushing the momentum Blair was in fact engaged in restraining Bush.

The U.S. Defence Secretary, Donald H. Rumsfeld, had ordered about 62,000 more U.S. troops to head for the Persian Gulf region in the coming days, doubling the size of the force now arrayed on the periphery of Iraq.

The moments make clear that the Pentagon intends to have sufficient force in place for an Iraq war as early as the first week of February 2003, although the White House says the U.S. President, George W. Bush, has not yet decided to attack.

CHAPTER - 3

Just hours after officials disclosed that Rumsfeld had ordered nearly 35,000 troops, including two large marine units, to ship out for a possible war with Iraq, the Defence Secretary signed another order to deploy 27,000 more troops mainly Army and Air Force combat units.

One senior official with access to the deployment orders said the units designated for deployment in the latest Rumsfeld order include a squadron of Air Force F-117 stealth fighter-bombers that played a key role in the 1991 Gulf War.

The order also includes thousands of marines and an Army air-borne infantry brigade. The troops actual departure for the potential war zone was planned to spread out over the rest of January 2003.

The Central command, the headquarters that would run any war against Iraq, had begun dispatching its battle staff to a command post in Qatar, and it was expected to be operational in fifteen days.

Eventually, the size of the U.S. force arrayed against Iraq could reach 250,000, but defence officials had said any attack ordered by Bush could begin with 1,00,000 or fewer troops in place. The rest could be brought to the fight later or held in reserve.

Sources said this means the U.S. could be positioned for an attack on Iraq by mid-to-late February 2003 with a force exceeding 1,50,000 soldiers, sailors, Marines and airmen. However, increasing pressure from allies for Washington to allow U.N. weapons inspectors to complete their work in Iraq had raised speculation in recent days about whether U.S. war plans might yet be slowed. Meanwhile, the U.S. military had begun an E-mail campaign urging military and civilian leaders in Iraq to turn away from the President, Saddam Hussein, a Pentagon official said, on condition of anonymity.

Iraqis began to receive the e-mails from about a week. Stating that "if you provide information on weapons of mass destruction or you take steps to hamper their use we will do what is necessary to protect you and protect your families." The message continued further saying "Failing to do that will lead to grave personal consequences."

The U.S. propaganda effort was in line with the Bush administration's policy of encouraging the Iraqi soldiers to topple Hussein or at least lay down their arms when the U.S. war machine starts rolling in.

"Iraqi chemical, biological and nuclear weapons violate Iraq's commitment to agreements and United Nations resolutions and Iraq had been isolated because of this behavior," this was another e-mail that was sent by United States.

The United States Assistant Secretary of State for East Asia and Pacific Affairs, James Kelly, held out the promise of a two-stage process of addressing the international crisis over North

Korea's withdrawal from the Nuclear Non Proliferation Treaty (NTP) and its declaration of intent to resume test flight of ballistic missiles that could deliver nuclear weapons of mass destruction.

The first step in the two-stage process consists of party's with the Democratic People's Republic of Korea (DPRK) or the North about its 'response' to the world wide demands that it eliminate its nuclear weapons.

The second phase was to address the DPRK's energy concerns "once we get beyond the nuclear weapons issue."

Kelly, was in Seoul to consult America's allies and interlocutor states in Pyongyang's neighborhood, said the U.S. was willing to talk to the North Koreans about their response to the international community, particularly with respect to the elimination of their nuclear weapons."

The purpose of his nuclear discussions in South Korea was to explore "some of the best was to do that kind of talking" with the DPRK Kelly defended his stand.

Although Kelly spoke of possibilities rather than certainties at this delicate stage of sorting out the nuclear puzzle, he made it clear that the U.S. did not want to slam the diplomatic door on the DPRK's face.

There was no immediate reaction from North Korea, which however, was now searching for a new "crack in the U.S. door" of nuclear protectionism.

In the early 1990s, Pyongyang had for the first time seen a "crack in the U.S. door" and entered into the Agreed Framework accord with the U.S. in 1994.

Articulating the new and evolving U.S. approach of telling the North Koreans about the basic in Washington's thinking, Kelly understood the importance of helping the DPRK tide over its huge energy crisis only after steps wore initiated to eliminate Pyongyang's nuclear weapons.

On the energy-related second phase too, of engaging North Korea, the American envoy reacted no words. "It may well be once we get beyond nuclear weapons, there may be opportunities with the U.S. with private investors in the other countries, to help North Korea in the energy area"

The linkage between the DPRK's nuclear weapons capabilities on the one side, and the energy needs of the North Koreans, on the other front, has much to do with the constant refrain from Pyongyang that its latest actions should be seen in the overall context of its compulsions to "produce electricity" by using nuclear reactors that could yield weapons-grade plutonium.

Kelly met South Korea's President-elect, Roh Moo-hyun, and other leaders in Seoul in resolving the crises.

Kelly had plans to travel to China and Japan too, during his visits to East Asia.

Roh told Kelly about the need to resolve the North Korean nuclear issue peacefully. The bottom line in Roh's thinking, as conveyed to his U.S. interlocutor, is that South Korea cannot tolerate or accept the North's attempts to possess nuclear weapons.

He conveyed South Korea's suggestion that the U.S. could consider giving the North some "security guarantee" other than a bilateral non-aggression pact as suggested by Pyongyang.

Reacting to the increasing pressure by the U.S., North Korea said its intention is not to produce weapons but to use nuclear activities confined only to peaceful purpose such as the production of electricity.

North Korea announced its immediate withdrawal from the Nuclear Non Proliferation Treaty. This move was in line with the Pyongyang's recent hints about imposing sanctions.

North Korea's action followed a series of steps that took in recent days to place itself on a trajectory out of the NPT's reach. The DPRK had joined the NPT in December 1985 at the behest of the former Soviet Union, Pyongyang actually pulled out of the treaty in March 1993. While North Korea, associated itself with the NPT, for the second time, after signing a deal with the U.S. in 1994.

With the strong decision taken by North Korea the international community now felt a new qualitative challenge. More precisely, the tone of Pyongyang's latest statement is hardly music to the U.S. which had been conspicuously portrayed by the regime of Kim Jong-Il as its new interlocutor in the place of the International Atomic Energy Agency (IAEA).

North Korea's decision to reactivate a 5-mw nuclear research reactor that could yield weapons-grade plutonium was the major concern for the U.S. and this was the reason that U.S. was avoiding North Korea from advancing its nuclear programme.

It was said that such a specific remark, which cannot be seen as a mere Freudian slip might than receive the prognosis about the future nuclear nightmare. A possibility that was envisioned, with reference to North Korea, by Leonard Spector, and others in the West.

U.S. President Bush, had telephonic talk with Jiang Zemin they both agreed that North Korea's announcement that it is withdrawing from the Non Proliferation Treaty is a concern to the entire international community. They also expressed that the North Korea continued to take steps in the wrong direction hurting only their own cause and the cause of the North Korean people.

Russia and Japan also expressed deep concern over North Korea's pullout from the Nuclear Non-Proliferation Treaty and urged Pyongyang to reverse its decision

Russia and Japan expressed regrets and profound concern over North Korea's nuclear programme and announced intention to withdraw from the NPT and refuse to honor its obligations under an agreement with IAEA on cooperation and guarantees, the two countries said in a joint statement.

Russia and Japan called on North Korea go back on its decision as soon as possible and pledged to work together to reduce tension on the Korean peninsula. The statement was part of an action plan on bilateral cooperation signed by the Russian President, Vladimir Putin, and the visiting Prime Minister, Junichiro Koizumi.

The Russian Foreign Ministry issued a strong statement expressing deep concern and warning to North Korea that its withdrawal from the NPT can only aggravate the already tense situation around the Korean peninsula and seriously damage universal international legal instruments of ensuring global and regional security.

Russia demanded North Korea to accept the unanimous view of the international community, its neighbors and partners and opt for honoring its international obligations in the sphere of non proliferation.

Russian President, Putin, called on North Korea to make a choice in favor of a fair and mutually beneficial dialogue with all parties concerned on issues of ensuring national security. Japanese Prime Minister's proposals for multilateral consultations on North Korea's nuclear issue involving the Five U.N. Security Council members along with Japanese and South Korea.

A leader of the Palestinian Militant group Hamas Abdul Aziz al-Rantissi urged Iraq to use suicide bombers to confront any U.S. military offensive. He called on Iraq to prepare an army of would-be martyrs and prepare and tense and thousands of explosive belts. He told 3,000 Hamas supporters at a pro-Iraq rally in the Jabalya refugee camp in the Gaza Strip.

"Blow yourselves up against the American army. Bomb them in Baghdad, I call on all Arab nations to burn the ground underneath the feet of the Americans in all capitals".

The rally was held against the backdrop of the U.S. preparations for a possible war against Iraq over its alleged weapon of mass destruction. Shouting slogans "Death of America" and Victory for Jerusalem to Baghdad, the demonstrators burnt the U.S., Israeli and British flags.

Iraq had paid millions of dollars to families of Palestinians including those of suicide bombers and Islamic fundamentalist organizations that had carried out dozens of suicide attacks in Israel before and during a Palestinian uprising for statehood.

Turkish Prime Minister Abdulla Gul, had given permission for a team of U.S. experts, to inspect a number of Turkish airbases and ports to go study whether they could be used by U.S. forces in any possible war against Iraq.

Prime Minister Gul said "I have signed the necessary decision regarding the bases every thing is under control".

Prime Minister Gul's decision came as a relief to the U.S. which had reportedly become concerned over Turkish foot dragging regarding both allowing the expert team into Turky and any eventual permission to use Turkish basser from which a northern front against Iraq could be opened up.

The Turkish government decision was with the fear of any economic fallout that may occur though majority of its people wore against the decision.

The imposition of sanctions against Iraq for ten years ago that had caused effects on Turkey and had lost billions of dollars trade and fears that its burgeoning tourist sector would be hit badly with any new war.

Turkey also feared that a war may lead to the establishment of a Kurdish state in Northwestern Iraq, a development that may lead to Turkey's own restive Kurdish minority once again calling for independence.

U.S. and British jets had already landed at the southern Turkey base of Incirlik from where they patrol the no-fly zone over Northern Iraq. Meanwhile, the Turkish Foreign Trade Minister Kursad Tuzmen flew to Baghdad for trade talks with Iraqi officials.

Before leaving Ankara's airport, Tuzmen said he had a special letter from Prime Minister, Gul for the Iraqi government and that there was still a chance to avoid war. Tuzman said that "if there was a last wagon on the peace train, it is necessary that we get on it".

Most European Union officials believe that the multi national organization is being dragged into the United States war against Iraq, for lack of an alternative popular opinion. It is argued that the E.U. needs a united foreign policy, to start with. There was also concern that the U.S. President George W. Bush, and his fellow White House Christians have woven elements of the Christian faith into his presidential vocabulary.

Bush critics in Europe feel that the "wall" between the Church and the state is being straddled, to dangerous effects. Many Europeans felt Bush's recent "axis of evil" speech linking Iran, Iraq and North Korea came as a new revelation.

As diplomatic pressure for dialogue over its nuclear weapons programme mounted around the world, North Korea agreed on to attend Cabinet level talks with South Korea the meeting that could help solve the dangerous stand-off.

Pyongyang said it wanted the talks held a week later than the South had proposed, the North did not explain the delay, however, it would allow the communist regime to digest.

South Korea which announced to host the Cabinet-level conference in Seoul, said the nuclear dispute will be on the agenda.

The talks were the ninth since a historic summit of the leaders of the two Koreas in 2000. That was also the highest level of direct communication between the two governments since the North's secret weapons programme was revealed in October 2002.

Meanwhile, other countries pushed hard for a diplomatic solution. France's Foreign Minister was in Beijing petitioning China which is one of North Koreas few remaining allies. The French President, Jacques Chirac, had said the North Korea has no other choice but to abandon its nuclear programme.

The Japanese Prime Minister also left for Russia another North Korea ally.

Although it said it is willing to talk with the South Korea Pyongyang has not yet replied to a separate offer for dialogue with the United States, which it accused of plotting to attack it, in creating the danger of a nuclear war on the Korean peninsula.

At the same time U.S. said it would not talk with North Korea regarding the issue until it scraped its nuclear weapons programme.

China being the permanent member of the United Nations Security Council and announced itself categorically on North Korea and Iraq, both being the two major global issues of important concern. France another permanent member of the U.N. also supported China and said the North Korea and Iraq is a sensitive issue.

China Called for a direct dialogue between Pyongyang and Washington as the best way to bring the de-nuclearisation of the Korean peninsula. The visit to Beijing by the Foreign Minister of France Dominique de villepin, stressed to maintain the frame work agreement which the U.S. and North Korea had reached in 1994 should be continued and carried out further.

Reacting to China and France demand for the U.S. to have direct talks with North Korea. General Powell had said that U.S. would adopt flexible methods in any manner with the DPRK on the nuclear issue

The Chinese President, Jian Zemin's suggested the next move towards the resolution of the current Iraq tangle should be decided by the U.N. Security Council on the basis of opinion of all the concerned parties and the on going mission of the international weapons inspectors in Iraq should be continued so that the fact on the issue would be clarified.

Based on the arms report submitted to the U.N by Iraq, both United States and Britain had raised objections that the report was incomplete.

Reacting to the objections raised by U.S. and Britain the Iraqi President Chief Scientific Advisor, Amir Al-Saadi, disputed charges and challenged both the countries to prove allegations that Baghdad is hiding weapons of mass destruction. Al-Saadi said there were no gaps and he could specifically tell where to find the answers in the specific pages or tables and information. He also said that those who wore making allegations on Iraq had not red the report.

Amir Al-Saadi said that the similar complaints or allegations wore not mentioned about the Iraqi report by Hans Blix or Mohamed El Baradei, both weapons inspectors deployed by the U.N. to look in for Chemical, Biological and nuclear weapons in Iraq.

Blix already had said Iraq's weapons report failed to support its claims to have destroyed missiles, war heads and chemical weapons such as VX nerve gas.

El Baradei had said he does not yet have enough information to determine that Iraq is trying to develop weapons of mass destruction.

On the other side North Korea vowed to increase the communist army's combat readiness amid accusations that the U.S. is focusing on disarming the North Korea.

South Korean diplomat lobbying Russia for help and officials started preparing to draft a compromise plan to the United States.

North Korea left open the possibility of other countries mediating in the dispute this was an indirect indication that North Korea was attempting to resolve the crisis in a diplomatic resolution.

North Korea said that if there are countries which are concerned for the settlement of the nuclear issue on the Korean peninsula, the proceeding from a far stand should force the U.S. to be committed to the international agreement so that it may stop its unilateral behavior.

Pyongyang blamed the U.S. for trying to disarm the isolated country with demands that North Korea scrap it nuclear programmes, and called the U.S. the main obstacle in Korean reunification.

The Russian Foreign Minister, Alexander Losyukov, agreed that it was important to get all sides to the negotiating table.

The frame work of the solution wore beginning to get started so that North Korea would not feel insecure and will be able to accept the proposal and give up its nuclear programme.

The details of Seoul's settlement plan wore beginning to appear in the media reports and the reports wore suggesting that the proposal would require concessions from both United States and North Korea.

Israel carried out its most ambitious test of the Arrow anti-missile system, firing several interceptors at once at simulated incoming rockets in which was described as a rehearsal for a possible attack by Iraq.

Israel Radio reported that the test was successful, but the Army Radio said the test results wore still being evaluated.

Israel in its nine previous launches only one Arrow was fired each time when it tested but this time several Arrows wore fired.

The test reportedly conducted in the presence of American experts, was seen as a signal to Saddam Hussein that any missile strike could be scuttled by the high-tech system.

While the international community wore trying to avoid a war in Iraq the allied commanders wore drawing up secret plans to fight a war against Iraq entirely at night mainly to avoid the burning heat of the desert summer.

The American front-line troops began to undergo intensive training in preparation for the night combat in the desert land.

As American generals believe that their ability to fight in complete darkness would prove to be an important factor in the out come result of the conflict, as such American troops posses the worlds most advanced battle night-vision equipment.

President Bush, was of the view to delay an attack such that all the military and political factors wore in his favor, mean while American Military commanders wore expecting surprise from the white house for a quick and successful attack against Saddam Hussein.

Saddam Hussein expected that Americans cannot fight a war in summer but it was proved possible with the high technology in the night. In the day times the temperatures could pass 104F (40C) and in such heat troops could easily become tired or dehydrated in case they have to wear heavy suits to protect against chemical or germ warfare.

American commanders chose to fight a war at night as temperatures drop to about 68F (20C) would avoid several drawbacks.

The American solders are trained to use night vision goggles which will enable the solder to view the night darkness in to day light. The U.S. front line solders are also issued with laser marker fitted with their rifles. The laser guided bullet will hit the exact target where the red laser dot on a target is settled and the trigger is pulled.

Night-Vision equipment is also a part of the weapon system in every American battle tanks armored troop carrier helicopters and fighter jet aircrafts.

It is found that only U.S. solders has the benefit of using the Night-Vision goggles with the laser guided rifles where as compared to Britain that provides these equipments only one to every three solders.

The 60,000 strong, Iraq Republican Guard Army is one of the worlds biggest and is equipped with Russian-made T-72 tanks which are fitted with the night vision equipment but majority of Iraqi troops depend on flares and illumination from artillery rounds during night battle is the biggest draw back of Iraq.

The United Nations Monitoring Verification and Inspection Commission (UNMOVIC) were planning to present the Security Council on January 27th 2003. The International community expected that in all likelihood lead to the adoption of another resolution authorizing a necessary means to bring about Iraq's compliance with the demands of the international community.

In case UNMOVIC were to convey to the Council its conclusion that Iraq did not posses and will not have in future the capability to produce WMD the Security Council would not be in a position to take or even endorse any punitive action against Iraq. The Burden of Proof was on Iraq but it was not possible for Iraq to produce such evidence in this case. Iraq got fixed in a no-win situation.

Hans Blix in his statement to the council on 19, December 2002 had said that the inspectors have no occasion behaved in a manner that the Iraqis would be justified in regarding as offensive.

As Blix described it UNMOVIC carried out an inspection on December 13, which was a Friday, the Muslim day of peace. The Iraqi staff was absent, doors were locked and keys were not available. The Iraqis offered to break the doors videotaping the whole event. Finally it was agreed to seal the doors and to carry out the inspection the next day.

The declaration submitted by Iraq on December 7, 2002 as required under Resolution 1441 of U.N. was 12,000 pages long. Hans Blix handed it over to the President of the Security Council in December; the U.S Ambassador of Columbia passed it to White House.

The Americans made copies and gave them to Russia and China in New York and to Britain and France in Washington. Out of the 12,000 original pages only 9,000 page documents was given to the ten non Permanent members.

Norway which protested and refused to accept the expurgated text but the other members did not mind this improper procedure.

Syria which refused to accept the expurgated text was meaning less since it had already voted in favor of 1441 resolution.

The secret behind the removal of three fourth of the declaration was that the removed portion contained sensitive information's. As the permanent members already have the expertise to make all the WMD.

Finally it was clear that the really sensitive information in the Iraq's declaration contained information's related to 150 companies that had business dealing with Iraq in the production of WMD. Iraq's declaration report contained 24 American, 17 Britain, 80 German, and countries such as France, Italy, Switzerland, Japan and Brazil companies.

There wore evidence to prove that most of the weapon development took place before Iraq's invasion on Kuwait in 1990 which led to gulf war one, while some foreign companies wore in business links with Iraq in 2002.

On December 19 Hans Blix informed the Security Council that Iraq had not furnished recent information's. Blix had expressed inconsistencies in Iraq's declaration which leads more clarification related to Chemical, Biological and missile technology that Iraq possessed.

Blix had expressed that despite all the support that technology could support the investigation, there was no guarantee, and that required evidence of secret materials which Iraq was in possession may not be found.

It is in this connection the U.N had given the extensive authority to the weapons inspectors as specified in resolution 1441 that could make Iraq very difficult to keep their weapons development secret.

As the deadline for Hans Blix finds it difficult to submit his report to the Security Council on or before 27, January 2003 regarding the inspection conducted in Iraq by him was yet to be completed, the intolerant America finds the efforts of United Nations inspection chief, Hans Blix, a major obstacle to its plans and wanted to stop inspections on 27, January 2003 and prevent weapon inspectors for producing a new report at the end of

March that could lead to cancellation of sanctions against Iraq.

The U.S. was planning to launch another massive campaign against Saddam Hussein, projecting him as the source of all evil. The U.S President George W. Bush going ahead with his war plans was unclear that January 27 which was seen as a crucial date after which the U.S. could take action over its threat of war against Iraq.

Blix had said that he plans to tell Iraq the situation was very dangerous but Saddam can still prevent war if he provides new evidence about his Nuclear Chemical and Biological weapons programme's.

The message that Blix gave out was that they are in a tense situation and would want Iraq to cooperate more on the substance in particular.

Blix had expressed that there wore major gaps in the 12,000 page declaration and Iraq needed to do a good deal more to provide evidence if there was any room to avoid any worse development. Blix in his findings was of the view that to complain about the list of scientist who worked on programs connected with the development of weapons of mass destruction as provided by Iraq.

Bush administration was attempting to meet the challenges in different ways even as it tries to keep up the military pressure on Saddam Hussein.

United States, President, George W. Bush, who was visibly irritated with some unusually blunt criticism from allies across the Atlantic over its attitude on Iraq, asked allies how much more time had to be given to the Iraqi leader, who in his view was not disarming.

Bush also went on to caution allies of their own history. "Surely our friends have learned lessons from the past. Surely we have learned how Saddam Hussein deceives and delays."

Bush's cautioning his allies was just a separate part of the broader strategy that his administration was resorting to an effort to win over allies at the United Nations Security Council and in the international view as a whole.

The U.S. Deputy Secretary of State, Richard Armitage, argued that, time was running out for any options except war. Armitage said "some people may say there is no smoking gun, but it is clearly visible that there is nothing but smoke."

Senior members of the Bush administration started one-to-one meeting with both permanent and non permanent members of the U.N. Security Council in New York

The Secretary of State, Colin Powell, argued that the Iraqi leader must be disarmed if not peacefully, then by force either one way or other Sadden Hussein must be disarmed.

The biggest problem was coming from France and Germany, and China which are opposed in some way or another to any military strike against Iraq. While France, Russia, China is veto-holding members, Germany was taking over the Presidency of the Security Council for the month of February 2003.

France was the only ally that had given clearest indication of casting a veto on any resolution that was sought on use of force.

The United States came away with unanimous backing in the

Security Council with Syria extending its support but the situation and support over the issue had developed beyond New York meeting.

One of the real critical periods in that ongoing tussle with Iraq wore three things that wore taking place. First, on January 27 the U.N. chief weapons inspector, Hans Blix was submitting his report to the Security Council and the Council had scheduled a session on January 29 to discuss the report in New York. And secondly Bush had scheduled his State of the Union address in Washington, which was his first reaction to the report of Hans Blix.

German Chancellor, Gerhard Schroeder, had hinted at a "no" vote in the United Nations over Iraq. Germany was in the mood or voting "no" or abstains in the situation of a U.N. resolution authorizing the U.S. to launch a military campaign.

The Europeans wore watching the changing situation that Iraq had failed to fulfill the U.N. resolutions and feel strongly that military action against Iraq should not be taken.

After France and Germany was leading the "no" campaign while Greece which was holding routine six monthly rotating presidency of the European Union was trying to evolve a consensus in the European Union forum.

Italy and Spain wore to go along with the U.S. and British line. French Foreign Minister, Dominique de Villepin, had appealed to Europe to adopt a common position and stand up to American pressure for an early military move.

Gerhard Schroeder was to face crucial state elections in the next month. So as to according to the political strategy Schroeder in an election campaign speech had said "We will not take part in a military intervention in Iraq, and that was exactly Germany voting behavior will be in all international bodies."

The German public opposition to war against Iraq had hardened and according to the opinion polls, more than 80% Germans believed an attack against Iraq was not justified.

"Blood for Oil" was the front page headline in the German magazine Der Spiegel, which carried front page news which was actually the feelings of the Germans.

As a regular strategy U.S. reconnaissance mission continued on the Iraq territory and as usual Pilot less Predator drone which entered the Iraq from Kuwait was shot down by the Iraqi anti-aircraft defence forces. This was the second drone which was shot down in just month duration

The Iraqi military spokesman addressing the media announced "the U.S. surveillance plane that violated Iraq's international airspace is used by the U.S. enemy to spy an Iraqi civilian and military installations and it is a very sophisticated spy plane with advance electronic equipment."

The moral of the Iraqi forces increased with the downing of the second U.S. drone. The Iraqi forces pledged to President, Saddam Hussein, that the Iraqi forces would strike any hand that wants to harm the security and sovereignty of Iraq's airspace, land and water.

The U.S. drone which fly at a low speed of about 240 km an hour or less. The Iraqi spokesman said at least three other drown had been shot down by Iraqi forces in the past two years.

The U.S. Under-Secretary of State for Arms Control and International Security, John Bolton, who was in Seoul to discuss the issue over the North Korea Nuclear Issue as the ninth round of Inter Korean ministerial meeting was going on. He held talks with the South Korean Foreign Affairs Minister, Choi Sung hog, and it's Defence Minister, Lee Jun. he said the threatening crisis over Pyongyang's actual disposition would be brought before the United Nations Security Council as early.

North Korea making assurance in the inter Korean ministerial meeting had assured that it was not thinking of fabricating nuclear weapons in the current situation. However it reacted strongly to the U.S. diplomat's suggestion that the puzzle over Pyongyang's nuclear weapons programme could be taken up by the U.N. Security Council soon.

The DPRK sought to reserve the right to resume missile tests in the new scenario. However North Korea did not make immediate reactions to the statement made by DPRK as North Korea was playing the issue very diplomatically and remained within the bounds of the Nuclear Non-Proliferation Treaty.

North Korean Nuclear Programme was in line with the U.S. led consortium and the Korean Peninsula Energy Development Organisation (KEDO) was working on the electricity needs of North following its Agreements of 1994 with the United States.

The U.S. President George W. Bush reacting to the North Korean leader Kim Jong II, had said that "no heart for somebody who starves his folks." Bush further said that he was confident a peaceful conclusion could be reached in the nuclear standoff on the Korean Peninsula.

The U.S. spokesman, Richard Boucher said "exile is the only options for Saddam Hussein." and considering it or not is left to him. "The certainty of coalition forces prevailing if it comes to military action should make him consider any other options he might have."

Speaking to journalists, in Texas, President Bush, kept skepticism, that Saddam Hussein, would voluntarily give up any biological, nuclear or chemical weapons. "He has to understand that his day of reckoning is coming".

President, Bush trident to make it clear, about his stand on Iraq that he was not on an inevitable path to war with Saddam Hussein. "I am hopeful we won't have to go to war, and hopefully Iraqi leader will realize we are serious and hopefully he disarms peacefully."

CHAPTER - 4

Comparing the tense U.S. relations with Iraq and North Korea, President Bush, said "the standoff with North Korea was a diplomatic issue and not a military issue". Bush expressed "I believe the situation with North Korea will be resolved peacefully".

President, Bush, pointed out at the economic situation of North Korea, he said "one of the reasons why the people are starving in North Korea is because the leaders have not seen to it that their economy is strong or they have to be fed".

North Korean Ambassador to China, Chow Jin-su, told reporters in Beijing that the nuclear arms controversy should be resolved by Pyongyang and Washington themselves diplomatically.

North Korea stressed for its diplomatic case for a new deal with the United States regarding its sovereign rights to posse's nuclear weapons.

North Korea had a different game plan to influence on the international community as the first step in any such situation.

However the diplomatic observers in the region believe that the South Korean, President, Roh-Huyn himself may not have not given a definitive shape to the concession that he might design a compromise draft that could be discussed and suitably agreed by U.S. and North Korea.

North Korea aware of the South Korean initiative, its envoy in Beijing Choe Jin su insisted that any unconditional talks between Washington and Pyongyang, if organised by other countries should be understood in the existing ground realities.

North Korea was of the view that U.S. hostile stance on DPRK was well understood and with its war style thinking is threatening Pyongyang with the possible use of nuclear weapons against it.

For the international community it appeared both United States and North Korea had locked themselves in to a chain of provocation which may lead to disastrous consequences as it revolves round the issue of North Korea acquisition of a nuclear weapon capability.

The regular provocation from the North Korea side had been its warning that it was not presently able to meet commitments under the Nuclear Non Proliferation Treaty (NPT) since the U.S. had threatened to launch a preemptive nuclear strike.

What was more worrisome was that Pyongyang specified that the commitment it would not be able to commit to the obligation of states possessing nuclear weapons to not use them against other states that do not have such weapons.

North Korea had already declared that it possess a nuclear weapon capability, this statement was understood that it was a threat to use such weapons against U.S. allies, South Korea and Japan, in a situation if Washington launched a preemptive strike.

Pyongyang's new threat had followed close to military action it had taken to evade international monitoring of its nuclear capability. North Korea had shown the root back to the weapons monitors who wore in North Korea representing the International Atomic Energy Agency.

The observers found that the cameras wore disabled set up to observe sites connected with the nuclear programme and broken the seals that has restricted the access to reach the facility for the technicians.

North Korean scientists had began work on making two facilities, one research reactor that can produce plutonium and the second one was a fuel reprocessing plant that was in progress. If the facilities wore put in to full operation capability, North Korea could produce weapon grade plutonium for five nuclear weapons in just six months.

The inclusion of North Korea in the "axis of evil" by President,. Bush had taken the U.S. administration more aggressive attitude towards Pyongyang taken a far more aggressive than any body had expected.

United States had forced a disclosure from North Korea that it has also tried to become a nuclear weapon state by the uranium enrichment process, slowed down the multi lateral programme to build light water reactors to generate electricity and cut all the fuel and oil supplies.

While United States took these measures by force and cap the North Korean nuclear programme back in to the bottle. However Washington was able only to realize Pyongyang that the U.S. administration was questioning on its commitments under the frame work signed by the two countries in 1994.

North Korea had strong motive that it can take a tough stance since it had reasons to understand that it is not in the vicinity to become the target of United States as in the case of Iraq.

The South Korean Capital Seoul and majority of the U.S. military camp in that country wore well in the reach of artillery range of North Korean target and Pyongyang was targeting Japan as its missiles could his any part of Japan in just minutes.

Probably the U.S. administration knew the fact that their troops and allies in East Asia wore in a dangerous position and an attack by North Korean forces had made Washington to move its strategy against North Korea in a cautious manner rather than the aggressive policy enforced on Iraq.

Understanding the Unites States vulnerable condition Bush said that his belief for bold diplomacy could solve the problem rather than confronting with North Korea. It was well understood that with this decision of President, Bush the imposition of economic sanctions on North Korea by the United States and its allies was the next step.

South Korea had declared that it will not enforce economic sanctions or participate in such activity against North Korea as such pressure and isolation tactics do not work with communist countries.

After going through all the pros and consequences the U.S. administration was forced to take the experiences from the past and decided to begin a new phase of diplomatic talks with North Korea.

The diplomatic process regarding the North Korean issue began again with China and South Korea coming closer together than at any time before. The diplomatic front meeting began in Beijing between the visiting South Korean Deputy Foreign Minister, Lee Tae-sik, and the Chinese Deputy foreign Minister, Wang Yi.

The effort of Beijing and Seoul to prevent further escalation on the current crisis over the North Korean nuclear issue was the highlight of the meeting. However, North Korea did not show any sign of coming out of its outburst against United States and Japan as it claimed was its sovereign rights to become a nuclear state.

Pongyang's argument was that Japan was going back on the commitment it had made in their joint declaration that took place between the Japanese Prime Minister, Junichiro Koizumi and North Korean Leader, Kim Jong-il, a few months ago.

While U.S. was preparing for a war with Iraq it was also making a last effort to disarm Iraq and to bring an end to the regime of Iraqi President, Saddam Hussein, without using military force.

According to diplomatic sources U.S. through Britain issued fresh ultimatum to Iraq to surrender its weapon of mass destruction or face war. It is said the Syrian President, Bashar al Assad, conveyed this ultimatum to Saddam Hussein.

The visit of U.N. Chief Weapons Inspector, Hans Blix, to Iraq in the middle of January 2003 to present Baghdad an opportunity to make its declaration. If Saddam Hussein did this fulfillment then he could live in exile in a country of his choice. In case Hussein rejects the offer the choice for U.S. was to build up military force against Iraq.

The U.S. preparation for a war was still incomplete as only two aircraft carriers wore present in the region however the U.S. needed another two carriers before a war against Iraq. Along with the carriers the U.S. was planning to position four army divisions in Kuwait.

Iraq surprisingly submitted a long list of 500 names of scientist involved in its missile development, nuclear, chemical and biological weapons programmes.

Along with the new list of scientists involved Iraq also showed the way to the U.N. weapons inspectors about a secret Iraqi nuclear project. This move by Iraq was seen as a signal to Washington to accommodate it's so called more proofs to avoid a war.

The British, Foreign Secretary, Jack Straw, statement in London came shocking to Iraqis as Britain had avoided linking Iraq with terrorism and the British government had kept distance from Washington's "axis of evil" theory, when he said Saddam Hussein regime and terror groups such as Al-Qaeda were part of the same picture and warned both posed a similar threat to world peace.

According to Jack Straw, Iraq, Iran and North Korea wore linked to terrorist groups and were quoted as "rouge" states. They wore the most likely sources of technology and knowhow for terrorist organisation. He quoted Iraq was a "litmus test" of the international community's determination to make sure that these states comes under the non proliferation treaty.

Jack Straw was of the view that terrorism and rough regimes wore part of the same picture and Britain's aim was to disrupt and eliminate terrorist groups which might attempt to acquire weapon of mass destruction and at the same time it was necessary to deter and remove the threat posed by hostile or unstable states which posses or pursuing weapon of mass destruction.

Jack Straw's statement was particularly and specifically on the threat posed by the rouge states and terrorism, the urgency to deal with both with equal severity. He made it clear that Iraqi disarmament whether achieved peacefully or by force was essential both for the world and the United Nations.

In Iraq the President, Saddam Hussein, finds something suspicious over the United Nations weapons inspector's functioning. He accused that the inspectors wore interested in collecting the names of Iraqi scientists, asking questions to them that indicates hidden agenda and wore gathering information's about military facilities instead of searching for nuclear, chemical and biological weapons though Iraq has denied possessing such weapons, but America and Britain had accused Iraq of hiding banned arms.

The Whitehouse spokesman, Ari Fleisher, denied Saddam Hussein's allegations, saying the U.N. had sanctioned the mission of the inspectors, the Iraqi leaders remarks wore unfortunate and the work of the weapons needed to continue until its findings wore over.

The U.S., President, Bush, had threatened to attack Iraq and bring an end to Hussein's regime if it did not eliminate all weapons of mass destruction as required by the U.N. resolution adopted after Iraq invade Kuwait in 1990.

The Iraqi Vice President, Taha Yassin Ramadan accused the new inspectors of gathering intelligence for Washington and Israel and their work is to spy on Iraq. In 1988, the previous U.N. monitoring program collapsed amid Iraqi-U.N. disputes over alleged U.S. spying within the U.N. operation.

As Ramadan's allegations continued a surprise search in one of Hussein's palaces went on.

Quickly a spokes man Ewen Buchanan, for chief inspector Hans Blix had made it clear that anyone found working for individual government would be fired.

The spokesman Melissa Fleming, for U.N. International Atomic Energy Agency said if the inspectors are gathering intelligence, it is intelligence for U.N.

President, Saddam Hussein speaking to his country men said truth and justice were on their side "we are in our country and whoever is in his own homeland and is forced to face an enemy that stands on the side of falsehood and comes as an aggressor from beyond seas and oceans will no doubt emerge triumphant". Speaking further he said "we shall thank the almighty if he guides the enemies to the right path and he also would be grateful if god destroys them.

Encouraging the courage of the Iraqi forces Hussein said he knew his military would stand by its oath to protect the mother land.

The United States was assembling a ground force for a possible invasion of Iraq that could exceed 1,00,000 troops and include three or four heavy armed divisions, an air born division and an assortment of Special Operations forces, U.S. military sources wore giving this information's to the selected media.

The U.S. army had summoned commanders of four of its best equipped and most capable divisions for an exercise called "Victory Scrimmage" at the end of the month, in which commanders will use computer simulations to run through Iraq war scenarios.

It could be understood that the size of the U.S. force could reach as high as 2,50,000 but the actual size of divisions wore not confermed.

The Iraqi Republican Guard had about 80,000 troops and President, Saddam Hussein's Special Republican Guard has about 15,000 troops. There wore an additional of 3,00,000 solders in Iraq's regular army.

The U.S. ground forces had enormous advantage in technology, firepower and mobility that would almost confirmed that any invasion with the advantage of total support of the air force.

The U.S. ground forces wore sure to have the benefit as the MIAI tanks of the first Armored Division had almost twice the range of Iraq's remaining 600 T-72 tanks, which could be targeted by laser guided Hellfire missiles from miles away from an Apache gunship.

The U.S. was preparing that it prefers the U.N. to deal with the issue but if it does not do so it will invade Iraq to disarm Saddam Hussein with the supporting allies.

After the one day consultation in Moscow, both Russia and South Korea rejected pressure tactics in solving the North Korean nuclear issue and called for a resumption of dialogue between Washington and Pyongyang. The pressure tactics cannot be accepted in resolving the standoff and the legitimate rights of all sides must be respected.

Both Russia and South Korea speaking to Itar-Tass news agency criticizes the U.S. which triggered the current crisis by halting fuel oil supplies to North Korea and this is in violation of the 1994 accord. Russia's Deputy Foreign Minister, Alexander Losyukov, said the Russia's involvement was essential as it was the only G-8 country having good relations with North Korea.

North Korea remained firm about its need for self defensive military capability, as the U.S. decided to give the communist nation a second chance to abandon is secret weapons programme. It also dismissed claims by U.S. that North Korea had made achievement further in acquiring nuclear capability and was a threat to the region.

The International Atomic Energy Agency's board of governors was to convene an emergency session to discuss the dispute. The North Korean Central News Agency coated that the IAEA officials saying it would like to give one more chance to North Korea to abandon its nuclear weapon's program and readmit U.N. inspectors expelled a month ago before the dispute was settled in the Security Council.

In responding to the twin suicide bombings in Tel Aviv in which 3 people died and 114 people wore injured the Israeli helicopters did target what was said to be a facility in the Gaza Strip that was manufacturing mortar shells with the support of Palestinian leader, Yasser Arafat's Fatah faction.

The militant organization in Palestine took responsibility for the attack in Tel Avive, but the Fatha denied any connection with the attack. In this connection Israel decided to prevent Palestinian delegates from attending a mid-January International Conference on West Asia in London.

The Palestinian Authorities sought International intervention to lift the ban imposed by Israel on vehicle traffic beside it had stopped transfer of money to the Palestinian Authority, so that the Palestinian security forces can take action against the perpetrators of this attack.

The Israeli Prime Minister, Ariel Sharon's office condemned the attack, and said Israel had no choice but to fight terrorism with a fury.

United States did not want to handle the Palestinian situation, which had Pan-Arab implications, which could worsen this time and could divert its attention from development in Israel.

The North Korean Ambassador to China, Cho Jn-su, announced in a news conference "we believe we cannot go along with the self imposed missile moratorium any longer because all agreements have been mollified by the United States side." With this North Korea increased its aggressive strategy against U.S. and announced its readiness to conduct the missile flight test that had remained stagnant for more than two years. This was also an indication to the U.S. that North Korea would conduct testing of ballistic missiles and the production of nuclear weapons.

North Korea announced that "if the U.S. drops its hostile policy to stifle the DPRK and stops Washington's nuclear threat to the DPRK, the DPRK may prove through a separate verification between the DPRK and the U.S., that Pyongyang does not make any nuclear weapon".

North Korean neighbors made a swift move for diplomatic action in a different level immediately after North Korea made its announcement and Japan was the first neighbor to make a move in this regard.

The phase of the negotiations was so quick that Russia and Japan held a summit; South Korea and Japan had consultations with each other. U.S. was in touch with China and France had talks with South Korea.

The Iraqi leader Saddam Hussein was not able to please the U.N. Chief Weapons Inspector in spite of disclosing all its weapons programme and handed over reports weighing several kilos to Hans Blix.

Hans Blix criticism was that the whereabouts of thousands of warheads filled with poisonous gas which includes mustered gas and anthrax which wore unable to trace by weapons inspectors. The particulars of these weapons wore not disclosed whether these weapons Iraq posses or claimed that those weapons wore destroyed.

Hans Blix was under the pressure of United States for not questioning of scientists who had worked on weapons programmes in Iraq and to find where the weapons of mass destruction are hidden. However the U.S. experts wore of the view on three theories: the weapons were hidden in Iraq, shifted to some foreign country or secretly destroyed.

United States experts wore of the view that they had proofs that Saddam Hussein had destroyed some parts of Iraq's biological and chemical weapons after the attack on world trade centre on September 11.

Though Iraqi leader Saddam Hussein had expressed that he had nothing to do with the attack on world trade centre, but Washington had the suspicion that the terror attack had the links to Iraq.

The real mistake that Iraqi's did was that they did not correctly document the weapons of mass destruction which was also the actual duty of the United Nations Monitoring, Verification and Inspection Commission.

Even today many Iraqis believe Saddam Hussein has stored the weapons of mass destruction in underground shelters under the Tigris River. Some believe that the weapons have been handed over to terrorist organization.

Regarding the questioning of scientists Hans Blix had not found a solution that satisfies U.S., U.N. or Iraq. Though several interviews of scientists had take place in the presence of an Iraqi official group, Hans Blix was of the view that it was difficult to get honest answers from difficult questions that to in the presence of Iraqi officials.

The United States suggested removing of scientists along with their families out of Iraq in case the weapons inspectors failed to "spill their guts" and find the answer.

United States was of the view that if scientist wore taken abroad or questioned in sound-proof conditions in Iraq the scientists wore expected to spill out the troths. However the U.N. was of the opinion and said "we cannot simply deport people against their will", or interrogated scientists or practice torture.

United States decided to build up more pressure on Iraqi leader and in this regard U.S. Defence Secretary Donald Rumsfeld, signed the single largest deployment order since the Pentagon began its forces build up in the Gulf region. Almost 35,000 American troops, including two large marine units wore getting orders.

The troop's departure for the potential war zone was getting ready and spreading of troops was planned to position at Camp Lejeune, North Carolina, about 7,000 marines wore ready to leave for the destination. The second amphibious task force of about 7,000 marines wore also ordered to be deploying for the West Cost.

Playing out the diplomatic cards in Washington, New York and world capitals apart, pressure was also kept on Iraq by the Bush administration and was taking a tough stance on Iraq and in the perceptions of allies, was then trying to soften its image for the domestic and foreign audiences and was creating the impression that it might be flexible on the time frame at the U.N. if that could be a way to win back support in the New York and later in the U.N. security council.

The Bush administration which was facing protest internally and from overseas was trying to play alone but had made the point that if nations such as France and Germany decided to sit on the sidelines it was their prerogative and business.

"I don't think we will have to worry about going to war along", the Secretary of State, Colin Powell, was of the view that he might get support from British counterpart, Jack Straw on the intentions of the U.S. that it reserved the right to act alone if the United Nations did not provide the lead in Iraq.

Colin Powell was of the view that if the United Nations did not take a lead role in the possible war with Iraq then "I am quite confident if it comes to that, we will be joined by many nations and I consider that it will be a strong coalition".

Referring to the report of the U.N. weapons inspector Hans Blix who was to submit his report in the next two days to the U.N. Security Council, General Powell had said that "this was the beginning of a debate and not the end of the debate and U.S. was prepared to listen to others and find a way for the crisis".

The U.S. administration was trying out efforts in a variety of ways on Iraq, particularly as it was aiming for a possible military strike against the Saddam Hussein regime in Iraq. Domestically the Bush administration was finding a major challenge by way of public opinion and sentiments on Capital Hill.

According to the poll survey nearly 63 per cent of Americans wanted the President, George W. Bush, to find a diplomatic solution and the inspections process run their full course and later on to support military forces to topple Saddam Hussein.

United Nations weapons inspector Hans Blix report was seen to be critical that the Bush administration could use the report as its final basis for launching a military strike against Iraq. The top weapons inspector was scheduled to give his report to the Council in the form of a speech and not a detailed point by point assessment of his mission that began in November 2002.

The assessment of Blix is subjected to some intense questioning by members of the Security Council where there was a clear and major split among the permanent members on how to proceed in the aftermath of the report.

The Bush administration went on to the extent of directing the U.N. weapons inspector Hans Blix what to do and what not to do, U.S. wanted Blix to confine his report to various aspects of Iraq compliance of Security Council Resolution particularly to weapons inspections and not look for a "smoking gun".

However the Assistant Secretary of State for Non Proliferation, John Wolf, is said to have argued that it was not the job of the weapons inspectors to look either for a smoking gun or a needle in a haystack. "I think there are a number of questions. We look forward to hearing whether there was anything from Baghdad that answers those questions. We have not seen it".

In Britain Prime Minister, Tony Blair was facing Public anger against his Iraq policy when he was surrounded at a Labour Party function in London, while anti war protesters shouted slogans outside the venue.

Blair was forced to use an indirect door to enter the building to avoid protesters who had gathered at the main entrance of the South Camden Community School where he later addressed party activists about his government's policy reforms.

The growing public anger was such a student of the London School of Economics; Ian Wilson interrupted and protested in the midway of Blair's speech that the Prime Minister was missing the point over Iraq. A section of the audience also supported his remarks.

Though visibly embarrassed, Blair had said "this is a democracy and you are entitled to make a speech but I am making my speech now. You can go and make our speech somewhere else".

Wilson was grabbed by security men and escorted him out of the building. This incident came as a new opinion poll trend that a majority of 81 percent of the people in Britain were opposing an attack on Iraq without a fresh U.N. mandate.

South Korea took the initiative of scheduling a mission to the North Korea by a presidential envoy, even as a top U.S. trouble shooter consulted Japan on ways to resolve the question of Pyongyang's nuclear profile through peaceful methods.

South Korean President, Kim Dae-jung, nominated his Special National Security Advisor, Lim Dong-won, to visit Pyongyang with a mandate to carry out a reality check in the specific context of the nuclear crisis between the two sides. The South Korean objective was to capitalise on the existing comfort level with North Korea to explore a realistic solution of the present crisis through diplomatic method.

Finally in the inter-Korean ministerial meeting the two sides agreed to cooperate actively in solving the nuclear issue peacefully. However the joint statement on these lines wore found short of the South Korea's expectations of being able to persuade the North Korean's to renounce its ongoing nuclear weapons programme.

The chief delegate and Cabinet Councilor of the DPRK, Kim Ryong Song, supported the joint statement and also stressed the South Korean acceptability. DPRK's general refrain was that the nuclear issue could be settled only through bilateral talks with the United States.

However the South Korea's unification minister and chief delegate, Jeong se-hyun, noted that the accord with the DPRK was not totally satisfying. The point underlined was that the two countries had agreed to continue the dialogue. The renewed inter Korean dialogue did not deliver either DPRK's preference for a bilateral talks with United States or the Japan-U.S. multilateral approach.

The Japanese Foreign Minister, Yoriko Kawaguchi, had dialogue with the U.S. Undersecretary of State, John Bolton, in Tokyo and insisted that the issue of imposing U.N. sanctions on the North Korea should be handled carefully.

Finally Japan and the U.S. agreed at the decision that Tokyo, Seoul and Washington would act jointly as regards Pyongyang's nuclear issue within the jurisdiction of either the International Atomic Energy Agency or the United Nation.

As public protest began in America over the possible attack

on Iraq by the allied forces the Bush administration started giving the impression that it is weighing options of allowing the weapons inspections process of Iraq run its full course, however the bottom line consideration will be if the inspections are productive.

The Change in the U.S. policy came on the eve of a report which was to delivered by the chief weapons inspector, Hans Blix, to the Security Council in the next 24 hours time and a discussion the matter was scheduled to take place the next week.

As Blix was to submit his report in the form of a speech his findings in the past 60 days in Iraq, the impression was that while the top United Nations official wore seeking Iraqi President, Saddam Hussein's cooperation, and would not interfere in the entire process as to avoid waste of time.

It was expected that Blix would be focusing on lack of sufficient data, Baghdad's conditions on U-2 spy flights and allowing inspectors to question Iraqi scientists and officials without much embarrassment.

Blix had said before that while Iraq had come clean on the volume of the date sent already but the substance was not enough. The investigation in the matter was going well in some areas like the access and prompt access. But there wore several areas in which the U.N. was not satisfied.

The Bush administration was in confusion on how much material and information it could gather on Iraq fearing that further this could hamper the intelligence gathering process and have to waste time in taking a decision.

Baghdad was helping the weapons inspectors looking for weapons of mass destruction inside Iraq. But on one thing that Washington was quite dissatisfied about it is Baghdad's refusal to fully cooperate on the interrogation of its scientist's and their families wore facing death penalty in the event of cooperation with the U.N.

The Bush administration was now thinking of changing its strategy and go on an early deadline for the start of military action against Iraq, it was not only on the reasons of objections from key allies in Europe.

Pressure from the senior Republicans started forming from the Capital Hill which the white house could not so easily brush aside. The Chairman of the senate Foreign Relations Committee, Richard Lugar, had said that he thought inspections would be continued to its full length.

Another Republican on the Committee, Chuck Hagel, had warned Bush administration against any rush to war in the absence of a multilateral coalition might lead to dangerous consequences.

In spite of all the talks of the U.S. forces being kept ready to carry out the strike, but the fact in and around Iraq was entirely different and transporting required military forces to the area was a big role to be played.

The first assessment was that the ground, navel and air force would not be in position for a full scale attack for another two months by giving the U.N. more time and the Bush administration was trying its strategy on both ways so that the allies would get the impression of listening to their opinions and at the same time giving more time to the war planners for preparation.

In Baghdad a man holding three knives tried to enter the building where U.N. arms inspectors wore housed, he was stopped by the Iraqi guards and the United Nations security persons. The intruder appeared to be an Iraqi in his 20s and was holding the knives in his hands.

The U.N. arms experts left the building after a short while and headed for at least five sites suspected of producing weapons of mass destruction. Another person jumped into one of the inspector's cars as it was moving and tried to grab documents before Iraqi guards seized him. Reuter's news agency reported.

To avoid a war in Iraq the Iraq's neighbors met in Turkey had held talks with Germany to coordinate a common approach. In seeking to expand the peace camp the Foreign Ministers of Turkey, Syria, ran Jordan Saudi Arabia and Egypt who held their consultations in Istanbul met the German, Foreign Minister, Joschka Fischer, who also began a visit to Turkey at the same time.

Fischer also held separate meetings with all the diplomats at Istanbul's Ciragan Palace hotel where the conference was held. His meeting with the Syrian Foreign Minister, Farouk al Shara, had special significance as both Syria and Germany wore non permanent members of the United Nations Security Council and could directly influence at the highest level in the U.N.

Syria opposed the unilateral attack by the United States on Iraq. Both Syria and Germany expressed that the U.N. alone can implement the U.N. Security Council resolution 1441.

Arab, Germany, France and Russia decided to work together to resolve the Iraq's disarmament through peaceful menace under the U.N. framework. Iraq's neighbors said that their consultations in Turkey should be seen as the beginning of a process which was likely to see more intensive consultations among themselves in further developments on the issue.

The meeting of the five Arab countries Foreign Ministers decided to approach France and Germany that the U.N. weapons inspectors in Iraq should be allowed to continue till their investigation is over. These regional players wanted United States to stop taking unilateral military action against Iraq and insisted that the U.N. Security Council pass a fresh resolution and sanction any other action to disarm Iraq.

The Secretary of State, Colin Powell, in some unusual observations about the attitude of France on the ongoing crisis expressed that Paris will come to the understanding of the need for such a strategy and the importance of such a strategy. Gen. Powell stressed that the U.S. would stick with that strategy.

Before the final formulation of Security Council resolution 1441, France held out for about eight weeks and has now made the point that any attempt by Washington to have its way in the Council later on the report of the weapons inspectors could be met with a veto. In the non permanent category at the Council, Germany was with France.

President, George W. Bush, responding to the international and domestic criticism beside showing frustration and irritation with allies who wore seeking more time for the Iraqi process at the U.N. "There will be serious consequences for the dictator in Iraq, and there will be serious consequences for any Iraqi general or soldier who wore to use weapons on our troops or on innocent lives".

The fact that, Bush was using every opportunity to warn Saddam Hussein, regime in Iraq, of serious consequences in the event of a war, this had been considered and understood that a war may just be a few weeks away.

The policies and attitude of the Republican administration was questionable and there was a growing feeling within U.S. that the Whitehouse had not fully proved justification and the reason for heading towards war.

Apart from all the adversaries and criticism the daily announcement of build up force in the Persian Gulf was indicating that U.S. forces are ready to strike.

Finally Chairman of the Joint Chief of Staff, General Richard Myers announced "We are ready now".

The Hans Blix mission was to achieve the two core objectives of the U.S. and that was to disarming Iraq and changing Saddam Hussein regime. In case Blix visit failed to make progress in the direction that U.S. was expecting the countdown for a war could begin.

The U.S. President after making such high voltage talks against Saddam Hussein was now firmly committing himself to a regime change in Iraq; Bush had no option, but to carry out the decision. In case he failed to take decision he would have to face grave political embarrassment both domestically and internationally.

Iraq's neighbors had subsequently steeped up the pressure on Saddam Hussein to go into exile voluntarily.

General Myers visit to Turkey signaled the U.S. commitment to give a final shape to the Northern Front that is likely to be opened up against Iraq in case of a war.

Protesters world wide wore shouting "No" to U.S. war plans against Iraq." I hardly see a threat from Iraq" said a poster of Plymouth Congregational Church in Washington. Another poster said "The threat is the United States being a bully, the bully on the play ground"

More than 3,000 Palestinians marched in support of Saddam Hussein in Gaza City, with Iraqi flags and pictures of the Iraqi leader Saddam Hussein. Shouting slogans, "our beloved Saddam, strike Tel Aviv".

In Sao Paulo, Brazil, hundreds of people shouted slogans in front of the American Consulate and burnt a U.S. flag. The student groups also burnt a flag outside the U.S. Embassy in Buenos Aires.

The U.S. armada carrying 10,000 sailors and marines set sail from San Diego navel base for duty in the Gulf for a possible war with Iraq. Already 60,000 U.S. troops wore in the Gulf region and the additional 67,000 troops to join in the coming weeks and the total size of the U.S. force against Iraq was about 2,50,000.

The amphibious transport ship USS Dubuque left next followed by amphibious assault ship and mini aircraft carrier USS Bonhomie Richard as well as the USS Cleveland transport ship. US Navy 3rd Fleet Commander Jackie Yost said "every thing is going smoothly so far", as his sailors left their families to the Gulf region. The amphibious assault ship USS Boxer and dock landing ships USS Anchorage and USS Pearl Harbor were set to flow the ships that wore already on their way for the Gulf.

Family members of U.S. military men crowded hugging each other as their loved ones sailed out into the Gulf region. "This was their job to fight for our country and a good cause" said the wife of a soldier who had lost count of how many times her husband had left home.

Iraq's neighbors met in Istanbul to find ways to delay and to avoid a war in Iraq. The two stage strategy was framed by the Foreign Ministers of Syria, Iran, Saudi Arabia, Jordan, and Egypt looking for a solution that could help Iraq to disarm as well as meet the U.S. demands to change regime in Iraq.

CHAPTER - 5

France one of the members of the Security Council had threatened to veto a war resolution without allowing the weapons inspectors to complete their course. With the disadvantage from France it was difficult for the U.S. to get the U.N. nod for military action; besides this Jordan had stated that it will not allow the use of its territory or airspace for military action against Iraq. Lack of cooperation from Jordan the U.S. was finding it difficult to open a western front against Iraq.

Turkey which is a North Atlantic Treaty Organisation (NATO) member was yet to come under the collective pressure of the grouping, as the military alliance itself was reluctant to come to an understanding in support of a war.

The Polarization of international politics and opinion on the Iraqi crisis became more disadvantageous to United States as China made a similar statement with France and Germany on the diplomatic side of the spectrum. China as the only Asian country among the permanent members of the United Nations Security Council was one among the group of nations which opposed individuality of using military force in disarming Iraq.

The Chinese Foreign Ministry spokeswoman, Zhang Qiyue, in Beijing expressed hopes to resolve the Iraqi crisis through diplomatic and political means under the guidelines of the U.N.

The Australian Prime Minister, John Howard, flagged of a batch of military personal that set sail on a mission of pre deployment of forcers for a potential war with Iraq. The opposition circles in Australia were of the opinion that U.N. should be first allowed to explore the possibility of a peaceful settlement on the Iraq crisis.

Activists of Turkey's Human Rights association conducted a demonstration out side the Incirlik town, the place where a major NATO military base was situated, which was used for implementing a no fly zone in northern part of Iraq.

The State Department's Assistant Secretary for eastern affairs, William Burns, held first discussions with the Syrian President, Bashar al Assad, and secondly with the King of Bahrain, Sheikh Hamad bin Issa Al Khalifa, along with the U.S. Central Command, Gen. Tommy Franks.

A 150 member delegation from the United States, team completed site survey of some airbase and ports in Turkey, which was later decided to be, modernized for the benefit of U.S. military purpose in case the war with Iraq was the ultimate decision.

Meanwhile Jordan had declared that it will not allow the use of its airspace and territory for launching of a military attack on Iraq. In this regard the head of NATO's Europe allied forces also arrived in Turkey to hold talks with the Jordanian leaders, with the intention that without the use of Jordanian support the U.S. would find it difficult to open the western front against Iraq.

The U.S. war planners wore working with the intention that the occupation of western Iraq apart from mounting military pressure on Baghdad was also seen necessary for avoiding Iraq to position Scud Missiles that could reach any part of Israel.

The Bush administration started working on to provide packages for Jordan, Turkey and Israel that the total package was $30 billions over a period of time. Out of the total package Turkey was expected to receive $14 Billion in the form of loan in exchange for cooperation in a possible war with Iraq.

Taking advantage of the situation Israel placed a request to the U.S. administration to provide $4 Billions in additional military assistance and $8 Billions in loan guarantees. Israel was already the highest beneficiary and aid receiver which amounted to $3 Billion in mostly military assistance every year. The new aid package was announced by Washington in addition to the existing U.S. commitments.

The Jordanian Prime Minister, Ali Abdul Ragheb, willfully expressed that Jordan would not take part in any military action against Iraq, even if sanctioned by the United Nations. He was of the view that Iraq's stability and its territorial integrity was extremely important for the Arabs in the region. Reminding the history he had said no foreign power has occupied an Arab Country after the disruption of the Ottoman Empire.

The French Foreign Minister Dominique de Villepin expressed "in the event of a second resolution we will not associate ourselves with military intervention that is not supported by the international community". He further said "if Washington want to war with Iraq without authorization of the Security Council that would be a victory for the law of the strongest".

A group of British nationals headed by Ken Nichols O'Keefe, which had no political affiliation and belonging to all races and ages spending their own expenses wore also collecting funds for the Iraqi people went on a 5000 km road journey that would lead nearly 10,000 people to Baghdad where they plan to form a human shield against any U.S. led military strike on Iraq.

The British group was planned to travel through Europe in a double-decker bus and two black London cabs as a peace convoys to show the solidarity of British nationals with common Iraqis. Following this another bigger convoy was expected to travel to Baghdad two week later.

Keefe, a former U.S. marine, who took part in the 1981 Gulf War, had since renounced his U.S. citizenship because of U.S. foreign policy and became a peace campaigner who has tapped into the widespread anti war sentiment and had decided to organize the largest symbolic protest.

The protesting volunteers before leaving London submitted a memorandum to the British Prime Minister's office with the list of their names and locations in Iraq where they would try and protect by forming human shield; the locations included Hospitals, Schools, Power instillations, and important oil fields.

Tony Benn, the veteran Labour leader who strongly opposed to British supporting the American military moves, was also on the convoy to Baghdad to explore the prospects of peace.

With just 24 hours left for the United Nations weapons inspector Hans Blix to submit his report to the Security Council the stage was set to make all the difference between war and peace of the crisis in West Asia.

Blix was to submit his assessment of the first 60 days of his inspection in Iraq followed by the question and answer session and 48 hours later the Security Council had scheduled the discussions on the report to find a peaceful resolution in the on going showdown with Saddam Hussein.

Blix was expected to be critical of Iraq over the questioning of scientists but it was sure that his criticism would fall short of what George W. Bush, was expecting. In fact the Bush administration wanted a wholesale condemnation of Iraq. On several occasion Blix had said that Iraq could have done much better in the cooperation with the weapons inspector.

Iraq had to give the explanations to the Security Council regarding the destruction of weapons that is capable of carrying chemical, biological weapons, this was the serious issue that was raised by the United Nations itself and the answers had to come from questioning the Iraqi scientists.

The Bush administration wanted Blix to list the violations by Iraq as much as possible so that those points could be used to clear other members who wore not supporting Washington. In fact the Bush administration did not want the inspections to continue further and wanted U.N. to authorize the use of force in Iraq.

President, George W. Bush, was frustrated with the attitude of Russia, Germany and France over the Iraq issue and he was sure that there was an attempt to delay decisions further into the future, and that could hamper the political, diplomatic and military calculations and he did not want to change his strategy any more.

Mean while the Pentagon was using this period to get fully prepared for any military action on Iraq in the Persian Gulf, though there wore warnings that U.S. would have to go along in the event of a showdown with Iraq, but the Bush administration was firm in its attitude and wanted as many as collision partners supporting U.S.

Britain after it announced a huge deployment of troops accounting for almost a quarter of the Britain Army and its commitment to an expected U.S. military action against Iraq. This move by Britain surprised because the size of the deployment was about 30,000 soldiers and a huge amount of weapons.

Defence Secretary, Geoff Hoon, defended that it was no ordinary measure though he was of the opinion that a war was not necessary. The experts wore expecting that this move by Britain was to give a clear message that there is a threat of war.

Prime Minister, Toni Blair, speaking to senior MPs said the Iraqi people would rejoice if Saddam Hussein was removed as well as the world and the West Asia region would be a better place without the Iraqi dictator.

The United States Secretary of State Gen. Collin Powell was of the view that North Korea had to be proving that it could be trusted as its nuclear programme was a danger to the Asian region and to the world.

"The United States is willing to talk to North Korea about how it will meet its obligations to completely dismantle its nuclear programme. Pyongyang's behavior affects the stability of both Asia and the World". Speaking at the World Economic Forum

Gen. Powell expressed "The U.S. stands ready to build a different kind of relationship with North Korea once Pyongyang comes in to verifiable compliance with its commitments".

Gen. Powell made his stand that the U.S. do not have any intention to attack North Korea and was willing to continue to support North Korean aid programme which had suffered economic collapse and famine because of it policies have dragged its people in to a dark cloud, hunger hell.

Finally North Korea was inching closer to its demand for a non-aggression treaty with the U.S. when Gen. Powell hinted that U.S. could provide a written security guarantee rather than a non-aggression treaty. This statement came as a softening stand towards North Korea and a new hope that North Korea and U.S. could sit across a table for a discussion.

Israeli military conducted eight hour long large scale assault targeting small weapons factories, moved deep in to Gaza City in the early hours killing 12 Palestinian gunmen in exchange of fire and wounded more than 50 people.

The Israeli troops destroyed more than 100 lathes that could be used for making rockets, with just two days before Israel's general election. Israel's Defence Minister even threatened Palestine that he was considering the reoccupation of the entire Gaza Strip.

The Gaza City raid came in response to the firing of crude, short-range rockets on the Israeli town of Sderot in the Negev desert near Gaza, by the Palestine militants to disrupt the elections in Israel.

In Palestine seven metal workshops wore destroyed in the Israeli raid, the military tightened travel bans on Palestinians completely sealing the West Bank and Gaza to prevent militants from disrupting elections. Prime Minister, Ariel Sharon was accused for ordering the raid with the intention to win more Votes in the Israeli general election.

The Israeli troops wore withdrawn a day after the election, and only then the 12 gun men dead wore give the funeral, a large gathering of 30,000 Palestinians joined the procession. This death toll was the highest in the past five months in Gaza.

Hamas, the Islamic militant group announced in fury that the Israeli's will pay the prize for every drop of blood shed. Abdel Aziz Rantisi, a leader of the Hamas shouted "Our battle will continue until we uproot this Israeli occupation from our holy land no matter what the sacrifice"

Egyptian sponsored mediated between the Hamas and other Palestinian faction was held in Cairo for stopping attacks on Israeli civilians but the Palestinian Islamic Jihad did not agree to the ceasefire.

The Qatar based TV channel Al-Jazeera had been criticized in Washington for making major news coverage of Al-Qaeda and Israeli-Palestinian conflict. In what is called as the secret signals to Al-Qaeda by the TV station being accuse of encouraging terror.

Adrian Van-Klaveren, chief of news gathering at BBC supported Al-Jazeera by saying that it had established itself as a major international broadcaster. Looking in to the progress of the Arab channel BBC signed a news gathering deal with Al-Jazeera which is been favored by Osama for their video broadcast to the world.

With the new arrangement, the two broadcasters would share facilities on the ground, BBC would be using satellite link in Kabul in return Al-Jazeera would get advice to its English language website, and get help with training. Al-Jazera became popular when its major coverage including filmed statements from Osama, after the 9/11 attack on the twin tower.

Finally Iraq announced that it would encourage its scientists to be interviewed by the United Nations Weapons Inspectors Privately. Saddam Hussein's advisor, Amir al Saadi, informed media about his meeting with the inspectors, Hans Blix and Mohammad El Baradei.

Iraq also promised to provide more cooperation to the U.N. weapons inspector; it also expressed forming its own team to search for the banned weapons. Till now all interviews conducted by the U.N. inspectors was held in the presence of Iraqi officials.

The U.N wanted 16 Iraqi scientists in its list for interviewing but wore unable to contact them till now. The U.N. officials suspected that these wanted scientists might have been kept secretly or sent abroad by the Iraqi President. The list of scientists was sent to Jordan, Kuwait, and Turkey.

Blix and El Baradei told media that Iraq would supplement a list of around 500 scientists who wore involved in the weapons programme, and hand over more documents to inspectors. At the same time inspectors had found empty chemical warheads which Iraq had failed to provide details in its report.

United States had demanded on the grounds that the interviews need protection from reprisals. Blix had said he was fairly confident that Iraq would honor its commitment. Speaking to media persons Blix said "we have solved a number of practical issues, not all". But was confident he would succeed in doing his job.

Blix and El Baradei were likely to influence strongly a decision on a U.S. led war against Iraq. The report of the weapons inspectors' team was likely to set in motion a chain of events that could result in a war.

Meanwhile, the "peace Camp" led by Iraqi neighbors had stepped up efforts to avoid a possible war. Realizing that conflict could be averted only if the Iraqi President agrees to go in to exile, Libya was a possible destination that suited Saddam Hussein.

Military tensions in the Gulf region was on the rise and most Israelis wore convinced that their country would benefit if Saddam Hussein is unseated. The Israelis wore of the opinion that the consequences of invasion of allied forces would be mixed but the out come result would be positive. Israel would find that a regime that has had a record of attacking it would be out of the way.

After the first Gulf War and the sanctions imposed on Iraq by the United Nations was failing to make any impact on Hussein's regime and the pressure had begun to lift the restrictions against Iraq. In case of a war with U.S. Israel was the first target for Iraq and during the first Gulf war Iraq had fired several scud missiles against Israel.

In Iraq Shias formed the largest community, and Sunnis wore playing a major role in Saddam Hussein's empire. In case of a change in the regime in Iraq this two communities wore in a position to clash each other for the domination in a new regime.

After the Iranian Islamic Revolution in 1979 it had been hostile to Israel which was a setback for Saddam Hussein, as Iran was supporting the Hezbollah group which was functioning against Israel from Lebanon.

The Consul General, Ri To Sop of North Korea had said that "we will go after our enemies, we will not mix up South Korea with the United States," The top North Korean official had clearly said that his country would not attack South Korea in case the United States pulls his country for a war.

The North Korean official also made it clear that his country dose not posses a nuclear weapon as alleged by the U.S. and with frustration the U.S. was making such allegation after North Korea withdrew itself from the Non Proliferation Treaty.

Speaking simple but tough in his State of the Union Address the U.S. President, George W. Bush, said "the world has waited for 12 years for Saddam Hussein to disarm, America will not accept the serious and increasing threat to itself, allies and friends". Bush also announced that Secretary of State, Colin Powell, would be present information and intelligence report about Iraq's illegal weapons programme in the next U.N. Security Council.

Bush also had given a clear message to the United Nations that "We will consult, but let there be no misunderstanding. If we lead a coalition to disarm Saddam Hussein if he does not fully disarm for the safety of our people and for the peace of the world".

For President, Bush, Iran and North Korea was also an irritating matter but Iraq was the most serious subject in his State of the Union Address. "the dictator who is assembling the world's most dangerous weapons has already used them on the whole village leaving thousands of his own citizens dead, blind or disfigured, if this is not evil then, then evil has no meaning".

Bush called Iraqi leader as the symbol of evil and a brutal dictator. He specifically accused Saddam Hussein for aiding and protecting the members of Al-Qaeda and not accounting for thousands of liters of anthrax and botulism toxin, as much as 500 tones of sarin, mustered gas and the VX nerve agent and 30,000 munitions that are capable of delivering chemical weapons.

For the first time Bush reveled through his intelligence sources that Iraq security officials wore hiding documents from the weapons inspectors and sanitizing inspection sites. He accused Saddam Hussein has developed in lengths, spent enormous amount, taken big risk to build and keep weapons of mass destruction.

According to Bush the only possible explanation Saddam Hussein could have for those weapons is to dominate, intimidate or attack his enemies. He maintained that America fights reluctantly because the country is well aware of the costs; but that sometimes peace must be protected.

At the end of his argument the President, Bush, said "Future lived in the mercy of terrible threats is no peace at all. If war is forced upon us, we will fight with the full force and might of the U.S. military and we will prevail".

The Iraqi Deputy Prime Minister, Tariq Aziz, denied the charges levied by the U.S. President in his State of the Union Address. Defending the Iraq's position, "I absolutely deny that and I challenge Bush and his Government to present any evidence of that. Everybody in the region and the world knows Iraq has no connection with Al-Qaeda".

"Americans can inflict damage on our country as they did in 1991, but this nation is brave enough and capable enough of protecting its sovereignty. If they dare to invade Iraq, they will suffer great losses, and they will lose in the end. These allegations have been raised before by Bush and this is not the first time he is doing this. Iraq was ready for war tomorrow and was prepared for the worst situation". Tariq Aziz called the U.S. President's motive assumed for war designed to control the economy of the West Asia.

However the Director General, of the International Atomic Energy Agency, Mohamed El Baradei, had said in an interview "do not forget that by 1998 we eliminated Iraq's nuclear programme so our focus right now is to find out has anything happened in the last four years". He had confirmed that in the past eight weeks the U.N. inspectors working in Iraq had been able to eliminate many of the important aspects required for the Nuclear Programme.

The French, Foreign Minister, Dominique de Villepin, welcomed the U.S. plans to present evidence that Iraq is harboring mass destruction weapons and has links with Al Qaeda, Without making any shift in its stand on Iraq Dominique, had said "The International community's responsibility today is huge the choice of war or of peace, and it's not a choice to be made lightly. The overthrow of the Saddam Hussein's regime by military means could be imagined".

Japan and South Korea took note of what they assume to be the logic behind Bush's uncompromising statement on Iraq and relatively soft tone on North Korea. However these strategic allies of the U.S. in the Asia Pacific region welcomed U.S. decision but wore in some sense not happy over the U.S. soft decision on North Korea.

China made their concerns that a U.S. led war on Iraq might only open Pandora's Box in West Asia. There was a discontent feeling against Bush's in taking unilateral action against Iraq.

The Australian Prime Minister, John Howard, raise the question "What hope we have got of controlling North Korea which is in our region, if the Security Council walks away from its responsibilities to deal with Iraq. Whether or not the Council decides in some kind of military action against Iraq while perhaps not approving the use of force, the onus was now on the U.N. to match its resolution with action.

North Korea changed its aggressive pact with the U.S. and renewed its call for a non aggressive pact. It also pledged to accept that Washington plans for a preemptive strike against its nuclear facilities. North Korea coming out with relief that Bush did not portray it in the strategic metaphor of "Axis of Evil".

The real meaning of the discussion on nuclear issue continues as different strategy on different countries adopted by the United States begins hear after in the world politics and any one questioning on their ideas were dealt with serious consequences. Even the United Nations was in no mood to go against the hard decision of United States.

It is clear that new nuclear weapons states have found it advantageous to exploit the threat potential of their assets. They do not see nuclear weapons as merely a means to deter. A new value was added to nuclear weapon that goes beyond deterrence. For some countries they have become as instruments of a policy that creates global fear and regional advantages. More over nuclear weapons have been used as tools to involve regional conflicts, it is been even used for getting economic and political advantages over the super powered nations.

Now for some countries Nuclear weapons have been used to fulfill other aims, they have been used for negotiating tables. This strategy has become a common agenda to influence politically and to achieve economic advantages and finally getting the military requirements by the smaller countries.

The Iraqi Foreign Minister, Naji Sabri, in a press conference had said Baghdad, had done all it could to convince the world it had no weapons of mass destruction and had provided full cooperation with the weapons inspectors. "We have done every thing possible to let this country and this region avoid the danger of war by the warmongers in United States and Britain."

He called Bush and Blair wore fond of exporting death and destruction to other countries, "they are the one who are exploiting the situation and making a lot of threats. Fabricating lies every day"

The U.S. and Britain's concern over the weapons of mass destruction was only a reason to invade Iraq. He alleged that U.S. was controlling the oil of the region and safeguarding the security of Israel. War was a reason for them to develop weapons of mass destruction which is their desire to experiment it on Iraq.

He accused Bush and Collin Powell of making repeated lies which no one believes that Iraq had links to Osama bin Laden's Al Qaeda.

The Iraqi Foreign Minister expressed that Hans Blix and Mohamed El Baradei, would confirm that Iraq is free of banned weapons and find that Iraq's cooperation with the inspectors was super.

Sabri was of the opinion "we hope that they will be fair and that they would present the facts as they are on the ground, that there wore no banned weapons or activities and the Iraqi authorities had cooperated effectively on a wide scale with inspection teams. We have done our duty and when there is a fair administration for the inspection process, and then it would definitely convey this image to the Security Council".

The real fundamental differences between the weapons inspectors and the Bush Administration is that Washington believes the inspection process is over, but the weapons inspectors say that it is incomplete. For United States the U.N. process in Iraq is over and was expecting an official announcement.

In fact Hans Blix had himself expressed his views that he would like to present a final report towards the end of March 2003. Blix had been seriously critical of the Iraqi regime; his negative comments on Iraq would be seized as proof by the Bush administration that Saddam Hussein had not lived up to the U.N. expectation.

The Permanent and Non Permanent members of the Security Council who wore in full confidence that Blix will not out rightly criticise Iraq and wore in hope that the process set in motion by the U.N. could be allowed to continue, at least for a short period.

Though the Bush administration was not in favor for the extension of the search in Iraq by the inspectors, but for political and military reasons some more time for the weapons inspectors was in the U.S. agenda.

Both Hans Blix and Mohammad El Baradei expressed the hope that the report submitted by them to the Security Council will give the international community an assessment of the situation in Iraq and the need full act to be done further. "How they want to use it is their prerogative".

At the time when Bush administration was trying to make the point that it had indeed made the case for military action against Iraq, Americans wore evenly divided on the subject with 49% maintaining the President has made his case and 48% saying that he has not.

The White House had been continuously making the point that Bush was not guilty by the result of the public opinion, but the political assessment was that Bush would decide whether to militarily strike Iraq or go by the public opinion.

The Senate Minority Leader, Tom Daschle pointed out that "The President needs to make a compelling case that Iraq poses a very imminent threat to the U.S. and secondly, that he had worked through the International community and exhausted all other options".

The options before Bush was to go in alone or with the so called coalition of the willing, increase pressure on the Security Council for a second resolution authorising the use of force, or go for other ways in which Saddam Hussein could be forced into exile, only then a war could be avoided.

In London the growing in-house opposition for Tony Blair to his Iraq policy began. Several of his senior cabinet colleagues had arguing against him a revolt was likely to take place among his MPs who say Blair is demeaning parliament by trying to plunge the country into a U.S. led war without parliament approval. Majority of his party opposed to his line there was a concern that he could be risking his political carrier if he backed the unilateral American action which did not have the United Nations mandate.

Blair was dragging the country without the support of the public this what the seniors in the parliament expressed and Blair was not in a position to make out a convincing case for risking thousands of British lives where there was no particular national interest at stake every one was wondering if Blair's decision on Iraq was in national interest or by a personal interest.

However Blair sticks to his point saying that it was Britain's interest to disarm Saddam Hussein as the weapon of mass destruction which he holds is likely to be in the hands of terrorists and finally when they have no business to do those weapons might be used against Britain.

The argument went throughout country that Blair was making Britain more vulnerable to a terrorist attack by supporting the U.S. led war. As the Israel and Palestine crises is increasing day by day the situation in West Asia false in the hands of militants.

The Egyptian President, Hosni Mubarak, strongly warned Saddam Hussein to avoid any missteps in dealing with the U.N. inspector. He cautioned the Iraqi leader to abide by the U.N. and stop obstructing weapons inspectors operations.

According to the weapons inspectors only two issues had to be resolved regarding U-2 reconnaissance flights and private interviews with scientists. Out of the 16 Iraqi scientists none of them had accepted the request for interviews without the presence of Iraqi officials for which U.S. had been demanding.

Meanwhile the inspectors continued their search for evidence of Chemical, Biological and Nuclear weapons in several suspected sites including weapons depot where empty chemical warhead wore found earlier.

The Iraqi, Deputy Prime Minister, Tariq Aziz, in an interview said that Iraq had no plans to attack targets inside the U.S. in the event of a war. Aziz warned that any one attack on Iraq would be bravely defended and they will have a great number of casualties. "We will fight within our territory", but those restrictions would not apply to Kuwait.

"American troops are in Kuwait and preparing themselves to attack Iraq. If the attack is from Kuwait then we will have to retaliate".

Russian President, Vladmir Putin warned Iraq that it would take tough decision if it did not improve cooperation with the U.N. disarmament mission. "The international weapons inspectors don't say that they are facing complications or problems in their work in Iraq. And if that is the case then the inspectors should be given the opportunity to continue to work in Iraq"

"At the same time Putin made it clear that "Moscow can change its stand and agree with the U.S. on other UNSC actions, tougher ones, if Iraq created problems for the U.N. inspectors. However he maintained the need to resolve all disputes on the basis of international laws and U.N. decisions".

China in clear terms urged Baghdad to enhance its cooperation with the IAEA to inspect the suspected sites in Iraq. China being the only Asian Country with full fledged Veto powers in the U.N. Security Council maintained that the U.N. Security Council should continue to support the unfinished work of the nuclear inspection in Iraq.

In its carefully designed comments to keep the U.S. guessing about China's strategy, China said there was no room for hasty conclusion at this point.

Japan a key U.S. ally in the Far East Asia emphasized the need for a peace full resolution.

Indonesia made it clear that it was against an attack on Iraq

Malaysia was of the view that U.S. had already gone overboard in its attempt to demolish terrorism.

The closed door session at the U.N. to discuss the substance of what Hans Blix and Mohammad El Baradei had to say at the Security Council asking the two more specific questions on their findings or assessment.

The German Ambassador, Gunter Plueger, giving his reactions to media said there was more scope for a better cooperation on the Iraqi side. In his view the inspectors should be given opportunity to achieve their goals in a peaceful way.

The French Ambassador, Jean Marc De La Sabliere, was in favor of pushing more time and not a specific time frame for continued inspection, according to him as long as the U.N. system is producing results the inspections should go on.

Hans Blix in being more critical of Iraq over the nature and scope of disarmament did not specifically ask for more time for inspection to continue their job. But his colleague Mohammad El Baradei, clearly did ask the Security Council for extra time, arguing that it was essential for inspection and preventing a war with Iraq.

According to El Baradei "these few months, in my view will be a valuable period in peace process, because it could help us avoid the war".

Gen. Powell, questioned from the speech of Blix "where is the missing anthrax? This is not just a question, but it is essential for us to know what happened to this deadly material and with respect to the VX, chemical and biological munitions, the mobile biological laboratories and the list of Iraqi personnel involved with weapons of mass destruction.

According to Powell "Passive cooperation is not what was called for in resolution 1441. We have made it clear from the beginning that we could not allow the process of inspection to string us out for ever" the process of consultation with allies will go on, and the time was running out. "But, what we cannot do is just keep kicking the can down the road".

The British Foreign Secretary, Jack Straw, was of the view that the weapons inspectors report clearly established the Iraqi President, Saddam Hussein, had reduced the inspection process and there was clear evidence that he was in material breach of the U.N. Security Council resolution on the issue. The case against Iraq has strengthened following the inspectors report.

He gave the hint that "The chances of resolving the crises peaceful means wore less then they wore because of Iraq's unbelievable refusal to comply with the U.N. terms."

Giving a call to the Iraqi leader Straw warned that the chances of resolving the crisis peacefully had decreased and it was up to Iraq to avoid any military action.

Labour, MPs, who wore opposed to a war, insisted that the inspectors should be given more time to complete their work. The MPs, prepared to set up pressure on the government not to plunge the country into a U.S. led war without a fresh U.N. mandate and a vote in Parliament.

In a statement Pakistan's position on Iraq continued to be based on a peaceful resolution and preventing further suffering of the Iraqi people must constitute the main objective. It said the UNMOVIC and the IREA are carrying out an important exercise to ensure that Iraq remains disarmed of weapons of mass destruction and they should be permitted to continue their work. It further said "in the interest of the Iraqi people, regional and international peace and security, Saddam Hussein had a heavy responsibility to ensure that the Iraqi authorities cooperate to fully implement the Security Council responsibility related to disarmament in Iraq"

Iraq's neighbors Turkey and Jordan wore now prepared to provide their territory as military base for an U.S. invasion on Iraq. The diplomatic efforts by the United States paid off at last with Turkish and Jordanian government's giving their nods for a multi front U.S. invasion on Iraq.

Both Turkey and Jordan had repeatedly expressed refusal to permit U.S. troops in its territory. Washington had accepted Turkey's claims on the northern Iraq oil cities of Mosul and Kirkuk. Turkey, which was an aspirant for getting the membership, of the European Union, and needed support from some of these countries, to fulfill its ambition.

The new understanding between the Turkey and U.S. was offered on conditional support for the U.S. to have a light division of about 15,000 troops rather than 80,000 as Washington had demanded to push its forces in to Iraqi northern areas from its territory. Turkish forces had agreed to pull back their forces that wore reportedly already inside Northern Iraq to their home bases before the U.S. invasion.

Turkey in return for its cooperation was to receive big U.S. support economically and bailout package after the war.

Jordan which said no to U.S. troops was ready to allow the use of its soil and airspace in return for a new compressive security guarantees. Jordan was positioned in between Iraq and Israel, wanted its national security as it could become a battle ground in a possible conflict between Iraq and Israel.

The U.S. wanted to have the western front across Jordan to prevent Iraqi's targeting Israel with Scud missiles. Apart from this aspect the western front was an advantage to a multi directional attack on Baghdad and the stronghold of Saddam Hussein on Tikrit.

In return Jordan, had given a proposal to U.S. Assistant Secretary of State for Eastern Affairs, William Burns, and the U.S. Central Command Chief, General Tommy Franks, for a new U.S. air defence system to safeguard its airspace.

British, Prime Minister, Tony Blair, while preparing to meet the U.S. President, George W. Bush, in Washington the leaders of Italy, Portugal, Spain, Poland, Hungary, Denmark, the Czech Republic supported the U.S. campaign to disarm the Iraqi President, Saddam Hussein by force if necessary.

Blair, and the leaders of the seven nations signed the appeal and the signatories included Anders Rogh Rasmussen (Denmark), Leszek Miller (Poland), Peter Medgyessy (Hungary), Jose Maria Aznar (Spain), Silvio Berlusconi (Italy), Vaclav Havel (Czech

Republic), Jose Manuel Duroa Barroso (Portugal).

Blair and the supporting seven nations were of the opinion that "The opportunity to avoid greater confrontation rests with Saddam Hussein, the leaders expressed that the Security Council would lose its credibility and world peace will suffer if Iraq was allowed to violate the United Nations resolution.

Blair and the seven nation leaders signed the appeal and it said "we must remain united in insisting that Saddam Hussein regime is disarmed. The combination of weapons of mass destruction and terrorism is a threat of incalculable consequences. It is only at which all of us should feel concerned".

The Secretary of State for International Development, Clare Short, warned against a preemptive action against Iraq. She said "We must deal with Iraq in such a way that minimizes any risk of further suffering for the people of Iraq.

The day after talking tough in his State of the Union Address that he would provide evidence against Iraq, yet another time Bush, said if the world did not support him the United States will go alone in the campaign to disarm Saddam Hussein.

President, Bush, argued "In my judgment, you don't continue Saddam Hussein; you don't hope that will somehow change his evil mind. I have thought long and hard about this. The risk of doing of nothing, the risk of expecting the best from him is just not a risk worth taking. So I call upon the world to come together and insist this dangerous man should be disarmed".

The Bush Administration was making plans to increase the speed of diplomatic activity including the Secretary of State; Collin

Powell's presentation at the United Nations Security Council would be a diplomatic win where final phase of the Iraq crisis was taking place. Bush was very much confident that with or without a second resolution, the United States was preparing a deadline.

CHAPTER - 6

The United Nations debated the Iraqi crisis for the whole day in two sessions. It was said that out of the 15 members 11 wore in favor of giving Hans Blix and his team more time and to continue their job to its full course. But U.S. Administration had told the council that the deadline for decision was fast approaching.

Washington had tough time at the Security Council, where a clear majority of permanent and non permanent members wore in favor of giving more time for the process to complete. It was Spain, Bulgaria and Britain wore in favor of United States.

"I will continue to plead for more time" the International Atomic Energy Agency, Chief, Mohammad El Baradei and the head of the United Nations Monitoring Verification, Hans Blix had expressed to complete the remaining part of the work if more time is needed.

The U.S. Secretary of State Collin Powell was to present additional information and intelligence to the council in the next meeting, in which Powell had to present compelling evidence to Council members and after the presentation Powell was to press for a resolution declaring that Iraq was in Material Breach and justifying U.S. demand for military action.

It was expected that Gen. Powell would be presenting in the Security Council as evidence the satellite images of mobile biochemical labs and the cleanup of operation of sites before the arrival of the weapons inspectors in Iraq.

Russia pleaded that what the United Nations was asking was the "undeniable proof" and that was needed as new evidence if any before the Security Council.

The Bush administration political commitment to oust the Saddam Hussein regime was the decision in the White House for regime change in Iraq was taken even before the tragic event of September 11, 2001.

North Korea had already begun to take full advantage of the crisis in the Gulf. Stepping back from the brink now would further weaken the international coalition that Bush had struggled to hold together.

For the Bush Administration, war with Iraq was not merely about removing Saddam Hussein. It involves a much larger dimension about the political transformation in the Middle East. Even before September 11. It was said the radicals in the Bush Administration had come to the conclusion that a major overhaul in American policy towards the Gulf region was necessary. And the war on terrorism declared after the attack on New York and Washington had reinforced this objective.

President Bush, attempt to define the war as liberation of the Iraqi people from the dictatorship of Saddam Hussein might be liked by some sections, but majority of the observers felt that this war as mere personal revenge but some facts reveals that Bush administration had secret agenda behind the war.

The frozen peace process between Israel and Palestine deteriorated and escalated and attempts to dictate rather than negotiate to resume peace talks was a never ending crises in West Asia.

In Hebron, tanks rumbled along the streets as Israeli soldiers patrolled on foot. Three bulldozers escorted by four tanks demolished more than 100 stalls in a vegetable market located in the heart of Hebron.

Israeli soldiers fired live rounds at Palestinians who threw stones and large objects during the demolition. The military said it carried out the operation in response to a series of shooting and ambushes in which 15-18 Israelis wore killed.

The Hebron crackdown came two days after the Israel, Prime Minister, Ariel Sharon's victory in the election was announced. This crackdown was an indication to Sharon's tough policies against Palestinian leader Yasser Arafat.

Sharon alleged Arafat encouraging attacks on Israelis with the support of militants and as a result this became the reason for Sharon's refusal to talk with Arafat and a reflection of the policies of the next government of Israel.

Germany which took over the Presidency of the Security Council for the month of February, which became a disadvantage factor for the Bush administration to plunge in to war with Iraq as Germany was in favor of giving more time to the weapons inspectors to continue their work searching for banned arsenal.

Germany wanted Hans Blix to come up with his second report, but the Bush administration did not want to give any extension to the inspection team after February 14, 2003. And after that it was anybody's guess what would be the decision of the U.S. President, Bush had specifically said that it would not agree to give indefinite period for the weapons inspectors to continue their work in Iraq.

The Bush administration was very much cautiously making decisions on how much information's to share with the Security Council and also with the international community, apart from the other organizations in the world which wore more skeptical of the additional information and intelligence which Gen. Collin Powell wanted to prove in the Security Council on 5th of February 2003.

In Washington hectic political activity on the Iraqi crisis was going on meeting world leaders. The Prime Minister of Italy, the Foreign Minister of Saudi Arabia, leaders of Portugal, Sweden had several round of talks with the President, Bush and Deputy Secretary of State, Richard Armitage.

The one discussion that was in serious nature was of the Iraqi leader Saddam Hussein, needed to go on exile so that the war in West Asia could be avoided. One thing that was very clear in the discussion was that Saddam Hussein, would not go in exile voluntarily and there needs a force to throw him out.

The British Prime Minister, Toni Blair and President, George W. Bush wore to take a major decision on the crisis and the strategy that had to be adopted in the crisis at the Camp David meeting. Till this time Britain was the only country that was openly supporting U.S.

The Russian President, Vladmir Putin, had bluntly reiterated his stand that he was looking for compelling evidence that cannot be undeniable proof to prove that Iraq was in possession of such dangerous weapons.

Maj. Gen. Hossam Mohammed Amin, chief Iraqi liaison officer with the weapons inspectors invited Blix and El Baradei that his country was interested in resolving outstanding issues before them and make their next report to the U.N. Security Council on February 14.

Gen. Amin suggested Baghdad would not oppose over flights by U-2 aircraft, as requested by the U.N., as long as the U.S. and Britain stop patrols over the "no-fly" zones of south and north Iraq while the spy planes are in the air. So that the Iraqi anti aircraft batteries would not mistake the reconnaissance plane for American and British jets fire at it. He also was of the view that it was up to individual scientist whether they wanted to speak to U.N. inspectors in private.

The Director General of the Vienna based International Atomic Energy Agency, Mohamed El Baradei expressed that "we need to make sure before we go that they are ready to move forward on these issues, we will have first to see what they are offering before we decide on the visit."

The debate of using a nuclear weapon on Iraq was another serious issue that was in the discussion at the White House as the news spread out in the American leading news paper (The Washing ton Times).

According to a document which was signed by the President, George W. Bush, in September 2002 specially allows the use of nuclear weapons by way of a response to chemical and biological attacks.

The White House declined to comment on the document. In the past, successive governments in Washington had deliberately been vague about the possible use of nuclear weapons, and have confined their comments to all options or response with overwhelming force. However it did not say much on what the response of he U.S. will be in the event of a chemical or biological attack on its forces.

The visiting Pakistani, Foreign Minister, Khurshid Mehmood Kasuri, in Washington apparently had told the President George W. Bush at White House that it would prefer any military action against Iraq to be approved by the United Nations

Pakistan was among the 11 nations in the Security Council which was pleading for more time for weapons inspections in Iraq, and had also been making its views that the Iraqi crisis would have to be handled under the supervision of the U.N.

It was also said that in between the meeting with Kasuri and National Security advisor, Condoleezza Rice, President, Bush had intervened and had praised Pakistan's support for the U.S. anti terror campaign.

Finally President, Bush agrees for second U.N. resolution though he and his administration believes that this was not necessary but under the U.N. resolution 1441 there is provision to provide additional political relaxation and this situation was used for tackling the Blair problem who was under strong pressure domestically for his full support to the U.S. led war.

For many permanent members and non permanent members the Bush tactics was some thing confusing, now the question arising was that if U.S had the extra evidence and proof why did they not present those information's to the council much earlier rather than waiting till 5th February.

The real technical point that U.S. was lacking was that out of the 15 members only two wore in favor of the Bush idea and the remaining 13 wore against and to pass a resolution in the Council a minimum of 9 votes was necessary against no votes. The Bush thinking is when it is time for showdown in the Council by that time with more evidence the other members of the council could be changed in his favor.

At the same time both the weapons inspectors had rejected the invitation from Iraq to visit the country on 10, February. On the grounds that unless Baghdad accepted the series of conditions that showed its commitment to disarm on the progressive work for the second report that needed to be completed by 14, February.

The Bush administration suspected that the Iraqi invitation was yet another tactics to divert the attention of the international community. The American envoy in the U.N. John Negroponte, expressed "We certainly don't see anything new in this initiation".

It is said that the word "Quickly" had become a code word in the Bush administration but none of them wore in a position to define. However the American media interpretation was that it referred to the military attack on Iraq after February 5, 2003.

Mean while the World Health Organization announced the world to be alert, in its 45 page report entitled "Terrorist Threats to Food". The WHO report warned of the possible inclusion of chemical, biological or nuclear agents in food as a way of intentionally harming civilian populations. The malicious contamination of food for terrorist purposes was a real and current threat and intentionally contaminated at one location could have global public health implications".

The Pakistan, Prime Minister, Mir Zafarullah Khan Jamali after returning from his Persian Gulf tour, at a news conference in Islamabad, expressed his opinion that the Gulf countries have a genuine concern for peace in the region and Pakistan agrees that Iraq on its part should fully comply with all relevant U.N. Security Council resolution.

Jamali's visit to United Arab Emirates, Kuwait, Qatar and Bahrain and consultations with the leaders of Gulf Cooperation Council (GCC) countries in the changing political situation was of much importance to Pakistan. However there was general agreement that if military action becomes inevitable let that be within the frame work of the U.N. and all efforts should be made to preserve and safeguard the territorial integrity, stability and independence of all nations in the Gulf region.

The U.S. National Security Advisor, Candoleezza Rice, reacting in Cairo made her comments over the latest developments on Iraq. "We believe that when Iraq has been liberated from Saddam Hussein regime, the Iraqi people will be perfectly capable of running their own affairs.

In Iraq Saddam Hussein was preparing his troops for defending his country against the invading U.S. warriors. He was confident that any one trying to invade on the ground will leave them counting casualties on their side.

In Britain fears persist because of the prevailing hysteria over asylum seekers fuelled by intelligence warnings that potential terrorists posing as Iraqi refugees might try to enter Britain ahead of a war. An estimated 3,000 Iraqis wore in Britain every month in search of asylum and the number was expected to shoot up once the war break out.

Meanwhile in Britain the Labour Party veteran, Tony Benn, flew to Baghdad, to talk peace with the Iraqi President, Saddam Hussein. Britain's largest trade union TUC, demanded the Prime Minister, Tony Blair, and the U.S. President George W. Bush to avoid a military confrontation with Iraq.

Both the Labour moments of Britain urged Blair and Bush to continue to lead the global fight against totalitarianism, and terror through the U.N. to ensure this fight is carried out by the broadest possible coalition, and with the strongest international legitimacy.

Located some where in the southern Kuwaiti desert, the United States and Israel ground force test fired about 10 to 14 Patriot missiles in what is termed as the simulated exercise in the Nagav desert was real that may spark in to a full fledged war between the two sides and there was all possibilities that Iraq would fire its Scud missiles.

With the possibility of a war increased, Iraq's neighboring countries had a conclusion that the war will lead to an invasion of American policy in the region wore beginning to find a new ally and E.U. was emerging as future ally. And in this regard the Iranian President, Mohammad Khatami, had talks with the E.U., External Affairs Commissioner, Chris Patten in Teheran.

The six Persian Gulf states that are part of the Gulf Cooperation Council (GCC) wore also looking at cultivating the E.U. more keenly. Qatar had invited the Foreign Ministers of France, Belgium, Spain and Luxembourg, to participate in what would amount to a Euro-GCC.

The Foreign Minister of Greece, George Papandreou, and the E.U. President had said that yet no decision had been taken in this regard.

On February 5th 2003 the stage is set for Gen. Collin Powell; to make his submission in the Security Council, in which he was, suppose to provide additional information which U.S. says as strong evidence. After Powell completes his presentation the permanent and non permanent members will get 10 minutes each to respond on the matter.

Interestingly the Iraqi envoy had appealed that he would ask for an opportunity to speak at the Council after Gen. Powell had made his presentation.

When the Iraq issue was a major discussion which was hunting the British Prime Minister, Tony Blair, domestically and in abroad, finally he admitted that "when people say why are you risking everything in a sense politically on this issue, I say to them in all honesty I do not want to be Prime Minister, when people point the fingers back at history and say you knew those threats were there and you did nothing about it". He said the campaign to disarm Saddam Hussein had entered its Final Phase.

The real objections came from the Iraqi side when Hussam Mohammad Amin, head of the National Monitoring Directorate, saying that Iraq could not take responsibility for the safety of the U-2 spy planes in northern Iraq because the United States and Britain had since the early nineties forbidden it to fly escorts in what he describes as "no fly zone".

Both U.S. and Britain had violated the no fly zone to protect Kurds in northern Iraq and Shias in southern Iraq from air attacks by Iraqis. He made it clear that Iraq could not do much to push Iraqi scientist for private interviews with the U.N. inspectors, because "we can't force them".

Reacting to the Iraqi statement the U.N. in its letter pointed out that the safety of spy flight U2 and private interviews with the scientists besides the U.N. also expects Iraq to provide data missing from a declaration on its weapons that Baghdad made on December 7th 2002. The U.N. wanted to know the whereabouts of previously established stocks of the Chemical agent VX and anthrax.

Amin in reply to the U.N. letter had said that Iraq had purchased a portable lab from a British company to test the validity of imported foodstuffs. While another lab did not meet the requirements and that would be returned and these two units had been visited by the U.N. inspectors.

Amin reacting to Gen. Collin Powell of having addition information, he said "they wont be rally proof, instead they will be fabricated space and aerial photos, if we are given the chance to look at these photos, we will prove they are lies,"

Russian President, Vlaedmir Puttin was to visit Lebanon to have discussion with the chairman of Arab League, Amr Moussa over the threat of U.S. led attack on Iraq.

The United Nations draft report, that gave a shock to the world, that in the event of a war in Iraq, the assessment was that there could be 1,00,000 direct and 4,00,000 indirect casualties. According to U.N. assessment the large scale ground and aerial offensive along with the conventional bombardments and in such case the devastation would undoubtedly be great. The report said nearly 3.03 million people need feeding including children and pregnant women. And eventually 9,00,000 Iraqi refuges required assistance, out of which 1,00,000 needs immediate attention. For the existing 1,30,000 refugees in Iraq, it is probably that the UNHCR will initially unable to provide the support required.

The document said that the electricity network in the country would be seriously degraded and would cause collateral reduction in all sectors, particularly water and sanitation as well as health.

Most Iraqi's wore in full employment and had cash and material assets available to them to cope with the crisis during the 1991 war, but today most have completely exhausted their cash assets and material assets.

Additionally, logistics, particularly the ability to move with any degree of freedom, would be a major constraint in Iraq the report said.

Saddam Hussein in an interview on television channel 4 questioned the British and American motives and had said that they wanted to destroy because the destruction of Iraq is a well planned idea to control the oil.

Reacting to the arms inspections by the U.N. he said "if the purpose was to make sure that Iraq is free of nuclear, chemical and biological weapons then they can do that". He had said that these weapons do not come in small pills that you can hide in your pocket. These are weapons of mass destruction and it is easy to work out of Iraq has then or not. He made it clear that he had no wish to push through to a confrontation and Iraq had no interest in war. It was the other side which was gearing up to a war against Iraq.

Saddam Hussein was of the view that America as the most aggressive compared to Britain, Iraqis do not hate the British people. "We hope the British people would tell those who hate the Iraqis and wish them harm that there is no reason to justify this war". This interview for which Channel 4 had paid huge amount to the London based Arab TV network Al Jazera.

Reacting to the interaction between Saddam Hussein, and veteran Tony Been, Blair was skeptical that Evidence did exist to prove Saddam had links with Al-Qaeda.

As the U.S. prepares for a military campaign against Iraq, the Turkish Prime Minisster, Abdullah Gul, in his statement had said that "we have tried all methods including a summit meeting to be held in one of Arab countries. Unfortunately we have been approaching to a possible war.

U.S officials and leaders of the Kurdish opposition parties had already gathered in Turkey for a brainstorming session to remove the bottlenecks in the way of opening a U.S. led "northern front" against Iraq. Jalal Talabani was representing the Patriotic Union of Kurdistan (PUK) while Necirvan Barzani was heading the delegation from the Kurdish Democratic Party (KDP).

The U.S. Secretary of State, Collin Powell, during his hour long presentation making a strong case against the Iraqi leader in the Security Council that the evidence he presented was undeniable to prove that Saddam Hussein was in possession of weapon of mass destruction.

Gen. Powell cautioned the Security Council that Iraq was in deeper material breach and would face more serious consequences. Appealing the Council that resolution 1441 was one last chance for Iraq to come clean on its obligation. And that Iraq is following the "evasion and deception" policy. He pleaded that he obtained the evidence material through "various sources". I cannot tell you every thing I know. Gen. Powell one of his evidence the playback of two audiotapes which was recorded on Nov.26th 2002 a day before the weapons inspectors wore getting in to Iraq. The second recording was on 30th January 2003.

The British Foreign Secretary, Jack Straw, argued that Gen. Powell, had made the most powerful and authoritative case against Iraq.

China's Tang Jiaxuan, made the case for continuing weapons inspection to continue as long as there was chance for political settlement, "we should apply our utmost effort to achieve that".

Russian Foreign Minister, Igor Ivanov, was of the view that the U.N. weapons inspectors must be continued, there need to be more analysis and study of the evidence presented by Gen. Powell.

The French Foreign Minister, Dominique de Villepin, expressed that inspection should continue, if necessary increase the number of inspectors, war should be the last resort.

The Australian senate passed an unprecedented vote of no confidence in Prime Minister, John Howerd, censuring a serving PM for the first time in Parliament's 102 year history. The No Confidence Motion was in deepening public interest and political displeasure with Howard's handling of the Iraq crisis and growing anger over his support to the U.S. led war.

The German government announced that it supported French proposal to intensify weapons inspectors in Iraq. It said the majority of the members of the U.N. Council wants a political solution to the conflict.

After the U.S. Secretary of State, Collin Powell, failed to impress the United Nations and to take the consensus of the Council members, the show for Bush administration ended what they wore saying that they had more evidence. But Washington had already decided to invade Iraq much before February 5th.

Though there were not many reactions from the world leaders regarding the failure of Powell's evidence case, the media in the

Gulf region took it as a big issue and commented in their own assumptions.

A leading Saudi Arabia daily said Washington was systematically engineering the war against Iraq to control its oil resources. America wants to control oil because who ever control these resources remains the most influential and Iraq has become the first victim in this wicked idea of the U.S.

A Syrian media report appeared as saying that the U.S. administration was seeking to build world wide empire and was trying to control the regions oil resources.

In fact every one in the world had assumed that Powell's presentation would ignite as a time bomb which many wore talking about. But in the conclusion they wore nothing but accusations and fabricated tape recordings and a smoke of lies and also blackmailing the public opinion in order to find an excuse for U.S. aggression against Iraq.

Saddam Hussein's reaction was that "this was a typical American show, complete with stunts and special effects; it is really below the level of a country leading the world now to come up with such allegations and ideas. What we heard was for the general public and mainly the uninformed in order to influence their opinion and to commit aggression on Iraq".

The Iraqi Information Minister, Mohammad Saeed al-Sahaf, expressed "we can confirm that these are hollow allegations that have nothing new to add to previous CIA reports and nothing different to cartoon films. Any third rate intelligence outfit could produce such recordings. It is nothing beyond their capabilities; it is simply untrue and not genuine"

The U.N. weapons inspectors conducted their first private interview with an Iraqi biological scientist on 7th February 2003 in a lengthy session of 3hours and 30 minutes. Iraq's reluctance to allow private interviews and its refusal to guarantee the safety of the U.N. authorized U-2 spy planes had become a major issue.

Blix who was to submit his report to the Security Council on 14th February it would be in favor of the France, Russia, Germany and China who are reluctant to endorse the use of force on Iraq.

The Iraqi Gen. Al Saadi made a point regarding the audio tape "I will not grace them with any more comments. They wore below the level of a superpower. One can fabricate anything in this regard and they are no evidence at all.

Iraq's Deputy Prime Minister, Tariq Aziz, denied any links with Al-Qaeda or Ansar-ul-Islam or with Kurdish rebel leader Jalal Talabiani. He made it clear that the point of sheltering Abul Musab al Zarqawi, an Al-Qaeda operative of Jordanian nationality who allegedly had ties with Ansar al-Islam group. He alleged that in spite of Baghdad making several request to Washington to cooperate in combating terrorism the U.S. had always failed to respond.

The U.S. President, George W. Bush, had signed the order, known as National Security Presidential Directive 16, in July 2002, but it was disclosed publicly only now for many reasons. The Bush administration was preparing the guidance amid speculation that the Pentagon was considering some offensive computer operations against Iraq in case Bush decides to go to war over Baghdad's weapon of mass destruction.

Until the Gulf war the cyber attack strategy warfare had lacked Presidential rules for declaring the circumstances under which such attacks would be launched, who would authorize and conduct them, and what targets would be considered legitimate.

The U.S. had the capability to go on cyber attacks and also had the organizations but did not have an elaborated strategy, doctrine, procedures. The extent of the U.S. cyber arsenal is among the most tightly held national security secrets, even more guarded than nuclear capabilities. Because of secrecy concerns, many of the programmers remain known only too strictly to a limited groups.

The U.S. had never conducted a large scale strategic cyber attack, the Pentagon had stepped up development of cyber weapons, envisioning a day when electronic might substitute for bombs and allow for more rapid and less bloody attacks on enemy targets. Instead of risking aircrafts or human casualties, military strategists imagine soldiers at computer terminals silently invading foreign networks to shut down radars disable electrical facilities and disrupt telephone services.

On the other side the Russian Foreign Minister, Igor Ivanov, expressed that he did not see any need now for a new U.N. Security Council resolution authorizing the use of force against Iraq and that an opportunity for a political solution still exists. "We have always underlined that the use of force is an extreme measure that would involve grave consequences for the country and grave international consequences and it should only be applied in extreme situation.

On a special BBC programme the British Prime Minister, Toni Blair, was grilled over his Iraq policy by skeptical public. He had a difficult time making a case for military action against Iraq but insisted that he was doing the right thing and would stand by it even if he was the last man left. Blair cautioned that the Anglo-U.S. campaign against states which are suspected to have weapons of mass destruction or links with terrorists would not end with Iraq.

United Nations, weapons inspectors, Hans Blix and Mohammad El Baradei after arriving in Baghdad, met the Iraqi President's advisor, Amaral-Saadi, and the chief of the Iraqi arms monitoring body, Hussam Mohammad Amin. Blix had said that he was hopeful about the outcome of the talks. El Baradei was of the hope that this visit was not the last chance to avert a possible war. "This is an important chance and certainly this will not be a last chance and there will be more chances".

Hans Blix welcomed Iraq's decision to allow its scientists to be privately interviewed by the inspection team. Four scientists wore already interviewed and similar interviews will take place in the coming days he said.

Britain's permanent representative at the U.N., Jeremy Greenstock, had indicated that Iraq was likely to allow U.N. flights of the U-2 spy planes, which the inspectors had demanded. An Iraqi legislation to outlaw development of banned weapons inside Iraq was also on the agenda.

At the same time U.S. was preparing for a war with Iraq continued without any interruption. The U.S. State Department had ordered on an essential diplomats and families to leave Jordan, Syria, Lebanon and Israel. The U.S. consular office at the Polish embassy in Baghdad was also closed.

Five U.S. aircraft carriers wore likely to be soon within Iraq's striking distance. The carrier Abraham Lincoln was on its way to join the Constellation in the Persian Gulf. The deployment of the Kitty Hawk in that area had also been ordered. The Theodore Roosevelt was linking up with the warship Harry S. Truman, which was already in the Mediterranean Sea.

The British aircraft carrier Ark Royal was reportedly close to the Suez Canal. Nearly 1, 50,000 U.S. troops wore expected to be deployed in Iraq's striking distance before February 14th the day when the U.N. inspectors submit their crucial report to the Security Council. The U.S. was yet to convince Turkey to use its air space and land so that would allow it to open up a northern front against Iraq.

President, Bush's special advisor, Zalmay Khalilzad was in Ankara to reconcile differences between Turkish Government and the ethnic Kurds residing in northern Iraq over the status of the oil cities of Mosul and Kirkuk. The Kurds feared that Turkey which had already indicated its intent to enter northern Iraq could occupy those cities.

Finally Khalilzad had accepted the Kurdish ambitions by declaring that all armed forces in northern Iraq would come under the overall command of the coalition forces.

The impatient U.S. President, George W. Bush while speaking to reporters in Washington had said that U.N. resolution 1441 should be upheld in the fullest purpose. "The Security Council needs to make up its mind soon, as to whether or not its decision means any thing. If the Security Council were to allow a dictator to lie and cheat, the Security Council would be weakened and this is a very defining moment for the U.N. Security Council".

It was said that Bush and Chirac did indeed had an excellent conversation and that Chirac took the opportunity to fully explain the reasons for what reasons it was not in this crisis. The world could easily understand that France is not opposed to the use of force, but it should come only after unmistakable signs that the inspections process is not going to work.

France, Russia and China, wore for going in for the political process some more time. However China had pointed out that weapons inspectors in Iraq had made some progressive development.

Britain and U.S. wore said to have worked on a document. At the White House, the spokes man, Ari Fleischer, had informed the media that the process of reaching an agreement on a specific language is just beginning.

The U.S. diplomats at the U.N. wore making the point that the kin of impression the top weapons inspectors, Hans Blix and Mohammad El Baradei, comes with from Baghdad would be critical in setting the stage.

At this point of time if Blix comes back on February 14th and reports of a positive change in the attitude of Baghdad, then the position of France, Germany, China and Russia would get strengthen. But if the inspectors tell that he still cannot find substantive change in the attitude of the Government in Iraq, it would be a clear victory for the U.S. as it demands for the second resolution.

U.N. Security Council when ask for division on the Iraq issue. Washington will be happy to get only the required minimum nine votes in its favor while Russia, China, Germany and France abstaining and not casting their veto.

Resolution1441 was passed by the Security Council last November 2002 with all 15 members including permanent and nonpermanent members voting in favor of it.

According to an UAE daily (Al Khaleej) The Arab intelligence was now by and large, was convinced that the U.S. was invading Iraq not just for its oil or for ridding it of its mass destruction. Along with getting hold of Iraqi oil, the U.S. after encroaching itself physically in Iraq, would begin to change the political ideas of the region that was defined after the world war1 break up of the Ottoman Empire, and in Iraq's case the Anglo-French Sykes Picot Pact and the San Remo treaty of 1920.

The Arabs suspected that unlike the first Persian Gulf War, which was to restore the statuesque in the region after Iraq had invaded Kuwait, the U.S. mission in Iraq this time in case it materializes, is aimed to achieve exactly the opposite to alter the statuesque.

Syrian analysts expressed fears that it would be surrounded by U.S. forces once they enter the position themselves in neighboring Iraq. The U.S. at its doorstop and Israel on the other side the pressure on it to increase anti-Israel Hezbollah offices would increase.

U.S. analysts, was of the view that Iran too complex and is likely to deal with it differently. According to some to few Arab thinkers, Saudi Arabia's ultimate nightmare scenario was to witness its three ways partition in what had been described by commentators as the Woolsey Plan, named after the CIA Director, James Woolsey. In this plan, the Saudi Kingdom could be divided into three separate states. Hejaz, Najd and the oil rich Shia Eastern province of Ihsa.

Though Ihsa would have most of the oil, but would be too small to defend itself, it could become a virtual U.S. protectorate on the lines of Kuwait. There wore two other lines of thinking related to Iraq. First, there wore those who are of the view that Arab people have been let down by their Governments. Therefore, the U.S. moves in Iraq and the region can only be beneficial as they will change the status quo.

The second, theory is that there was a recognition that the U.S. intervention in Iraq will cause political changes in the region and encourage terrorism. But, U.S. dominance of the region would undermine Israel's importance and encourage the emergence of an independent Palestinian state.

"United State's idea was to transform Mesopotamia (former Iraq) into a bridgehead for redrawing all the contours of West Asia, be they political, economic, ideological or cultural" according to its detailed information in "Al Khaleej".

According to the Pan-Arab "Al-Quds al-Arabi", Gen. Powell could mean many things, such as "drawing new geographical and demographic maps, partition along racial and ethnic lines, and nurturing the emergence of brand new entities, just like the Sykes-picot and San Remo agreements did during World War I.

The Bush, Ambassador to the U.N. Jeremy Greenstock, echoing the Prime Minister, Tony Blair's impatience, said, "Its 600 weeks since we started the business of asking Iraq to disarm. And now it is time to cut the knot and take action".

In Britain as anti war Labour MPs stepped up their campaign ahead of party conference where Blair was expected to face a hostile audience. The expression of MPs was that "the Government is not prepared to sit ideally by and those who argue otherwise should look long and hard at themselves". A potential revolt was said to be brewing among backbench party MPs who formed a cross party alliance with opposition members to demand a vote in Parliament on whether Britain should back a U.S. led war against Iraq without a specific U.N. mandate.

Russian President, Vladimir Putin, in his last minute effort to avert a war against Iraq began his tour to Germany and France. "There is no legal basis for use of force against Baghdad, because Iraq continues to cooperate with the international inspectors. Putin urged the U.N. to take additional steps towards improvement of cooperation with the international community and clarifying up remaining unresolved questions"

Indonesia's prominent organization leader Muhammadiyah, Chairman, called upon his followers not to take retaliatory measures against foreigners in Indonesia, in the event of a war against Iraq at this time, Indonesians were advised to remain calm in the circumstances and not put themselves in harm's way by trying to travel to Iraq to resist any U.S. move there.

According to the Malaysian Foreign Minister, Syed Hamid Alber, the Non-Aligned Moment (NAM) would have a grater justification to meet even if Iraq were to be attacked by the U.S. ahead of the scheduled conference.

For Tokyo, an additional source of concern was North Korea's profile as proliferators of nuclear weapons and ballistic missiles in Japan's immediate neighborhood.

China as a permanent member of the U.N. Security Council, had told the U.S. that the Iraq issue could still be looked at through the prism of the international weapons inspectors and that the North Korean question could be sorted out by the joint efforts of all parties concerned.

The U.S. President, George W. Bush, speaking in his weekly radio broadcast had said "the United States along with a growing coalition of nations will take whatever action is necessary to defend our selves and disarm the Iraqi regime. The Iraq regime's violations of Security Council resolutions are evident. They are dangerous to America and the world and they continue to this hour".

Bush continuing focus on Iraq that the Secretary Genera; of the United Nations, Kofi Annan, stressed the need for acting within the frame work of the Security Council and the consequences of going alone.

Secretary General, Kofi Annan advised that "war is always a human catastrophe, a course that should only be considered when all other possibilities have been exhausted and when it is necessary that the alternative is worse".

The Secretary General in his warning to the United States reminded "this is not an issue for any one state but for the international community as a whole. When states decide to use force, not in self defence, but to deal with broader threats to international peace and security, there is no substitute for the unique legitimacy provided by the U.N. Security Council".

Even after the international pressure and advise from the U.N. Secretary General, Bush administration's decision on Security Council resolution 1441 had not changed. Bush was of the opinion that Iraqi material breach of its obligations is more and has been brushing aside suggestions that the Security Council should be given more time to the weapons inspections the process which was under way.

The real fact is that the next few days wore very critical in the sense that much depends on what the top weapons inspectors Hans Blix and Mohammad El Baradei wore going to tell the Council on February, 14th 2003.

CHAPTER - 7

The Weapons inspector in Iraq wore on their duty and wore expected to have a third round of discussions before leaving Iraq. As more cooperation to the weapons inspectors Iraq, handed over documents related to the nuclear field to the two inspectors. The discussions were expected to tackle two key U.N demands private interviews of Iraqi scientists outside Iraq and surveillance flights by U-2 flights could be solved.

France and Belgium decided to block the sanction of a NATO military cover for Turkey could affect Turkish cooperation with the U.S. to open up a northern front against Iraq. With this U.S. had to encounter fresh difficulties in opening a possible invasion route in to northern Iraq. The Kurds wore seen as the core of a U.S. commanded invasion force in northern Iraq, after the war breaks out. But their military utility, without their most experienced commanders, was likely to get undermined. Because the assassination of entire top military leadership of the pro-U.S. Patriotic Union of Kurdistan (PUK) was a big blow to the U.S. plan to attack Iraq from the North.

The Ansar al Islam that allegedly had links with the Al-Queda and the Iraqi regime was being blamed for those killings. Because of its Al-Qaeda trappings, it was suspected that a similarity between these killing and the assassination of the late Commander,

Ahmad Shah Masood, in Afghanistan, which took place two days before the 9/11 attacks.

Apart from the gaps in the Kurdish military leadership that had emerged after those assassinations, the U.S. was finding it difficult to arrive at the right political formulation that would bring both Turkish Government and ethnic Kurds on board a plane to invade Iraq

Turkey had decided that it would like to position its own forces in the northern Iraq to prevent a flood of refugees entering into its territory in the aftermath of an Iraq war.

The Turkish decision had alarmed the Kurds, who fear that the real purpose of the Turkish forces in Iraq would be to fulfill Turkey's historical ambition of establishing control over the Kurdish oil cities of Mosul and Kirkuk.

Just a few days back the U.S. through its emissary Zalmay Khalilzad, had announced that all armed forces including Turky, PUK and KDP in northern Iraq would function under a single coalition commander in case of a war. This formula however had evoked a sharp response from Turkey military and had expressed opposition to subjecting itself to a foreign military command.

The PKK leader Osman Ocalan, the brother of Abdullah Ocalan, who was in Turkish Jail had threatened to reopen attacks in case the Turkish army enter northern Iraq. It was estimated that around 5000 PKK fighters wore still operating in northern Iraq and their activation could be of considerable damage to the forces that invaded northern Iraq.

U.N. weapon inspector, Hans Blix who had returned from Baghdad had expressed to the media persons who had met him that he saw no new evidence about Iraq's weapon during his visit to Baghdad. "This time they presented some papers to us in which they focused upon new issues. Not new evidence really as for as I can see, but they have never focused on the real issue and that is welcome".

The U.S. Ambassador to NATO, Nicholas Burns, expressed that the crisis of credibility had risen after France, Belgium and Germany blocked the alliance from supporting Turkey in the event of a war against Iraq. "This is a most unfortunate decision by three allies".

The NATO ally which would be on the frontline of any war in Iraq, formally invoked a key article of NATO's founding treaty aimed at putting pressure for agreement to defend its territory,. NATO criticized the European trio's position as illogical and politically motivated." These wore political calculations which wore driving the strategy. There wore many contradictions behind these three countries positions".

In London the crisis within NATO over Iraq, led to speculations in the media and the spokesman of Blair's government had said the question of beefing up Turkeys defence in the event of a U.S. led war was still up for debate.

Secretary General, George Robertson, of the alliances had said that the deadlock was very serious buy a solution could be at hand.

Turkey formally sought NATO support for defence of its territory in the event of a U.S. led war in Iraq. France, Belgium, and Germany had blocked proposals to start planning for the deployment of AWACS plane, Patriot missiles and anti chemical and anti biological warfare teams to Turkey.

Robertson in a news conference had said "I think people are focusing on it now in a very determined way. Turkey has asked for support under Article 4 of the NATO treaty and many of the countries concerned believe that now the situation was an unavoidable way on Turkey and its defence", that may well help to lead to a solution to a present problem.

The Russian President, Vladimir Putin, touring France and Germany at a time when the two NATO members voted out a U.S. plan to boost Turkey's defences in case of a U.S. led war on Iraq. He called for closer unity within (NATO) the anti terror coalition. "The way the world is evolving today, we are going to face many threats of universal nature and we need to unite efforts, not divide nations, to effectively handle these threats. I think we all have a stake in taking care of the U.S. does not adopt an isolationist stance. This would not help us build a new world order. I do not think it was worth inciting anti American sentiments. We agree that pressure should be put on Iraq. Russia has been uniquely positioned to act as a bridge between Europe and the U.S. on the issue of Iraq as the most influential member of the anti terror coalition out side NATO". At the same time the Russian leader said that more international inspections should be sent to Baghdad for more effective monitoring.

As Germany and France plan to avoid the chances of a war in Iraq it plans a three fold increase in the number of U.N.

weapons inspectors in Iraq, extensive deployment of U.N. troops across the country, extension of no-fly zones, the use of American, German and French reconnaissance planes in aerial search of Iraq's alleged arsenal of weapons of mass destruction and a host of other measures to strengthen the arms monitoring process.

The Russian President, Vlaedimir Putin, was of the view as saying that his country was almost completely in agreement with the ideas put for word by Germany and France.

Now out of the five permanent members two wore in favor of the Russian idea that the plan amount to effective handing over Iraq to the U.N. through the Iraqi President, Saddam Hussein, would be allowed to remain. Idea backed by Russia which like, France has a veto on the U.N. Security Council and can shoot down any British-U.S. resolution seeking a mandate for a military action.

The United States and Britain wore quick enough to under stand the Russian plan to shoot down when division takes place and decided to dismiss the plan to push for military action in the Security Council.

The opinion in the British government was that the number of weapons inspectors would not help unless Iraq was serious about cooperation. That means Iraq's compliance with the U.N. resolution 1441 which directed Baghdad to disarm fully.

The U.S. Secretary of State, Collin Powell, considered the plan as "diversion and not a solution". For Defence Secretary, Donald Ramsfeld, the preferred solution was for Saddam Hussein to go on exile.

The new resolution, which was likely to be cosponsored by Britain, would find Iraq to be in material breach of the demands and obligations and would seek authorization to use military action.

In case if U.S. and Britain push for new resolution than Russia, China and France all the three which are permanent members in the Security Council would exercise their veto or choose to abstain, in that event, the United States would be looking for nine votes in the 15 member Security Council of the U.N.

The other plan was the extent of the determination of the U.S. was that, despite the maximum diplomatic pressure of France, China and Russia Veto the new resolution, which the Bush administration was planning to go about on its own with its so called coalition of the willing to disarm Iraq as it has been saying all along. What the Bush administration have been saying in the past one week would be any thing to go by, Washington was determined for a conflict with or without the backing of traditional allied and friends in the Council.

The Bush administration was aware of the widening negative image that it was getting in Europe and commented that Belgium, France and Germany blocked NATO from planning for the defence of Turkey in the event of a war with Iraq. "I think their decision is short sighted, in my judgment I hope they will reconsider" President, Bush expressed his opinion.

The Turkish Foreign Minister, Yasar Yakis, expressed "Germany, Belgium and France did not veto the protection of Turkey. These countries have problems with the timing. Problem could be overcome because that was not disagreement on principle".

Section of the Arab countries appreciated the stand taken by France and Germany. The Yemeni Foreign Minister Abu Bakr Abdullah Al Kurbi was of the view that "Whether or not it succeeds in convincing the U.S. to abandon the use of force, France will be perceived as country that has defended the U.N. resolution till the end".

Regarding the stand taken by France and Germany, a representative of the Patriotic Union of Kurdistan (PUK) had said "I cannot understand their position; they want to let Saddam Hussein, stay in power. Unfortunately the position of some of the European countries gives the impression to the Iraqi people that these countries wore trying to prevent Saddam from being overthrown".

The real heat began in Turkey when its political leader of ruling Justice and Development Party (AKP) Tayyip Erdogan, objected to the Turkish forces fighting its neighboring Iraq under U.S. command as a national insult, and a shameful decision. Erdogan made it clear that Turkey opposed such a move as humiliation.

Turkish Top brass in the military who respect Erdogan with his background in politics wore reported to agree. The Generals wore of the view that Turkish forces must be free to act on their own.

However the White House frequently said that all military activity in or around Iraq should be carried out under the command of an international coalition.

While Turkey was edging towards allowing its NATO ally, the U.S. to use the country as a launching pads for an attack on

Iraq. Turkey stressed it will not join the fighting and would only use its troops to prevent a humanitarian disaster in northern Iraq.

The French Prime Minister, Jean Pierre Raffarin, expressed "it is up to us pursue the cooperation and to do every thing possible to prevent a conflict that could seriously threaten regional and international stability". France, Russia and China along with Germany wore among the strongest countries which took initiative for a peaceful solution to the Iraq crisis. He made a point that "we have interest in working hand in hand" on the Iraq crisis.

Putin along with Jacques Chirac, the two leaders issued a join declaration in which France, Russia and Germany proposed strengthened U.N. weapons inspections in Iraq, part of a diplomatic initiative aimed at disarming Saddam Hussein without war.

Putin made his point "We are against the war, both of our countries insist on the need to solve the problem and the crisis diplomatically and we consider that careless action could lead to unknown results". He also said that his country was ready to contribute equipment and aviation to any efforts to enhance inspections. Supporting Putin's commitment Chirac also offered to send Mirage-IV surveillance aircraft.

The Chinese President, Jiang Zemin, expressed support for the declaration in a telephonic conversation with Chirac. He had said that China supports the declaration by Russia, France and Germany that calls for strengthening U.N. weapons inspectors in Iraq and stressed the need to solve the crisis diplomatically. It is understood that in his telephonic conversation had said that his country maintains its long time stand that every thing possible should be done to avoid a military conflict.

The Chinese government news agency, Xinhua reported "the inspection in Iraq was effective and should be continued and strengthened. Warfare was good for no one, and it will be our responsibility to take various measures to avoid war".

Chinese government announced that it was withdrawing some staff from its embassy in Iraq personal whose presence was not necessary.

The British Foreign Secretary, Jack Straw, Publicly rejected the French, German, Russian and Chinese proposals to defuse the Iraqi crisis by allowing the U.N. weapons inspectors more time and increasing their strength to make the inspection process more effective. He questioned the logic of their proposal saying even a thousand fold increase in the inspection regime would not help in the absence of Iraqi cooperation. "Saddam refuses to cooperate then how will higher numbers help".

U.S Presidents, National Security Advisor, Condoleezza Rice, had a discussion with the Top Weapon Inspector, Hans Blix. Bush administration was very much concerned that Hans Blix might soften his comments in his second report which then could weaken the case for Bush. And in this regard it was suspected that Rice could have influenced on Blix to make a negative comment on his visit to Iraq in the Security Council against Iraq in his second report to be presented on February 14th 2003.

Hans Blix was strong minded and did not yield to any pressure tactics by Condoleezza Rice, though Hans Blix or Condoleezza did not make any statement on their meeting at the White House, but the facts of the matter was glaring on the face of Condoleezza Rice. It was clear that Rice had failed to convince Hans Blix to get report what White House wanted the report in Favour of U.S. This attempt by Condoleezza was a big failure not only for herself but to the entire White House radicals.

The next day when media persons asked Defense Secretary, Donald Rumsfeld about the matter related to the meeting between Rice and Hans Blix, Donald said Hans Blix was wasting time and prolonging to give his report "you know why, because he is a homo".

The entire media was shocked to listen to Donald Rumsfeld making such a nasty statement against weapon inspector Hans Blix.

One thing was clear that the Bush administration was very much disappointed by the facts of the matter between Condoleezza Rice and Hans Blix and had come to a conclusion that Hans Blix must be demoralized and that could lead to his resignation as weapon inspector so that U.S. could go faster in its strategy to go for a war with Iraq as the entire U.S. military mechanism was well prepared in position and waiting for orders to Invade Iraq.

Japanese Prime Minister, Junichir Koizumi, indicated in Tokyo that the question of war and peace in Iraq would depend on his actions of its leader, Saddam Hussein. "It is for Iraq to explain itself" as the U.N. weapons inspections could not be construed as a form of investigation.

North Korea had not met its obligations under the international nuclear accords, and the U.N. watchdog agency had said that "it remains unable to verify that there had been no diversion of nuclear material for weapons use by North Korea. The IAEA urged the North Korea to comply but also said it that "its desire for a peaceful resolution of the nuclear issue and its support for diplomatic means to that purpose.

The International Atomic Energy Agency's, 35 nation board of governors had made the decision, its last resort after months of intransigence by North Korea in an emergency session at the agency's headquarters in Vienna.

Russia and Cuba abstained from the vote, which sets the stage for possible sanctions. "We consider the sending of the question to the U.N. SecurityCouncil to be premature and counter productive step said Russia's representative in a statement.

The Philippine Government had told an Iraqi diplomat allegedly linked to the Muslim extremist Abu Sayyaf group to leave the country within 48 hours.

The Philippine Foreign Secretary Blas Ople, had said that he confronted the Iraqi charged affairs, Samir A-Masih Bolus, with the detailed intelligence report.

Ople said he expected retaliation from Baghdad. Most of the Philippine embassy staff in Baghdad had already left for Jordan in anticipation of U.S. military action.

Osama bin Laden, the head of Al Qaeda terror network in an appeal that was made in a voice tape aired by the Al-Jazeera television satellite station throughout the Arab world and believed U.S. officials to be authentic. It was broadcast as U.S. officials warned of devastating attacks within the U.S. and the Gulf, where U.S. forces are accumulating for a possible attack against Iraq. The speaker urged the Iraqis to draw the Americans into urban combat. "We stress the importance of martyrdom operations against the enemy, those attacks that have scared Americans and Israelis like never before. We advise about his importance of drawing the enemy into long, close and exhausting fighting, taking advantage of camouflaged positions in plains, farms, mountains and cities".

The U.S. officials said the call proves the world must fear the Iraqi President, Saddam Hussein's ties to the Al Qaeda terrorist network.

In Washington U.S. secretary of State Collin Powell, said "the nexus between terrorists and states that are developing weapons of mass destruction can no longer be looked away and ignored".

Israeli soldiers shot and killed two armed Palestinian infiltrators in the Gaza Strip, in which an 8year old Palestinian boy was also killed in the shooting between the Palestinians and Israeli army. Israeli tanks rumbled down the streets in Bethlehem after a Palestinian sniper killed an Israeli army officer who was standing in front of the Church of the Nativity, the traditional birth place of Jesus. The Israel army had said soldiers were checking a suspicious vehicle when a Palestinian fired from a nearby alley and killed the officer.

The violence flared as the army kept a tight closure on the West Bank, making it difficult for Palestinian Muslims to move about during the Eid al-Adha holiday.

The British Prime Minister, Tony Blair, ordered deployment of troops to protect the world's busiest airport after he was informed about the possible missile attack on a low flying plane. It was described as the most serious terrorist threat since 9/11 attack in U.S., and the police said they were not ruling out the use of troops in Central London even as security was stepped up at Manchester airport.

The British army intelligence stated that the information's wore specific, very real and solid. "We would not do this without extremely good reason. Our aim is to avoid a potential terrorist attack". At one stage, there were reports to shut down Heathrow airport completely but the idea was dropped for fear of causing panic among the people. It was also felt that this could be regarded as a victory by terrorists.

Security agencies pointed the finger at Al Qaeda for the threat saying it was known to have an interest in airports and possess shoulder launched missiles.

The surrounding Heathrow airport looked like any army camp as tanks rolled pas the complex and soldiers stopped and searched every vehicle which passed that way.

In a dramatic change that could benefit the U.S. decision in the Security Council was under way when the experts appointed by Chief Weapons Inspector, Hans Blix, announced that the Iraqi missile Al Samoud - 2, exceeded the maximum 150 km range allowed by the U.N. The findings would undoubtedly boost the position of the U.S. which had been saying that Baghdad had not been confirming to the terms of the Security Council's resolution.

The top U.S. diplomat, John Negroponte, in the U.N. said "this is something that our own intelligence sources had been saying us for long time but apparently, it is a matter of decision among the experts.

Al Samoudh - 2 and the Al Fatah, wore the two missiles that kept the U.N. inspectors worried about Iraq's missile development and wore trying to find more details about its capacity.

In India, Prime Minister, Atal Behari Vajpayee, expressed that India will not mediate in the on going tussle between Iraq and the United States.

The Egyptian President, Hosni Mubarak, after meeting the Libyan President, Moammar Gadhafi and Syrian President, Bashar Al Assad, and the Saudi Foreign Minister, Saudi Al Faisal, announced that Arabs could do nothing to prevent or avoid a war on Iraq and it was up to the Iraqi President, Saddam Hussein, to do some thing about.

The concern of the Arab countries wore that if the arms inspectors work continued in Iraq then they had a chance to make their effort. It was understood that with 1,20,000 U.S. troops already in Kuwait, and the Gulf Cooperation Council (GCC) countries had no business to do or interfere as another 1,00,000 U.S. troops wore to take their position in the Gulf region.

Gen. Powell said the United States would not be deterred by U.N. Security Council opposition of using force. "France and Germany are resisting. They believe that more inspections, more time. The question I will put to them is why more time and more inspections and how much more time. Or are you just delaying for the sake of delaying in order to get Saddam Hussein off the hook and no disarmament. This is a challenge I will put to them".

Chinese President, Jiang Zemin, stated over North Korea's suspected nuclear programme is important on account of Beijing's substantive strategic equation with Pyongyang. Being a veto empowered permanent member of the Security Council, China is in a position to determine the U.N.'s view of North Korea's Nuclear non Proliferation Treaty (NPT). China voted in favor of the resolution that raised the North Korean issue onto the Security Council's court.

Japan also called on North Korea to dismantle its nuclear weapons programme in a manner that the world body accepts.

The Top American envoy to the U.N. John Negroponte, had said that a final decision on Gen. Powell attending the Security Council's session had not been made but in all probability, he will attend. "We believe that Iraq has simply failed in every respect to cooperate sincerely either the inspection process. So adding a few inspectors is not going to serve purpose, and in our view, going to have much meaning if you don't have that essential ingredient, which is Iraqi compliance".

Gen. Powell indicated that he may be present in the Security Council saying he planned to ask the Foreign Ministers of France and Germany if they wore trying to get Iraq, off the hook. "We are reaching moment of truth with respect to the relevance of the U.N.S.C to impose its will on a nation like Iraq and we are reaching a moment of truth as to whether or not this matter will be resolved peacefully or will be resolved by military conflict".

Soon after chief weapons inspector, Hans Blix, completes his presentation in the Security Council, both U.S. and Britain was expected to immediately introduce a resolution demanding for the use of force to disarm Iraq. The real showdown would take place with U.S. and Britain on one side and China, Russian and France on the other side.

At the United Nations Security Council, the Chief Weapons Inspector, Hans Blix made his statement that access to inspection sites was almost and always prompt and that there were no indications that the Iraqi's knew in advance of the inspections. Axes to the inspections had improved, and Iraq had cooperated on private interviews with scientists, and more over the inspectors had found no weapons of mass destruction, but there was no account of many prohibited weapons. Even the Chairman of the IAEA, had said this, his agency had moved from reconnaissance to the investigative phase, and Iraq continued to provide access to its sites.

As Blix was still yet to complete statement on his report, the impatient United States, started its high profile diplomacy with the intention of pulling the other members on its side like France,

Russia and China. The doubts in the minds of the members, was that the weapons inspectors may once again, like in the previous report might be critical of Iraq, but would not criticise it completely.

The United States desperately wanted the Security Council to go on record that Saddam Hussein had not disarmed and therefore faces serious consequences.

The entire content of the weapons inspectors report left for the members to debate on the final element of the report. While Russian, France and China looked for a positive element where as the United States and Britain pointed on the criticism in the report. That Saddam Hussein had not lived up to the U.N. resolution 1441 and he had deliberately pushed aside the final chance to come out of the case.

The United States, President, George W. Bush expressed that his country would use every ounce of the power to eliminate terror. As America is facing the greatest danger in the world and the rouge state regime that possess weapon of mass destruction would use such weapons for blackmail, mass murder and terror.

Iraqi President, Saddam Hussein passed an authoritative order banning the import and production of weapon of mass destruction (WMD). Neither companies or individual or any other organizations wore banned from importing any of the material related to WMD. This move by the Iraqi leader had influenced the debate in the divided Security Council. The new declaration increased the momentum of anti war protests around the world. Saddam had also ordered the concerned minister to take necessary steps to implement the new declaration.

The U.N. Secretary General, Kofi Annan, told the Security Council, the extent to which the world body was planning for contingencies in the event of a military strike with Iraq, especially as it related to humanitarian aspects.

Annan had taken steps to help the population and a task force had been set up to draw up contingency plan to deal the devastation situation. The task force headed by a Pakistani national, Rafeeudin Ahmed, who had been associated with the United Nations, Development Programme.

The United Nations Development Programme estimated rebuilding Iraq could involve $30 billion in the first three years, increasing to $100 billions.

It was estimated that out of the 27 million People in Iraq 4.5 million to 9.5 million would immediately need outside food for their survival.

The Iraqi Deputy Prime Minister, Tariq Aziz held talks with Pope John Paul II and promised to follow the requirement of the U.N. resolution and fulfill its demands. In his long conversation with Pope he also assured the Iraqi government's willingness in its cooperation to the international community. Aziz had another longer meeting with Vatican's Secretary of State, Candinal Angelo Sodano.

In response to the meeting with the Iraqi Deputy Prime Minister the Vatican had announced that the pope had repeated the need to follow the resolution of the Security Council with respect and faithfully.

The Vatican reiterated its opposition to a U.S. led war, saying that the military intervention would worsen the situation and the long suffering people who wore already facing embargo. The Pope had pointed out that the war with Iraq would be a defeat for humanity.

The United States, President, George W. Bush, in his message to the world body had said "United Nations Security Council, can now decide whether or not it resolve to enforce the resolution. I am optimistic that free nations will show backbone and courage in the face of true threats to peace and freedom". The Iraqi President, Saddam Hussein, is not disarming, he is deceiving. He once again reiterated that if Security Council did not rally behind U.S. it would go along with the coalition of the willing".

France was planning to handle the Syrian issue in a different way as it was the only Arab country out of 15 members in the U.N. Security Council. France backed by Russia and Germany was considering introducing a new resolution in the U.N. Security Council for the supporting continuation of inspections in Iraq. This method could effectively put on hold a possible U.N. move by the United States and Britain to authorize the use of force against Iraq.

The experts pointed out that in case Britain or the U.S. veto's the tripartite initiative then that could paralyse the Security Council and pose an existential threat to the United Nations. Knowing the facts of the risk involved the ambassadors of France and Russia got in touch with the Lebanese Foreign Minister, Mahmoud

Hammoud, ahead of a meeting of Arab League Foreign Ministers scheduled in Cairo. This method could evolve Euro-Arab anti war front on Iraq.

The French led initiative to avert war among the Arab countries, this effort might not benefit much as leaderships in Iraq's neighborhood, with the exception of Syria, Lebanon and Iran, appear to be lining up behind the U.S. Jordan and Kuwait wore expected to serve as launch pads for an attack on Iraq from the west and the south, while the six Persian Gulf countries, apart from giving base facilities to the United States wore also contributing troops to defend Kuwait. France which became the biggest negotiator of peace made all efforts contacting Arab leaders individually to convince then to avoid a war on Iraq.

France, Germany and Belgium wore opposing the U.S. demands that the Alliance should start contingency planning for Turkey's defence guarantees

After weeks of trying to change the three countries minds, diplomats announced the NATO Secretary General, George Robertson, had decided to wait till the U.N. Security Council debated on the Iraq crisis.

As a frontline ally of the U.S. led coalition in the war against terrorism and the mounting criticism by the religious parties of the Pakistan government support to the U.S. the government was caught in a dilemma. Joining the Council for a two year period beginning January 1st had only led to difficulty.

There was little doubt that Pakistan's initiative of joining the United Nations Security Council as a non permanent member had proved to be short lived. Islamabad was seriously worried over prospects of war in Iraq where it would be called upon to vote in the Council.

The U.S. military's presence in the Asia-Pacific region had come under criticism in the evolving contest of the North Korean nuclear Issue. There wore 37,000 American military personnel in South Korea, and Seoul's statement acquired importance in the context of the increasing crisis over North Korea's nuclear weapons programme.

In connection with the North Korean nuclear crisis China expressed it would not like the U.N., Security Council, to take cognisance of the North Korean issue at the present situation.

The DPRK reaffirmed again that the only way to come out of the present crisis was to accept its proposal for a non aggression pact between Washington and Pyongyang. It also said that it would not tolerate any attempt by the U.S. to overthrow the Kim Jong-il regime in North Korea.

The Japanese Prime Minister, Junichiro Koizumi expressed that a new resolution was necessary in the Security Council authorizing any military strike against Iraq in the present circumstances at the same time he called for international unity on the issue. The intention of Japan was to demand the same action against North Korea after the Iraq issue was over.

With the Security Council now totally occupied with the Iraqi crisis, the U.S. said it would discuss with other members of the Council on when to bring up North Korean issue for discussion.

The Director of the CIA had informed Congress that North

Korea had an untested ballistic missile that could reach parts of the U.S. The Bush administration is to some extent backing on China to deal with the problems in North Korea, but for the time being it was not clear that Washington had ruled out any direct dialogue with North Korea.

China and Russia had reacted favorably to U.S. idea that sanctions would not work out and the situation would be worst and will not work.

In the case of Iraq the United States was taking unilateral decision to go for a showdown with Iraq but in the case of North Korea the Bush administration was keen to go on the Security Council root to deal with the issue understandably that the matter was not within the bilateral range and it had to be handled multilaterally and was an international issue.

North Korea had stated that it would consider sanctions as an act of war.

Anti-war protesters throughout the world united in their opposition to a dangerous United States led strike against Iraq. In London at least one million people participated to bring pressure on the British Prime Minister, Tony Blair, who has been the main supporter of the U.S. bullish policy.

Several thousands marched in Berlin supporting the anti-war decision by the German Chancellor, Gerhard Schroeder.

In Syria nearly two lakh protesters marched through Damascus

In Bulgaria, Romania, Hungary, Brussels, South Korea, Malaysia, Thailand, Bosnia, Hong Kong, Bangladesh, Kazakhstan, Russia and Australia and India, though there wore no huge gathering the participants wore in good numbers.

In Baghdad thousands of Iraqis carrying machine guns demonstrated in support of Saddam Hussein. Many Iraqis displayed giant pictures of Saddam Hussein while some burnt American and Israeli flags. Anti-war speeches wore more attractive to the crowd in all these protests.

The U.S. President, Bush, had some strong words for Saddam Hussein in which he said "This war requires us to understand that terror is broader then one international network, that these terrorist networks have got some connections in countries run by dictators. And that's the issue with Iraq. When I speak about the war on terror, I not only talk about Al Qaeda, I talk about Iraq. Because after all Saddam Hussein has got weapons of mass destruction and he's used them, Saddam Hussein is used to deceiving the world and continues to do so and that's why he will be disarmed one way or the other".

After an embarrassing session at the Security Council, the Secretary of State, Collin Powell, insisted that the issue on Iraq would be decided in a few weeks and a resolution in this regard would be made. Powell who had to listen to all the members, through out the day, along with anti-war sentiment was quite frustrated. But was firm on his attitude that the Security Council would have to decide in the very near future regarding the serious consequences of Iraq. The Bush administration short term agenda in the form of a second resolution may have suffered set back for the time being but the larger Iraqi policy and objectives wore the same.

In the United States a group of U.S. soldiers including their parents and some member of the congress had filed a suit to block any invasion of Iraq unless the U.S. congress issues an outright declaration of war.

"The President Bush, is not a king, he does not have the power to wage war against another country without a declaration of war from Congress". Bush and Donald H. Rumsfeld, wore named as defendants in the suit which asks an injunction barring a war in Iraq.

Reacting to the law suit a spokesman had said that the President in his role as Commander-in-Chief and the Congress had passed a resolution in October authoring the President to use force in Iraq, but the plaintiffs insist the U.S. constitution required a declaration of war.

In the northern Gaza Strip in an attack by the Islamic militant group Hamas blue up an Israeli tank in which all the crew members wore said to have been killed. Hamas militant had videoed the entire operation. The group had said the tank had blazed for a full hour after the blast and was completely destroyed.

The Israel radio said that the ambulances and helicopters arrived at the scene to carry the bodies of he soldiers.

The Chairman of the Arab League, Mahamoud Hammoud, announced that any aggression against Iraq would have direct consequences for the entire region he warned "Arab countries might not be able to stop this war but then have responsibilities to consider steps toward taking a unified and clear stand against those who are beating the drums of war. Arab countries should refrain from giving any military assistance in any aggression to ward Iraq. If the war is launched, this will be considered as a unilateral act in violation of international legitimacy".

Iraqi Foreign Minister, Naji Sabri, said that Iraq wanted fellow Arab states to do more to avert war. "We are satisfied with the public's position, but so far Arabs have not crystallized an official position".

Most of U.S. launch pads for the military strike on Iraq are located in the Persian Gulf states, while Egypt is known to be a close ally of Washington. Syria opposes war as it fears that the emergence of a pro-U.S. dispensation in Baghdad after a war can be detrimental to its interests.

As the fallout of the European efforts to avert a war spreads in the Gulf region, it had found a reflection in the pro-U.S. Kurdish parties that have begun to sharpen their attack of France and Germany.

The reason that Kurds wore supporting United States is that in the past Kurds have been victims of an Iraqi chemical weapons attack in Halabja in northern Iraq. It is therefore the wishes of the Kurds to see that Saddam Hussein is overthrown in Iraq.

In New York City 3,50,000 protesters braved the chilling winter and wore peacefully opposing the military action by the Bush administration for trying to wage a war against Iraq. The United Nations police denied permission for the marchers to be any where around the U.N. headquarters.

For the Bush administration after it found that they do not even have the require nine votes in the Security Council and the realization is that, along with Britain would have to show a significant change in attitude if China, Russia and France would have to agree on a text. This was under the assumption that Russia, France and China do not exercise the veto and abstain.

At the same time by using pressure on some of the non permanent members the Bush administration could ensure that the French proposal of expanding the inspections mechanism also did not have the required nine votes.

The outcome of the next Security Council meeting to hear non permanent member's views seemed to be a formal conclusion. The Bush administration and its key ally would suffer more embarrassment than what they did in the previous meeting when they wore taken to task for their current attitude and stance on Iraq.

One thing was clear that the Bush administration whether would it wait for the second resolution or not but one thing was certain that the result would be short of what Washington originally wanted.

Now that the members in the Security Council wore aware of the facts after the reports from the heads of the two inspectors show that they have been expanding their activity to cover an increasingly wide area of Iraq and the number of sites visits had also increased significantly. While these report did underline that Iraq's cooperation with the inspection process had not been up to the required levels, its overall content suggest that Baghdad can be trusted to move in the desired direction. And in these circumstances the conclusion leads support to the position taken by France and a majority of the members in the Security Council that an expansion and intensification of the inspection process is not only necessary but will produce results. It also rejects the U.S. arguments that Iraq cannot be rid of its Weapon of Mass Destruction potential by any means short of war.

CHAPTER - 8

North Atlantic Treety Organisation (NATO) broke the month long impasse, reaffirming alliance solidarity while supporting U.N. efforts for a peaceful solution.

NATO, Secretary General, Lord Robertson, stated "we have been able to collectively overcome the impasse. Alliance solidarity has prevailed".

Germany and Belgium drooped their objections to starting planning for Turkey's defence immediately, it was said that France kept away from this meeting.

Belgium, insisting on linking any eventual NATO deployment to developments, at the U.N. Security Council, but in the end it said "we continue to support efforts in the United Nations to find a peaceful solution to the crisis".

All the NATO members in the meeting wore united that Iraq must disarm. However with Washington pushing for military action, differences remained over how much more time to give to the U.N. weapons inspectors.

The E.U. foreign policy chief, Javier Solana, expressed "I think everybody has recognized that war is the last resort, I think everyone agrees war may be necessary at a given moment but we have not at this point reached the time for that.

Britain and Washington stood firm saying 'Time is running out". British Foreign Secretary, Jack Straw defending his idea said that the "U.N. setout very clearly that this was the final opportunity for Iraq to comply, that involves hard decisions for everyone across Europe. It is only by fighting tyranny that we are able to enjoy the freedoms that we do".

At the same time the Prime Minister of Turkey, Abdullah Gul, hinted in Ankara that the U.S. might yet have to wait for the permission it urgently seeks to deploy troops on Turkish soil for a possible war on Iraq. There are certain points we give importance to the present issue and without reaching an agreement on those points I believe it will be difficult to persuade parliament".

Continuing their search the United Nations weapons inspectors visited three more sites to determine whether Iraq possessed any weapons of mass destruction. Al-Mutaseem one of Iraq's important facilities in which final tests on the "Al-Fatah" missile was carried out. This mission by the weapons inspectors was on the suspicion when he said in his statement in the Security Council that Al-Fatah missile had a range beyond 150 km

After the 1991 Gulf War the U.N. had imposed on Iraq the ceiling that Iraq's liquid propelled Al-Samoud 2 missile violates the U.N. norms as it had a range beyond 150 km. the responsibility will then be on Iraq to destroy these systems. The inspection team had also visited Al-Haithem factory north of Baghdad and the Al-Nida facility where missile parts were manufactured.

The U.N. experts had also conformed regarding Blix's opinion that casting chambers refurbished by Iraq could produce engines for missiles capable of flying beyond the limits.

Iraq, however maintained that the Al-Samoud missile marginally exceeded its range ceiling only because it was tested without payload.

The Russian Foreign Minister, Igor Ivanov, warned "the use of force is an extreme measure that can only be applied if all other opportunities were exhausted. The last session of the U.N. Security Council had shown once again that opportunities for a political settlement are for from being exhausted. The work of the international inspectors in Iraq had proven their efficiency and ability to fulfill the task set by the U.N. Security Council. The international community must exert all necessary pressure on Baghdad to make it cooperate with the international inspectors and comply with the U.N. Security Council resolution. Ivanov, reaffirmed that Russia was ready to consider a new Security Council resolution if it's necessary to strengthen the efficiency of the inspectors work and help the political settlement".

U.S. National Security Advisor, Condoleezza Rice, expressed "we are in a diplomatic window but one that can't stay open much longer is continuing to talk about more time and more time and more time is simply going to relieve pressures on the Iraqi leader to do what he must do. We have not drafted the resolution. We are working it with different parties, with our friends. Sooner or later, we believe sooner, the Security Council is going to have to say that Saddam Hussein has not taken that final opportunity to comply, and the Security Council is going to have to act, or the United States will have to act with a coalition of the willing. Putting this thing off is not an option".

Israel said it would intensify its hunt for Hamas militants, who have carried out many of the bombings and other attacks against Israeli targets in the past several months of fighting. The Hamas fugitive, Riyad Abu Zeid, was seriously wounded in the Israeli raid and later died at an Israeli hospital, Israeli radio reported.

"Peace! Peace! Peace!" cried Bishop Desmond Tutu, the former Archbishop of Cape Town. "Let America listen to the rest of the world. And the rest of the world is saying. Give the inspectors time"

The weekend in Australia witnessed anti-war protests where nearly half a million protesters went round the streets of Sydney, protesters in Adelaide, Brisbane, Canberra, Hobart, Perth and Melbourne witnessed huge gathering of protesters.

In U.S. the United for Peace and Justice organization organised the demonstration and over 1,00,000 demonstrators, people of all ages bearing the zero temperature near the United Nations building and demanded more time for the weapons inspectors. "Just because you have the biggest gun doesn't mean you must use it" the protesters shouted.

Protesters also took to the streets in similar but smaller demonstrations in other cities including Philadelphia, Seattle, Chicago, Detroit and Miami.

Europe was one among the most concentrated destination where in Rome; over one million people participated in the demonstration.

Germany after 1945 saw the biggest protest in which half a million demonstrators participated.

British, Prime Minister, Tony Blair, was shattered with the domestic pressure not to push for war with Iraq had increased after massive peace protest in London and the Foreign Secretary, Jack Straw, admitted that it would be 'very, very' difficult to take military action without public support.

The Labour party's image in the minds of the British citizens was gradually fading and wore loosing hopes on Blair's Iraq policy. In the Labour Party meeting the Ministers acknowledged the depth of public opinion and had said Blair was aware of the risks. "Every body recognizes the enormous political dangers to the Government and this party. No one is more conscious of that then the Prime Minister and the Cabinet".

In the open letter from People in the United States against war several valuable write-up's wore found out of which few comments wore extremely good it said, the U.S. for setting itself above the law "in part because the United States insists on a prerogative of using nuclear weapons, and because it may have ulterior motives, unrelated to the use of disarmament."

"I believe the open letter from the people of the United States to the rest of the world states the case against war as persuasively as any I have seen", said Professor(emeritus, Boston University).

"People around the world and in the United States are opposing U.S. policy on Iraq because we seek a peaceful resolution of conflicts", said Dr. Micheal Klare, who is Five College Professor of Peace and world Security Studies, based at Hampshire College in Massachusetts.

Colorado Cowboy, Clergy, immigrants, peace activists, local elected officials and environmentalists. In reaching out to the world, they cite Mahatma Gandhi's rejection of the kind of patriotism that "sought to mount the distress, or exploitation, of other nationalities" and affirm their determination not to "allow the ill-considered and short-sighted military and energy policies of the U.S. Government to separate us from the fellowship of other human beings across national borders".

"I don't want to be despised as a warmongering person when I travel abroad just because the government of the United States is bullying the rest of the world", said Roxanne Turnage, Executive Director of the CS fund and one of the Charter signatories of the letter.

"Double standards regarding the rule of law and about weapons of mass destruction are not only wrong they are downright dangerous", said Arjun Makhijani, President of the Institute for Energy and Environmental Research.

The European Union (E.U.) delivered a surprisingly though warning to the Iraqi President, Saddam Hussein, to either seize the last chance to disarm or face war.

The European hawks led by Britain, includes Italy, Spain, Netherlands, and Portugal. The doves, besides France, Belgium, Germany, Luxembourg, Greece and Austria. At the middle wore Finland, Ireland, and Sweden.

The final out come of the E.U. was that "Baghdad should have no illusions; it must disarm and cooperate immediately and fully. Iraq has a final opportunity to resolve the crisis peacefully"

The French President, Jacques Chirac, also insisted that France would veto a second United Nations resolution, to explicitly authorize an Anglo-American initiated U.N. sponsored military action against Iraq, He said "There is no need for a second resolution, which France would have no choice but to oppose".

The E.U. leader's statement followed an earlier warning by the U.S. Secretary General, Kofi Annan, that the E.U. should avoid internal rift. The E.U. leaders agreed that the U.N. weapons inspectors be given more time and resources they needed to complete their job in Iraq.

The British Prime Minister, Tony Blair's popularity had decreased as he went the U.S. routs on Iraq, which the E.U. did not like, particularly France and Germany.

The Israeli troops had reoccupied all of Bethlehem, along with other West Bank towns, in an offensive against militants.

With the complete take over of Bethlehem area the Israel's security cabinet approve the construction of the wall through Bethlehem in Septembers 2003, as part of a series of barriers around Jerusalem that are intended to keep out Palestinian militants.

The order said 3.5 acres wore being taken by the Israeli army.

Later on Israel distributed notices to Palestinians living near the tomb that the neighborhood is formally being seized by Israel.

Over the past several months of fighting, Palestinian stone throwers and gunman had frequently clashed with soldiers guarding Bethlehem.

Palestinians complained that Israel grabbed the land illegally and was dividing the town in violation of previous peace agreements.

Israel said the wall is necessary to protect Jewish worshippers and keep Palestinian militants out of Israel.

On March 1st, the chief weapons inspectors, Hans Blix and Mohammad El Baradei, return's to report to the Security Council.

In addition to this, the French had proposed for a Ministerial Meeting of the Council meeting on March 14, but the Bush administration had rejected the idea.

The fact is that when the resolution is ready to be put to vote, it would be specific in its language on the expectations from Iraq including a statement that this was the last opportunity to the regime in Baghdad.

What the Whitehouse was not interested was further debates in the Security Council that would come after additional reports from the weapons inspectors.

The indication from Washington was that the Bush is not about to rush into a war with Iraq and was willing to give diplomacy some more weeks.

The French counter-intelligence service had found no evidence of links between Iraq and the Al Qaeda network, the chief Pierre Bousquet de Florian head of the DST agency said that "one thing is clear that there was no links between the regime of the Iraqi President, Saddam Hussein, and Al Qaeda, But he said that though the Al Qaeda leader, Osama Bin Laden, despises Hussein "some times they have interests in common".

The British Prime Minister, Tony Blair's at his monthly press conference at Downing Street came after an opinion poll showed that his personal standing among British voters had taken a huge blow.

Blair stick to his decision that he would not be deterred by public opinion from supporting a U.S. led military action against Iraq if he believed that was the "right thing" to do.

Blair also made it clear that a military action could well involve a regime change, though the main aim was disarmament. He said if it were a benign regime, things would have been different but given the "brutal nature" of the Hussein government the Iraqis would be the happiest people if it was removed.

The French move to bring home its aircraft carrier Charles de Gaulle from the Mediterranean Sea, setting back the possibility of its participation in a war against Iraq. French move came at a time when the United States was engaged in positioning its aircraft carriers in the Persian Gulf and the Mediterranean Sea for possible attack against Iraq. Britain had also sent in its effort by deploying its carrier Ark Royal in the battle zone.

The North Korean People's Army said in a statement, that "if the U.S. violates and misuses the Armistice Agreement, there will be no need for North Korea to remain bound to the Armistice Agreement". North Korea aware of the suspected move by the United States to impose sanctions on the Kim Jong-II regime by acting along or in conjunction with other countries.

In an authentic version of his latest remarks Kim Jong-II, noted that the important thing was the U.S.-North Korea talks. He also identified that U.S. as South Korea's most important ally in these circumstances and context that the U.S. Ambassador to South Korea, Thomas Hubbard, declared in Seoul that Washington "emphatically disagrees with North Korea's contention that this nuclear issue was strictly a bilateral dispute between North Korea and the U.S".

In India the Union Finance Minister, Jaswant Singh, in the Vajpayee Government while replying to a question in the Parliament had said that a War should be avoided and that all the parties must cooperate to find a peaceful resolution to the issue. He was answering the question on behalf of the Defence Minister Yeshwanth Sinha, who was in Russia on an official visit.

The Indian Parliament, believed in maintaining the U.N. relevance in matters relating to international security and the need to implement Resolution 1441 and avoid a humanitarian crisis in Iraq and in the Gulf region, at the same time it was also the importance of maintaining international and regional stability.

During the Discussion in the Indian Parliament on the Iraq issue majority of the speakers wore extremely critical of the U.S. and no one in the house supported military action against Iraq.

After 54 year of struggle finally Turkey was to get NATO cover for safeguarding its territory. NATO brought to a close the Turkey's security request one of the long pending issues. The decision was taken by the Defence Planning Committee in which 18 nation alliances on which France does not sit. It agreed to deploy AWACS early warning aircraft, Patriot air defence missile systems and chemical biological response units in southern Turkey, a launch pad for any U.S. led strike on Baghdad.

The U.S. Ambassador to NATO, Nicholas Burns, welcomed decision at a sign that the alliance had lived up to its responsibility to respond to an ally in a time of threat. "Alliance solidarity had prevailed".

Washington was unhappy with the Turkey delaying in passing legislation that will unable it to position its forces in Turkey and use the Turkey territory to transit troops into northern Iraq. By sending in its forces quickly, the U.S. was keen to establish control over the northern Iraq oil fields spread out around the oil cities of Mosul and Kirkuk soon. Information's about Iraqi plans to blow up oil fields in this area ahead of a U.S. attack appear to have added a sense of urgency to Washington's war plans in this area.

Turkey was running short of time hardly 48 hours was left to decide whether or not it will allow its territory to be used as a staging post for the U.S. attack on northern Iraq. Because the U.S. would consider contingency plans to position its forces to northern Iraq from an alternative allocation.

For allowing the U.S. forces to operate from its soil Turkey had openly demanded a $30 billion package as the price. This was nearly twice the aid package that the two sides had been discussing for some time. Turkey was of the opinion that this amount was necessary to compensate losses in case the U.S. attacks Iraq. Without such a hefty package, Turkey dose not feel inclined to be dragged in to a war. With over more than 90% of its country men opposing alliance with U.S. along with this Turkey had to face regional terrorism since the last Gulf war, which was planned by some sections of Kurdish refugees that fled from Iraq during that war.

The U.S. had agreed to the Turkish proposal to push its forces in considerable depth into northern Iraq. Along with this the U.S. had also agreed to the Turkish demand of not posting its forces on Northern Iraq under a U.S. led coalition command. Both sides wore believed to have agreed on opening a joint command centre at Diyarbakir located on the Turkish Iraq border.

One of Britain's leading news paper (The Independent) carried sensational news that British and American intelligence were tracking three giant cargo ships on suspicion that they may be carrying Iraqi weapons of mass destruction.

The front page news quoted as "authoritative" sources as saying that the ships had aroused suspicion because they had maintained complete radio silence and their captains had refused to provide information in their cargoes or destination. This was in breach of international maritime laws.

The report claimed they were chartered by a shipping agent in Egypt and had berthed in a handful of Arab countries, including Yemen.

It was said if the ships were really carrying Iraqi arsenal they could provide Britain and America the smoking gun that they had been looking for to justify a military action on Iraq. According to "The Independent" the ships wore thought to have set sail from a country other than Iraq to avoid interception by Western navel patrols in the Gulf region.

However the experts wore of the opinion that if those ships wore carrying weapon of mass destruction, those could have been smuggled out through Syria or Jordan.

These ships which was said to be flying the flags of three nations, had been sailing for three months after they reportedly left port in last November 2002 after the U.N. weapons inspectors arrived in Baghdad.

In case the ship was carrying chemical and biological weapons or fissile nuclear materials, and if there was any damage to the ship and the materials wore to be sunk in the sea then the environmental damage could be catastrophic. With this concern the British and American military forces wore believed to be reluctant to stop and search the vessels for fear that any intervention might result in them being scuttled.

The Chinese President, Jiang Zemin, expressed the hope that the Korean question could be resolved through dialogue among all the parties concerned. There was no direct or explicit reference to the United Nation's Security Council. This, according to regional diplomatic observers, was significant; the fact was that China had at a meeting with the International Atomic Energy Agency (IAEA) supported its move to the U.N. Security Council. The intention of China was looking clear that the issue could be sorted out even outside the direct involvement of the U.N. Security Council. It was in this aspect that China had said that its recent vote at the IAEA Board meeting did not imply any support for a U.N. intervention.

Zemin also informed that the inspections route was still our direction of efforts.

With this it was clearly understood that China was in complete tune with the French wavelength in the ongoing confrontation between Paris and Washington over Iraq.

The Toni Blair's government suffered an embarrassing blow against its tough asylum policy. The High Court blocked the government's decision and said the new measures requiring refugees to lodge their asylum claims as soon as they entered the country or forego their right to state funded food and shelter breached the European Convention on Human Rights. It said that insufficient consideration had been given to the issue and the decision as it applied to the other refuges who had challenged it must be quashed and reconsidered if that has not already happened.

The Home Secretary, David Blunkett, however, said the Government would challenge the ruling. He said he was deeply concerned and warned that the Government would continue to be tough on illegal immigrants.

In an overnight raids by the Israeli troops on militant stronghold in the Gaza strip, killing at least 11 Palestinians.

The raids suffered a setback on the ceasefire dialogue between the two sides but the army had decided to intensify operations against Islamic militants after a landmine blast that gutted an Israeli tank and killed its four crew members in northern Gaza.

The weapon inspectors in Iraq continued their search in the Ibn al-Haithem facility, located in the north of Baghdad, which produces missile parts, and the Al Samoud-2 factory, which makes liquid propellant engines for the missiles. They also visited the Al-Kudus company involved in explosives research and development and the Al Basil Company which makes chemicals. Under the U.N. resolution, the inspectors can order the missiles destroyed or rendered harmless. But U.N. diplomats wore saying on condition of anonymity that Blix was likely to send a letter to Iraq in coming days asking it to destroy all Samoud- 2 as it exceeds its range capacity.

On February 14th 2003: Hans Blix and Mohamed El Baradei, told the Security Council, that they detected some improvement in cooperation by Saddam Hussein's government. But Blix also said inspectors found that the Al Samoud - 2 exceeded the permitted range and blamed Iraq for not giving a full accounting of chemical and biological weapons programs.

Saddam Hussein said that Iraq doesn't want war with United States but at the same time peace cannot be kept at the expense of "our independence, dignity and freedom. Iraq does not want war" but peace "at any cost was unacceptable.

While the U.S. and Britain wore trying to pressurise the non permanent members of the United Nations Security Council there wore also indications that France was doing its best to put its views forward among the non permanent members and matter was expected to come before the Secretary General. The formal voting declaring Iraq to be in material breach of trust would not come before the top inspectors Hans Blix gets before the Council on February 28.

While France had demanded for a Ministerial Meeting of the Council on March 14 but that was getting nowhere due to the objection of Washington.

The second resolution was being worked on at a fast pace and a full text would emerge when once U.S. and Britain have agreed on the final language.

Now what the Security Council was asking Iraq says no to hand over weapons of mass destruction rather to handover documents and evidence that Iraq was free of weapons was free from mass destruction. This is what the Iraq is doing." The bush administration remained totally unimpressed by the arguments of the international community. That the weapons inspectors should be given time or the inspections process should run out its course.

Defence experts point out that U.N. weapons Inspectors wore looking for greater cooperation from Iraq for curtailing its Al Samoud-2 missile programme and allowing confidential interviews of Iraqi scientists outside the country. Blix reportedly plans to send a letter to Iraq demanding the destruction of the Al Samoud-2 missiles and related machinery as its range exceeds 150 km that Baghdad had been permitted. Iraqi officials, however counter his conclusions by pointing out that the missile marginally exceeded its range in flight tests because it was not mounted with a guidance pack age and payload.

Two French Mirage IV planes, which had the capacity to undertake surveillance missions, wore on their way to expand the aerial search for alleged unconventional weapons hidden in Iraq.

Russia had also pledged to send its planes that specialize in carrying searches at night.

Iraq had submitted a list of 83 people that wore reportedly involved in the destruction of material from its biological and missile programmes. But U.N. officials said Iraq had still not provided enough information about nuclear, chemical and biological and long range missile operations.

Even Buchanan the spokesman for the chief U.N. weapons inspector Hans Blix said "Iraq needs to do more by way of cooperating particularly on unresolved disarmament issues, which are clearly issues of substance,"

However the Iraqi Ambassador, Mohammed Al Douri, expressed that his government was doing the maximum cooperation with inspectors. Iraq for the second time in a week had allowed a U.S. surveillance plane to scan for banned weapons and the U-2 spy plane flew for six hours and twenty minutes over Iraq territory.

The U.S. President, George W. Bash's agreement was that endless delay with Iraq is not an option. "Military action is this nation's last option. But let me tell you what not an option is, trusting Saddam Hussein is not an option. Denial and endless delay in the face of growing danger is not an option".

As Blix was rigid to his stand on Al Samoud- 2, the conclusion was that the U.S. and Britain would be presenting a resolution at the Security Council but this resolution would not be put to vote until the Council had heard from Blix and his colleague Mohammad El Baradei.

The new date for the new report had been put at March 7th. The resolution that was being prepared would be a tough one, the language being very specific both in terms of Iraq non cooperation and the consequences.

The resolution was expected to say that Iraq was in further material breach of its obligations and commitments. But first indications wore that the U.S. would not be insisting on a definite timeline to be a par of the resolution.

The U.S. Secretary of State, Collin Powell, said the resolution likely to be tabled in the next meeting would summaries the situation as it exists and reflect the concern over Iraq's persistent refusal to cooperate fully with the weapons inspectors.

The British Tabloid, (The Daily Mail)reported that Tony Blair and Bush had put in place an end game giving a 21 day ultimatum to Iraq to fall in line or face the consequences . Blair had a long telephonic conversation with Bush to discuss what was described as the when and how for a second resolution would move.

Gen. Powell said being considered but he confirmed that here would be no demand authorization for force. He was of the view that the proposed resolution would lay down a time frame for Iraq to comply with the existing U.N. resolution on disarmament.

Iran made its scientific achievement when it announced that it started mining uranium for the first time and will soon open a facility to process the one in to fuel, vowing to move ahead with a nuclear programme it said the nuclear is for energy purpose.

The new tactics adopted by the U.S. administration in the new resolution was aimed at gaining more support for it in the Security Council where the majority was opposed to the military intervention in Iraq and may not support a resolution that indicated authorize the use of force.

The new countries that enter the nuclear zone is Iran and the United Nations atomic energy chief arrived in Iran to tour nuclear facilities Tehran stated that its nuclear programme was for peaceful purpose but Washington claimed that it was part of the Iran secret weapons programme.

The IAEA chief Mohammed El Baradei arrived in Tehran accompanied by two officials from the IAEA head quarters. El Baradie was expected to travel to Natanz about 320 km south of Teheran to visit the site of an under construction facility. However Iran stated that the construction was for nuclear enrichment. Further El Baradei was expected to inspect another nuclear facility in Arak in central Iran.

The U.N. Chief Weapon Inspector, Hans Blix in his four page letter ordered Iraq to begin the demolition of dozens of its Al Samoud-2 missiles that violated the U.N. limits, beginning the process from March 1, deadline.

In his letter to Amer al-Saadi, an advisor to the Iraqi President, Saddam Hussein stated "the appropriate arrangements should be made so that the destruction process can commence by March 1, 2003". Blix handed the letter to the Iraqi Ambassador, Mohammed Al-Douri, at the U.N. headquarters.

March1 is also the date of Blix's next report on Iraq compliance due to the Security Council.

Blix demanded that Iraq eliminate the Al Samoud-2 missile system will test Baghdad's willingness to disarm as negotiations enter a crucial stage. Washington had strongly pushed for the destruction of these missiles and all their components.

Blix order to destroy the Al Samoud-2 missiles confronts the Iraqi government with a serious question whether to give a valuable weapons system its military would almost certainly use against a U.S. led coalition, or refuse to comply and face war that it is not cooperating with U.N. inspectors.

Blix also ordered that fuel, launchers, testing equipment and all software and documentation about the Al Samoud-2 program be destroyed but not the factories as the U.S. wanted.

Blix told Iraq to handover to inspectors for verifiable destruction all Al Samoud-2 missiles and warheads, SA-2 missile engines configured for use in those missiles, machinery to produce missile motors, and other components.

However there was no immediate response from Iraq on Blix letter.

The ball is now in Iraq's court they have to say, Blix not only had detailed the range of the missile but also the manner he projectiles had to be erased.

If Iraq follows the guidelines of the deadline, it would be undoubtedly strengthening the arguments of France which had been demanding for the inspection process to continue.

France position had hardened since the last presentation by Blix and Mohammad El Baradei. France had objected to the idea of going for an invasion on Iraq.

Washington argued that the Iraqi intentions on Al Samoud-2 missile were not honest from the beginning; it said Baghdad wanted a missile that would travel a longer distance with a similar pay load.

The Bush administration was more curious and very much concerned whether Saddam Hussein regime would be willing to destroy a whole arsenal of missiles under the supervision of the U.N. in fact one of the first thing to be agreed upon was the numbers.

According to one estimates, Iraq had declared 76 Al Samoods in June 2002 and had said that some had been used for tests. According to U.N., Iraq had between, 100 to 120 Al Samoods in its position.

There wore two important reasons that Saddam Hussein had to think much about was that he had spent huge amount on the acquisition of the missile technology and secondly that in case of a war with U.S. he wore to be in need of these missile to defend the country.

The situation was such that if Saddam Hussein disagrees with Blix to destroy the Al Samoods then the Bush administration will have a strong case in the Security Council against France, China and Russia. And then there was an advantage for Bush to get nine votes from the non permanent members.

In case if U.S. wish to go for a war with Iraq it was very much necessary that Bush wanted the support of Turkey and in this regard Turkey wanted the financial package to come over its losses on account of the derailment of its trade with Iraq on account of the war, apart from its tie up with the IMF in the past, Turkey had been demanding that U.S. should not link its financial package to under take any economic reforms. Along with this Turkey wanted the U.S. also account for the weapons that wore being currently described among ethnic Kurds after the war was over.

Turkey had placed its demands to the U.S. in view of its unhappy experience in the past during Gulf War in 1991. The Kurds with U.S. weapons then had used these weapons against Turkey forces after the war was over. Turkey was also insisting that the U.S. must prevent Kurds from using the U.S. supplied weapons against the ethnic Turkomans. The final demand that Turkey placed was that it wanted assurance from the U.S. that ethnic Kurds do not declare an independent Kurdish State when others are busy in the war.

Turkey fear was that the creation of an independent Kurdistan could become the nucleus for encouraging secession among its own Kurds who wore in large number along the Turkish-Iraqi border. Turkey wanted its hold on Mosul and Kirkuk in Iraq and for this it demanded the U.S. to seize the oil cities of Mosul and Kirkuk on its own and prevent them from falling in to the hands of the Kurds. Turkey was worried that possession of Mosul and Kirkuk would provide the Kurds with the economic muscle that would encourage them to form a viable independent State. Other than that Turkey since the historic days of the Ottoman Empire had it own claims over Mosul and Kirkuk.

In its final demand Turkey pointed out that its military should be allowed to move into northern Iraq to a considerable distance.

The Secretary of State Collin Powell, expressing his views on the latest development on Iraq he said "People are expecting that war can be avoided, I hope it can be avoided. But the one who has the power in his hands to decide whether there will be a war or peace is Saddam Hussein". The Bush administration is going on a diplomatic way in view of an impending second resolution in the Security Council that will seek authorization for the use of force to ensure Baghdad's compliance on disarmament.

"Gen. Powell said "if Saddam Hussein complies, or if he leaves the country tomorrow there will be no war".

U.S. Under Secretary of State John Bolton was expected to meet the Russian side at the earliest to seek the Russian support at the Security Council. The U.S. needed nine votes in the Security Council.

President Bush, in an interview said "that is very hard for me to tell. Even if I knew that date, I would not share it with the Iraqi leader" this indicated that Bush was not ruling out the possibility of a war at the earliest.

Gen. Collin Powell was in Tokyo on his way to Beijing and Seoul, besides other engagements he was expected to announce a new installment of U.S. food aid to North Korea. He was also expected to have consensus on how to deal with North Korea's suspected nuclear weapons programme. Which China and South Korea would prefer to see settled through direct Washington - Pyongyang talks?

The Iraqi Gen. Hossam Mohamed Amin said at news conference "we received the letter from the Chief Inspector Hans Blix on the Al Samoud-2 and this issue is under study. We are serious about solving this. We hope this issue will be resolved without interference from the Americans or the British, I think we will be able to resolve this issue without the interference of people with bad intentions".

At the same time the U.N weapons inspectors visited two sites involved in producing and testing the Al Samoud-2 missile, which the inspectors had ordered Iraq to destroy,

The inspectors visited Al Fatah facility on the northwest outskirts of Baghdad which produces components of Al Samoud-2 guiding and control systems as well as parts of the engine and the airframe.

They also visited the Al Rafah facility, 130 km south of Baghdad where Al Samoud-2 engine is tested.

The Director of the Al-Haithem company, Owayed Ahmed Ali, pointed his views "I asked the inspectors you would destroy a defensive weapon now that we are threatened by the Americans, who might strike at any moment".

Some inspectors said "You are right but we have orders". While other said "You have other means to defend yourself".

The Britain, Spain and Italy, decided to issue a joint ultimatum to Iraq to destroy weapons of mass destruction within three weeks or face war. they issued the deadline as March 14, for Baghdad even though diplomats at the United Nations wore quoted as saying the opposition to war is hardening among Chile, Angola,

Mexico, Cameroon, Guinea and Pakistan on the U.N. Security Council.

The diplomatic countdown for the war had begun. The 15 European Union Foreign Ministers meeting in Brussels was to decide the timing of the war.

The weapons inspector Hans Blix would submit a report to the U.N. and at the same time the Arab League was begin its summit in Cairo to discuss various aspects of the Iraq crisis and Saddam Hussein who was facing the deadline for destroying banned missiles by U.N.

White House had already announced that on March 3, the U.S. and Britain would deploy heavy military equipment in the Gulf region.

On March 7, was expected to report to the U.N. in person and a vote on a second resolution could follow swiftly.

On March 11, the Arab OPEC meets in Vienna to ponder on a new oil strategy

On March 14, would be seen as the deadline for Iraq to comply with the U.N. obligations.

Now it is more or less certain that by the middle of March, Iraq will be facing an American military force of 2,50,000, and Britain is to contribute another 43,000 troops.

These Anglo-American forces would be facing an Iraqi force of 4,00,000 troops, equipped with 2,000 Soviet T-72 tanks. Along with this Iraq had a reservists with the capacity of 4,00,000 persons.

It was expected that the allied forces would first cripple the Iraqi communication network and leave the Iraqi forces blank.

In all probabilities this war would be four times larger than the previous war in 1991.

Gen. Collin Powell's visit to China had some significance on North Korea but above that Powell's intention was to urge the Chinese President, Jiang Zemin, to veto a joint U.S.-Britain bid for U.N. Security Council approval for a resolution authorizing the use of force against Iraq.

With reference to North Korea, Gen. Powell said "Time is passing and we are trying to use the time to the maximum, but at the same time, we are not going to let time become a weapon to be used against us. China has a role to play, and I hope China will play that role".

Gen Amer Al-Saadi in a statement to the media said that "it is being studied very carefully and the channels with U.N. arms inspectors wore still open between us and we will come to a conclusion very soon".

CHAPTER - 9

Baghdad, denying the charges that Hans Blix, had made regarding the Al-Samoud-2, missiles that those missiles had been designed to stay with in the stipulated range. Iraq said Blix's demand was under serious study and that it hoped to settle the issue through cooperation and agreement between the two sides.

Iraqi President, Saddam Hussein, now had a very tough time and the handling of the situation was very critical as there was no time more over denying the charges technically was a bit of tedious job.

The response from the Iraqi side to Blix's directive was been seen as a case of challenge across the world that could take the debate on whether the Iraqi President Saddam Hussein, was complying with the U.N. Security Council resolution 1441.

While Iraq signaled that it was willing to disarm after hosting and seeking the advice of a South African team of experts that had earlier worked with the U.N. to destroy Pretoria's atomic arsenal built under the previous regime.

In the on going scrutiny by the U.N. weapon inspection the inspectors also visited at least 12 sites including four missile related facilities around Baghdad. For nearly over a week the ballistic team had been busy taking an inventory of the Al Samoud-2 missiles and components.

Mean while Iraq was trying to convenience hard with countries belonging to the Non Aligned Movement to put across its point of view.

The Iraqi Vice President, Taha Yassin Ramadan, carried with him documents and tapes to convey to the leaders of the world and show them what was happening in Iraq, inform them of Iraq's cooperation with the U.N. disarmament inspectors.

Russia sent its former Prime Minister, Yevgeny Primakov, to Baghdad for talks with Saddam Hussein. The former attorney general of United States, Ramsey Clark, also met the Iraqi leader who had been opposing the war against Iraq.

Saddam Hussein challenged the U.S. President; George W. Bush whom he said was behaving without manhood and concern towards Baghdad. He also said hat U.S. would fail to humiliate Iraq.

Saddam Hussein expressed "the Iraqi's wore angry by the behaviors of their enemy which had no humanity". He told a visiting Lebanese delegation "tell you brothers that the Americans can damage and destroy buildings and facilities but they will fail to humiliate Iraq". He expressed his hope that Iraqis would emerge victorious in the war against U.S.

Later in the day at a cabinet meeting Saddam Hussein said "fighting a war against U.S. led forces would settle a number of things and will enable Iraq to regain its previous prosperity.

Finally the Turkey's Cabinet agrees to the deployment of tens and thousands of U.S. combat troops ahead of a possible war in Iraq, the decision was later sent to the Parliament, where it was expected to face a vote.

With Turkey, taking a tough decision and calling an end to a high stakes diplomatic silence regarding its support to the Bush administration which was rearing to go for invading Iraq.

The U.S.-Turkish talks with long standing diplomatic deliberations between the two sides was finally approved when the announcement came after a six hour long Turkish cabinet meeting, in which the passing of U.S. troops through Turkey was a big debate. The deadlock was finally broken amid tens negotiation.

With this Cabinet decision Turkey was assured by U.S. to provide $5 billions in aid and $10 billion in loans to compensate the Turkish economy for the impact of war with Iraq.

Hans Blix and Mahammod El Bardei wore in no mood to start a lengthy debate with Baghdad with a view to arriving at a compromise of sorts and simply put the message as the missiles would have to go.

The U.N. Secretary General, Kofi Annan, was of the view that "they have to destroy the weapons if they refuse to destroy then the Council will have to take a decision on that".

France, which went out of its way said "it is necessary for Iraq to act and meet its obligations, in this case the destruction of these prohibited missiles".

The Bush administration which had been saying that time is running out said what is not before the Security Council could be the final days before a military showdown.

China said it was eager to play a positive role in helping to resolve the crisis over the North Korean nuclear weapons programmes.

Gen. Collin Powell made his case for Chinas support in the U.N. Security Council to the resolution on Iraq that would authorize military action. He was of the view that "the U.S. had seen some setbacks; Washington had been deeply concerned by the execution of a prominent Tibetan, the detention of more than a dozen pro-democracy activists and the continuation of pattern of inconsistent and irregular legal and judicial procedure".

The former Russian Prime Minister, Yevgeny Primakov, made a lightening visit to Baghdad to discuss the Iraq crisis with Saddam Hussein. Primakov was in Baghdad on the President, Putin's instruction to explain the position of the Russian Federation on the Iraq and receive assurance that Iraq will strictly fulfill U.N. completely and unconditionally and cooperate with the international inspectors.

Saddam Hussein, in an interview to the CBS TV that, "we do not have missiles, which go beyond the prescribed range." However he said the decision on the missile is being studied. We are ready to face the aggression that doesn't mean we should stop our political and diplomatic work"

Saddam Hussein had clear confirmation hat U.S. President, George W. Bush is on the war track and was ready for any eventualities, he had said no matter what the Iraqi's performance is but was ready to face the attack.

In the TV interview he was coated as saying "we will die here, we will die in this country and we will maintain our honor the honor that is required in front of our people. Whoever decides to forsake his nation from whomever requests is not true to his principles. I believe that whoever offers Saddam asylum in his own country is in fact a person without morals. Iraq will not burn its wealth and it does not destroy its dams. War is not a joke, why don't we use this opportunity. I am ready to conduct a direct dialogue, so that I will say what I want and he will say what he wants".

In Moscow the Iraqi Information Minister, Muhammad Said Kazim Sahhaf in an interview to 'Vremya Novostei' was quoted as saying "there was no talks about Saddam Hussein's exile, they are simply dirty rumors, no Iraqi leader intends to leave Baghdad, and no normal self respecting man would ever propose that to our President".

The U.S. fighter jets raided three Iraqi ground and air missile sites near the oil city of Mosul. This air raids launched from Turkish bases wore being interpreted as part of preparation to demolish Iraqi defences before the U.S. led coalition launches a full scale ground attack and seize Iraq's northern oil fields.

The oil resources in Iraq are the second largest in the world after Saudi Arabia. U.S. had been conducting air raids around Basra in a move that it could capture Iraq's oil fields and undermine the possibility of Iraq positioning its surface to surface missile launchers in this area.

The U.S. had intensified its air raids by justifying that they wore meant to enforce the no fly zone with the provisions of the early nineties in northern and southern Iraq.

The Turks and Kurds had pressurized the U.S. to implement the plan with some urgency as there wore reports that Saddam

Hussein might order to blow up the oil fields in the north and the south soon after the war breaks out. It was said that it was in this intention U.S. air raids wore conducted as there was also a general agreement between the U.S., Turkey and the Iraqi Kurds that the U.S. troops should quickly establish direct military control over Mosul and Kirkuk soon after the war begins.

At the United Nations Security Council, Britain moved a one page resolution signed by the United States and Spain, demanding the Council to say the Iraqi leader Saddam Hussein had failed to take the final opportunity offered to it by resolution 1441 and one that was adopted unanimously on November 9, 2002.

However the final demand in the draft did not formally call on the Council to authorize the use of force, adopting the new resolution, the intention of the new resolution was exactly what they wanted.

France, Russia and Germany which had opposed military action moved a counter proposal calling for a peaceful disarmament of Iraq through the strengthening of the weapons inspections. It was said that if the new proposal was accepted then the weapons inspectors would continue their investigation till June. That means Saddam Hussein would get another 90 days of time to tackle with the U.S. administration.

It was suspected that if the voting in the Security Council on the U.S. backed resolution was unavoidable then China would abstain instead of casting its veto.

The U.S. had four votes in the 15 member Council which includes Britain, Spain and Bulgaria. For the resolution to pass it requires nine votes and no permanent member casting a veto. China and Syria wore against any use of force and the six non permanent members Angola, Cameroon, Chile, Guinea, Mexico and Pakistan, who wore said to be just observing. (Fence Sitters).

Washington was in focus on this six members and that strategy of winning support was through a variety of means including economic incentives, profile lobbying and many other means of political strategy.

It was said that President, Bush, may be inclined to wait until the March 7, report of the Top weapons inspector Hans Blix, and then ask for division.

The indications at this juncture was that March 7, to March 15, would be a crucial determining period after which Bush would go the military rout.

As the news of new South Korean President, Roh Moo-hyun, after he was sworn in as President in Seoul came out, North Korea's launch of missile into the sea between Korea and Japan sent a new wave of anxiety through in Asia and the stock market made a big nose dive.

The Australian Foreign Affairs Minister, Alexander Downer, who was in Seoul to attend the new presidents swearing in ceremony busted out his comments on the North Korean missile launch "To have done it on the day of the inauguration of the new President is an exercise in drawing attention to themselves, and trying to crate a sense of crisis when none is necessary, I regard it as entirely unnecessary and provocative".

The U.S. Secretary of State Collin Powell, who was also in Seoul to attend the ceremony, however, expressed fears over the test. "It looks to be a fairly innocuous kind of test".

Japan was calm however it said "there is no indication that a long range missile was tested. But it is important for us to find out why this occurred.

North Korea in August 1998 fired a multistage missile over Japan and into the Pacific. That was an indication that Japan was under North Korean targets. Probably a nuclear attack could be the intention.

Later on the North Korean leader, Kim Jong-II promised to freeze such tests.

The U.S. Secretary of State, Collin Powell, announced at the end of his visit to Asia with the concern about North Korea's nuclear programme and disagreements. That U.S. had planned to give North Korea 1,00,000 tons of food aid for that year but decided to reduce it to 40,000 tons of food supply, a sharp reduction in assistance that it said was not related to North Korea's suspected nuclear programme.

The Russian President, Vladimir Putin, dismissed as "unacceptable' that any resolution that would grant the right to automatically start a war". He said that Russia would reject the U.S. draft resolution calling for war on Iraq.

Our position remains unchanged, it is necessary to continuously continue the quest for peaceful settlement of the crisis and ensure that Iraq fulfill all its obligations to the U.N.

Stating that the previous Security Council, resolution 1441 had not exhausted its potential, the Russian leader said he was ready to discuss a new resolution. "We had talks about the new U.N. Security Council resolution. We are ready to work with our colleagues talks serve to bridge position, we are ready to talk, but we are not ready to go to war.

Pakistan had signaled to the Bush administration that it is willing to back a new resolution at the United Nations Security Council on the disarmament of Iraq. "We are not asking any price for our support" said a spokes man.

Pakistan in favor of United States would be a major boost to the U.S. as it looks to picking up at least five out of the six undecided in the non permanent category of the Council. "Pakistan was reported to have said "we are very good allies of the U.S. and value our relationship and want to see that blossom. The issue of Iraq will not become a problem between us".

The Bush administration had been putting in place an elaborate mechanism to win votes in New York political and diplomatic pressure with economic incentives. But Pakistan from the past which was heavily dependent on military and economic assistance from the U.S. was denying that any deals have been struck.

China and Russia decided to stand firm against the United States over its move towards a declaration of war. With regard to the U.S. view on war as a viable option, China and Russia reached a consensus on the feasibility of asking the international weapons inspectors to continue their work. They agreed that the

U.N. Security Council should intensify its guidance and support to the inspection.

China and Russia wore working on besides a host of earlier resolutions on this issue and have provided the necessary legal basis for handling issue

Russian Foreign Minister, Igor Ivanov and Chinese President, Jiang Zemin, expressed that North Korea's suspected programme of making weapons of mass destruction, would push for a dialogue between the Democratic People's Republic of Korea (DPRK) and U.S.. The two leaders emphasized the need for an equal and constructive dialogue between Washington and North Korea.

U.S. President, George W. Bush was now trying to make the point that getting rid of the Iraqi leader Saddam Hussein, regime had more benefits to the world other than on the terrorism front that it could pave the way for democracy in the Gulf region. In Washington the president expressed "acting against the danger wall also contributes greatly to the long term safety and stability of our world. A liberated Iraq can show the power for freedom to transform that vital region by bringing hope and progress into the lives of millions. A new regime in Iraq would serve as a dramatic and inspiring example of freedom for other nations in the Gulf region. It is presumed and insulting to suggest that a whole region of the world or the one fifth of humanity that is Muslim is somehow untouched by the most basic aspiration of life. Human cultures can be vastly different, yet the human heart desires the same good things everywhere on earth. Success in Iraq could also begin a new phase for West Asia peace and set in motion progress towards a truly democratic Palestinian state. The passing of Saddam Hussein's regime will deprive terrorist networks of wealthy citizens, which pay for terrorist training and offers rewards to families of suicide bombers. America will seize every opportunity and pursue the peace. And at the end of the present regime in Iraq would create such an opportunity. That choice belongs to the Iraqi people, yet we will ensure that one brutal dictator is not replaced by another".

The communist government in North Korea blamed the United States of planning to send reinforcements into its coastal waters in advance of an invasion. It fired a short range missile in to the sea which further escalating tension in the region.

In a statement the North Korean Foreign Ministry accused the United States of planning massive war games in South Korea so it could attack the North Korea.

The present situation that had been created by the U.S. clearly indicates that "this compels the army and the people of the North Korea to keep themselves in full readiness by using all means and possibilities necessary to cope with it"

U.N. weapon inspector Hans Blix was telling the Security Council of his three months of inspections experience in Iraq. At the same time the Iraq's leader Saddam Hussein received the letter regarding the weapons inspector's remarks on Al-Samoud-2 that wore in violation of the U.N. stipulations.

Even as the report was presented in the Security Council the draft copies of his March7, report to the Council members who finally wished to look into those sentences and paragraphs that fits according to their views.

The U.N. had given Saddam Hussein the ultimatum until March1, 2003 for the start of the Al Samoud-2 missiles destruction.

The fact that Iraq had now agreed to destroy the missiles reflects a change in policy for, only that week the Iraqi leader, Saddam Hussein, had said that the missiles wore not in violation of U.N. resolutions.

If Baghdad starts destroying the missiles it further complicates the Bush administration's war agenda.

If Saddam Hussein for any reason avoids destruction of his missiles then there will be Britain and U.S. ready to invade Iraq. More over the Bush administration had been saying that the Al Samoud-2 is only a small part of the overall issue.

President Bush had said that "the missiles wore just the tip of the iceberg. The only point at hand is total and complete disarmament which he is refusing to do".

Canada a non Permanent member in the Security Council put forward it opinion to extend the date for compliance to Iraq till March 31, but immediately it was brushed aside by America and Britain. In fact France, China and Russia had demanded to extend the time till June 1, however the lobbying of non permanent members continued.

The 29 Arab nation leagues which include Iraq moved the annual meeting location to Egypt on the prospects of a U.S. led attack on Saddam Hussein. The Ministers had rejected a draft resolution that expressed without pointing out at Iraq "absolute rejection of any illegitimate foreign aggression against any Arab Country.

The other agenda were Palestinian-Israeli violence and a Saudi proposal for political reforms in the region.

The U.S. Secretary of State, Collin Powell, urged Arab leaders to issue the strongest possible statement and the league to urge Saddam Hussein to step down and get out of Iraq and give way for some responsible leadership take over in Baghdad.

To General Powell's statement the Iraqi Foreign Minister, Naji Sabri, reacted "This is one of the silly and trivial ideas involved in this dirty psychological warfare staged by American administration. The one who should step down is the reckless dictator Bush himself because he is endangering his own nation. He has made the U.S. the No.1 hated ugly nation in the world because of its colonial war like policy.

All the other Arab nations also supported Sabri's statement saying it was not U.S. job to interfere in Iraq's internal affairs.

The Egyptian Foreign Minister, Ahmad Maher, said "we are not in the business of changing the regime of one country or another. We cannot start talking about changing regime that will definitely be interfering in internal affairs. We can only ask all countries to abide by international resolution in order to avoid war".

In London, British Prime Minister, Tony Blair, said, "the moment I heard earlier in the week that Saddam Hussein was saying that he would not destroy the missiles was the moment that I knew later in the week that he would announce just because Blix reported that he would indeed destroy these missiles" he said that Saddam Hussein was playing games.

Tony Blair said that he respected the views of the British People and all others who disagreed with him but justified his bellicose stand on grounds of national security and world peace. Earlier his cabinet, collogue, Jack Straw, had admitted that the Government was facing "a difficult moment in handling the Iraq crisis".

Blair said the Commons revolt, when 122 Labour MP's defied the party whip to vote for an Opposition proposition. People would support if there was a second U.N. resolution. "We are attached to the principle behind the resolution but we are up for negotiation on it.

The position and evacuations began as war clouds increased on Iraq. The neighboring Iran had sealed its entire border with Iraq. While Russia and Turkey had started withdrawing their nationals from Baghdad, apart from closing its borders Iran had deployed its troops in the border region while Iraq was in combat redness, while Turkey had evacuated its diplomats.

The U.S. Presidential address about the future of Iraq under a new political dispensation had been the opinion here as a major indication about White House having made up its mind to go to war.

The Pentagon made its warning to media organizations that the U.S. will not give any guarantee and the safety of journalists who wore interested in covering the happenings in Iraq. Pentagon pointed out that the War covering Journalists wore in great danger, because the intensity of the bombing will be more than in 1991. Pentagon also announced that it would not make any second warning to journalist to evacuate quickly.

The United States Air force for the first time had ordered the deployment of B-2 Stealth Bombers outside the country at a location close to Iraq at the British island of Diago Garca in the Indian ocean which the U.S had recently constructed special hangers for those radar evading B-2 Bombers.

The Chief Weapons Inspector, Hans Blix, had argued in New York, that Iraq was very active but had also said that it was still too early to come to a conclusion what that meant. He was also making statements that the Iraq's decision on the Al Samoud-2 missile would be referred in the next Security Council on March 7,

At the same time, Blix in his quarterly assessment referred to the council on February 28, stating that the total disarmament efforts had been very limited. With this statement from Blix it was evident that on March 7, the expectation was that there would be mixed bag of conclusion praising Baghdad on the Al Samoud-2 and at the same time, listing several instances of non cooperation with the inspectors.

Russia since the beginning had been in line with the France statement that it would vote a resolution that came anywhere the use of force against Iraq.

The United States at this juncture was lobbying for the nine votes and its allies and friends wore tired and irritated by the way things wore shaping.

The Syrian President, Bashar Assad, in his speech during the opening session of the Arab League summit said it was a mistake to identify the Iraqi leadership as the source of the crisis. He accused the U.S. of being interested not in toppling a dictatorial regime, but in securing Iraq's oil and redrawing the region's map and destroying Iraq's infrastructure.

Bashar made a point "We are all targeted we are all in danger".

The 22 member Arab league summit ended with a Pan-Arab declaration on how the Iraq crisis should be solved. The Arab, Foreign Ministers, rejects any attack on Iraq that was not sanctioned by the United Nations and proposes a last ditch peacemaking efforts.

Sheik Zayed bin Sultan Al Nahyan, President, of the Gulf nations, in his letter circulated to the media at the summit stating that the "Arabs should play a major role in persuading Saddam Hussein to step down and leave Iraq. Regional and international binding legal guarantees should be given to the Iraqi leadership so that it would not be subjected to any form of legal action".

Russia with a population of Muslims of over 20 million and though there wore no information about volunteers in other predominantly, Muslim leader says there number may be unpredictable if the war breaks out. More than 8,000 men in that muslin republic Dagestan located in the south of Russia had signed to go to Iraq to defend it from American aggression. During the 1991 war in the Persian Gulf dozens of children in Dagestan were named after the Iraqi leader, Saddam Hussein.

Pakistan, President, Pervez Musharraf, had to do more than what he had expected about the tight rope walk with United States. For the second time in just a month he advised the U.S. against war. In a telephonic call with the U.S. President, Bush, he had said that war was not a good option. He was of the view that the Iraq should be settled in the frame work of the U.N. resolution.

The Bush administration was willing to go to extra ordinary lengths to ensure that its objectives wore met in the Security Council. The fact is that deals wore not in signed papers rather in promises or economic handouts, flexibility on issues and in some instances even enhanced military cooperation.

Over the shadow on Iraq the Bush administration had given every indication that it was going down to win vote at the Security Council, abstentions for non permanent members could come along with a high price.

The spokesman of he U.N. Hiro Ueki, said meeting would be for the quantitative verification of VX and anthrax that it had unilaterally destroyed would be discussed.

Iraqi decision wore likely to strengthen the peace camp led by France, Russia and Germany as they wore demanding the U.N. inspections to disarm Iraq peacefully wore working, these countries wore pointing out that the use of military force was not necessary.

Blix commented that Iraq's decision to destroy the missiles was a significant piece of real disarmament.

Turkish Parliament rejected a motion that would have allowed the U.S. forces to assemble and transit through Turkey into northern Iraq for an attack. This was a major blow regarding its war plans to open a second northern front against Iraq for U.S.

U.S. was confident that Turkey would give all necessary support for its troops but confronted by the unexpected Turkish decision, the U.S. military planners would have to look at contingency plans, mainly by airlifting personnel directly into northern Iraq. If not the U.S. had to attack only from its southern launch pad in Kuwait and along the Jordanian Iraqi border in the west.

Iraq held talks with the U.N. weapons experts on the VX and anthrax stocks, which Iraq said it had destroyed, Baghdad began destroying some 120 Al Samoud -2 missiles meeting a key deadline set by the U.N. chief arms inspector, Hans Blix who said their range exceeded the 150 km limit allowed by the U.N.

The U.N. spokesman for the weapons inspectors told that "Iraq will be providing a report on the VX and anthrax in a week's time".

The chief weapons inspector Hans Blix said destruction of the missiles would be a significant piece of real disarmament. Iraq scrapped six more banned Al Samoud-2 missiles a senior official said bringing the total in three days to 16.

Amer al -Saadi an advisor to Saddam Hussein said Iraq had destroyed important quantities of banned VX and anthrax substances.

The U.N. spokesman had said "the destruction of Al-Samoud-2 missiles as well as casting chambers continued and was under way and in 24 hours the destruction of the casting chambers would be completed".

In Jerusalem, Taha (65), a hardliner ideologue and close associate of the Hamas spiritual leader, Sheik Ahmed Yassin, the founder leader of Hamas who was arrested since September 2000, even though the group has been responsible for most of the attacks on Israelis since then. Taha and his five sons all senior Hamas activists were caught off guard by the Israeli arrest raid on Gaza's Bureij refugee camp. Taha and his son Ayman, wore wounded in fighting that erupted when soldiers surrounded the family's home which was demolished later.

The Bangladesh, Prime Minister, Khaleda Zia, while talking to the visiting U.S. Assistant Secretary of State, Christina Rocca, had said that whether it is Iraq, North Korea and Israel, Bangladesh is against the proliferation of weapons of mass destruction. Iraq must comply with the U.N. resolution 1441 and other violations like Israel should also be pressured to comply with U.N. resolution.

Khaleda said "it is also important to find a joint solution to establish an independent Palestine at the earliest".

She said Rocca's visit to Dhaka is being considered significant against the backdrop of a growing anti war campaign against the possible U.S. led war on Iraq.

Iran suggested an U.N. supervised elections in Iraq and urged the divided Iraqi opposition to reconcile with the President,

Saddam Hussein, as part of a plan aimed at averting a U.S. led war on Iraq.

Kamal Kharrazi, the Iranian, Foreign Minister, expressed the plan "we want a referendum to be held in Iraq and the Iraqi opposition reconcile with the current regime in that country under the supervision of the U.N. The Iraqi government should accept this plan; we believe this is the only way for a peaceful change of Government in Iraq, which will prevent the break out of a war in the region."

On the eve of Islamic New Year, Iraqi President, Saddam Hussein, said in referring to Bush, "the despot imagines that he is like God, capable of controlling the universe and doing whatever he wishes, but the devil has pushed him in to the abyss of blasphemy. Things that he is capable of enslaving people, and besieging their freedom, their decisions and their legitimate choices, it is without doubt, that the faithful will be victorious against aggression and against all things, against those who are faithful".

Apart from Saddam Hussein's allegations, the Iraqi officials destroyed four more Al Samoud-2 missiles. However, warned that it would stop further destruction of these weapons in case it was confronted with a U.S. military attack.

The first batch of B52 landed on the British soil as MPs expressed concern over reports of a significant increase in British and U.S. attack in the Iraqi no fly zones and accused the two countries of having already embarked on an undeclared and unauthorized war. The British government had allowed the RAF station to be used by Americans apart from protests from peace activists who stormed the U.S. facilities a few days ago, and had threatened more demonstrations.

Russian President, Vladimir Putin, praised the Turkish Parliament, decision as the "most important development. This decision may have come as a surprise to somebody but not for Russia".

The Pentagon, announced that four North Korean, fighter jets intercepted a U.S. Air Force reconnaissance plane in international airspace over the Sea of Japan and came within 50 feet of the American Jet while shadowing it.

The closest point they came was within 50feet of the RC135 Pentagon said the Air Force plane was on a routine reconnaissance mission.

Later, MNI news agency, in India, received confirmation through its sources that two advanced MIG-29 fighters and two others believed to be MIG-24 intercepted the U.S. sophisticated four engine RC135 reconnaissance aircraft 240 km off the coast of North Korea and shadowed the American jet for about 20 minutes.

The U.S. officials in Washington would formally protest over the incidence, they said once the intention of such a move had been identified United States and North Korea would not have diplomatic relations.

Pentagon accused North Korea "this is particularly provocative and has the potential to frighten our allies even more than previous provocations".

Israel had criticized the draft constitution prepared by a Palestinian team, saying it sought to perpetuate conflict and did not reflect an attitude of peace and conciliation. It also rejected Article 2 of the draft, which said the Palestinian state will be established within the June 4, 1967 resolution or according to international decisions.

The Israeli government reported to have admitted that the article concerning refugees is relatively easy for Israel to accept, since it does not refer to a mass return of refugees to Israel.

However there wore reservations regarding the authority vested in the president, giving him veto powers over laws.

The Bush administration was making the point that a positive out come by way of a second resolution is desirable, it was not necessary in fact; a growing perception in the last three days had been that in case Washington was unable to round up nine votes it neither may nor press for a formal showdown at the United Nations.

Gen. Powell was of the view that Bush was keen on finding out what the weapons inspectors would say, in their conclusion in the Security Council.

It was also said that during the second resolution process was going on at the U.N. Washington was planning for another option that was giving the Iraqi President Saddam Hussein a very short deadline which was said to be the final chance for the Iraqi leader.

While the Bush administration was calling on members of the U.N. Security Council to vote on the new resolution and at the same time it was keeping up the momentum in the military build up giving every indication that a war in the Persian Gulf, was nearing. However the military strategists and designers wore making the point that the huge build up of force in the Persian Gulf was well understood and that an attack on Iraq without the military bases in Turkey would be a multi dimensional attack on Iraq.

The U.S. army had given the orders for its oldest armored division to head to the Persian Gulf. With this the total number of U.S forces that would participate in action against Iraq accounted to 3, 00,000 or even more which the military strategists said was necessary for a multi dimensional attack.

Tommy Franks, who was managing the war against Iraq, had a meeting with the Defence Secretary, Donald Rumsfeld.

President Bush, spoke to the Indian Prime Minister, Atal Behari Vajpayee, regarding the American conclusions on the situation in the Gulf region.

Gen. Collin Powell said, "we have already planned that will allow us to conduct any military operations that the President might order. We will still be able to accomplish our mission".

Yet another surprise came when German, Foreign Minister, Joschka Flischer's decided to join Ivanove of Russia, and De Villepin of France was described as unexpected and sudden. Ivanov had come to Paris from Britain where he reiterated Russia's hostility to a second resolution on Iraq.

France further increased its pressure and insisted that Blix report be heard at a ministerial level and in public. The procedures had to be followed that the presentation of the report was to be followed by consultations among Council members. Now that De Villepin had said he would attend the meeting, obliging the Council to change the format of the meeting and so the previous plans had been left out.

According to the new plans Germany, Russia and France had circulated a counter proposal they describe as a memorandum that calls for a listing of items of the inspector's priorities with a checklist of targets to be reached. The memorandum also calls on the Security Council to give the inspectors a four month delay to achieve these goals.

Ivanov had said that Russia does not rule out a use of its vote. "We cannot but be concerned by plans to force democracy onto whole people. Not only does this contradict the U.N. charter, but will have heavy consequences". He also made a point that any attempt to force Arab states in a particular direction will only help extremists.

After an aerial incident involving United States and North Korea over the Sea of Japan, South Korea dismissed the possibility of any pre emptive strike by the U.S. against North Korea.

Regarding the Sea of Japan, incidence and the demand of North Korea, for a bilateral non aggression pact with the U.S., The U.S. made it clear that "all options remain on the table" to deal with North Korea.

The live television broadcast of the Organization of Islamic Conference (OIC) summit's opening speeches was put on hold as the shouting began and the Kuwaiti delegation walked out quickly.

Izzaat Ibrahim, the second in command of the Iraqi Revolutionary Command Council, told a Kuwaiti delegate who tried to interrupt his address. "You are insolent. You are traitor to the Islamic nation".

This reaction by Ibrahim was with the recent announcement that came from one of the leaders of the Muslim countries recommending Saddam Hussein, to step down and leave Iraq. This incident is unlikely to help in persuading Hussin to step down, so that, Iraq can be ruled under a U.N. administration as proposed by the six Persian Gulf states ahead of the OIC emergency summit on Iraq.

The OIC special summit had received a lukewarm response from member states as only one fourth of the countries out of the 57 nation grouping had sent their delegations to Doha.

After Ibrahim had ended his verbal assault, the Kuwait Information Minister said "these are all live. These are the words of an infidel and a charlatan. Ibrahim's behavior proves that Iraq still continues enmity toward Kuwait". He said Kuwait would lodge a formal protest with the OIC but was not pulling out of the daylong summit.

Israel at the same time was stepping up its defense against a possible missile attack from Iraq by completing the deployments of the Patriot anti missile systems in the Tel Aviv area. The Patriot missiles, was to form a second line of defence as Israel was having its own Arrow missiles, was capable to counter any Iraqi missile attack

CHAPTER - 10

United Nations, Chief Weapons Inspector, Hans Blix, told a news conference that he had made contingency plans to evacuate the inspector's within 48 hours if necessary. He said it was only under intense military pressure in the last month or so that Iraq had become active even proactive in addressing disarmament issue. It was not too late to avoid the war between U.S. and Iraq. If war breaks out of course, I think, that it is serious failure for the approach through inspection to disarmament. The Security Council, and divisions may follow from this. Everyone agrees that Iraqis have a much smaller capability than they had in 1991".

Blix was of the view that in Iraq the inspection process had to be continuing for a few months more, but he said that he would not demand for the continuation of inspections, but it was left to the Security Council to ask for the continuation of Weapons inspectors job in Iraq.

Mean while about 150 Russians wore being evacuated from Baghdad, on the orders from Moscow and another 450 wore to leave within a few days. They wore to leave on a chartered flight bound for Moscow.

The Iraqi Ambassador, to the U.N., Mohammad al Douri, said that the two Iraqi diplomats Nazih Abdullatif Rahman and Yehia Naeem Suaoud expelled wore security guards and lives in the basement of the mission. It was also said that they wore expelled because they refused to defect. "All of our diplomats were pressurized and asked if they would like to leave the Iraqi Government right now, to stay here in the United States. And those people who refuse those kinds of proposals have been expelled.

Al Douri said this is the kind of vengeance the Americans are doing because the Iraqis didn't accept what has been asked by Americans, he accused CIA, FBI and the state department are indulging in this activity.

However the U.S. State Department said "the two attaches' were engaged in activities outside the scope of their official function. Federal law enforcement authorities deemed the activities deemed the activities to be harmful to our national security".

In yet another incidence the Bush administration ordered an Iraqi journalist working for the Iraqi official news agency out of the country saying he was harmful to U.S. security.

United States is also requested some 60 countries to expel about 300 Iraqis, saying these are undercover agent, who are possibly poised to attack American interests over seas.

The State Department had made similar requests of foreign government before the 1991 Gulf War.

The North Korean state central Radio and Radio Pyongyang, said the reinforcement wore preparations for invading the communist state. A group of long range bombers deployed as a show of U.S. military's might landed in Guam amid tension over

North Korea's nuclear programmes, and more bombers were scheduled to arrive

China taking note of the North Korean, disavowal of any intention to make and deploy nuclear weapons., It was in this context that China had noticed, too, that North Korea might be willing to allow inspections of its suspected nuclear facilities if such an arrangement could be worked out with the U.S. through bilateral channels this substance of a new offer from North Korea acquires unusual importance in the context of Pyongyang's recent expulsion of the inspectors belonging to the International Atomic Energy Agency (IAEA).

The Chinese, perception of the new thinking, in the North Korea, on the nuclear issue came. The Chinese Foreign Minister, Tang Jiaxuan, reaffirmed Bejing's belief that the issue of weapons of mass destruction on the Korean peninsula could be resolved only through a direct dialogue between North Korea and United States.

The U.S. Ambassador to Moscow, Alexander Veershbow, warned Russia that the Bush administration could also retain cold war era trade restrictions against Russia and lock it out of a post Saddam Hussein, Iraq. The threat came immediately after the U.S. Ambassador and Russian, Foreign Minister, Georgy Mamedov discuss Russian decision to torpedo, jointly with France and Germany, the Anglo- American war resolution.

The White House Spokes man, Ari Fleischer, in his remarks said "you will continue to hear various statements by various people around the world. What you are observing is a fluid structure as different nations make different statements that all lead up to the one day which is the most important day, the day of the vote. The Bush administration is convinced at least outwardly that when push comes to show, it will have nine votes with or without France, Russia and China".

The top weapons inspectors, Hans Blix and Mohammad El Baradei due to appear before the Security Council, on Friday March 7,. Washington was leaving no stone unturned in trying to pressure the permanent and non permanent members of the Council. One thing was that even if Washington had the support of nine members, it would start the military operations even in the face of a veto from France Russia or China.

The rationale that the Bush administration would use was that it had the support of a majority in the Security Council. One count here is that the Bush administration may have no more than four votes perhaps even three if Bulgaria opts to sit on the fence or abstain. The three sure votes in the 15 member Council wore the nations who sponsored the Second Resolution, namely the U.S., Britain and Spain.

The Chinese, Foreign Minister, Tang Jiaxuan, said at a press conference in Beijing that it was unnecessary to table a new resolution which the U.S. was known to be keen on introducing with a view to securing an absolutely explicit mandate to wage war against Iraq so as to disarm it.

However he did not indicate whether China would indeed exercise its veto in the event of the U.S. wanting to pilot such a new resolution in the U.N. Security Council in the face of opposition from Russia and France, and two other permanent members and Germany a proactive non Permanent member as regards the issue at that stage.

Tang indicated that Beijing would cross the bridge when necessary and do so in accordance with Chinas own independent foreign policy of peace. However that was still too early to think about any veto power over the matter.

Tang made it clear that China would still prefer to sort out the Iraq question through political means under the U.N. auspices.

Shocking and also surprising information was found in one of the Pakistan's English daily "Dawn". Quoting sources the English daily said that evidence also indicates that Khalid Shakh Mohammed, had a meeting with Osama last month. "There is now no doubt that he is alive and well. We have evidence that shows he is alive" the paper said. Based on the information gleaned from the documents, Pakistani officials believe that. Al-Zawahiri, slipped back into Pakistan after fleeing Afghanistan.

It was said that the documents, CD's and a computer recovered by the investigative agencies after Khalid Shaikh Mohammed's arrest indicated that Osama bin Laden was alive however the Pakistani government denied Osama's presence in Pakistan.

While speaking on Iraq in Washington at the Center for Strategic and International Studies, Gen. Powell, stressed that American intelligence had found that Iraq has been hiding machinery to convert other kinds of engines to make the same Al Samoud-2 missiles. And the Bush administration official was also patently dismissive of Blix's contention that the Iraqis have been forthcoming on the interview of scientist." The question simply is, has Saddam Hussein made a strategic, a political decision that he will give up these horrible weapons of mass destruction and stop what he is been doing for all these many years. That's the question. "There is no other question. Every thing else is secondary".

Rejecting the contention of France, Russia and China and others that more time should be give to the inspections process in Iraq, Gen. Powell, once again remarked that time was not the essence; rather it was that of the intention of Baghdad.

Gen. Powell's thesis based on 'New Intelligence in Formation', that Iraq is going about with the Al Samouds-2 would be treated with a great deal of skepticism at the Secretary Council where some, especially France, Russia and China have not been swayed by the assessments of American intelligence agencies. In his argument Powell further said the intelligence is showing that Iraq is shifting chemical agents to the borders of Syria and Turkey.

Gen. Powell said "Iraq's too little, too late gestures are meant not just to deceive and delay action by the international community, he has as one of his major goals to divide the international community, to split us into arguing factions". He had said Saddam Hussein, had not taken decision to strategically and politically disarm and had accused Baghdad of trying to hide machinery to make the Al Samoud-2 missiles.

Gen. Hilmi Ozkok, Chief of the Turkish General Staff, said the war would be short against Iraq if opened from the north. He pointed that Turkey would be better off in any war than out of it.

According to experts who pointed out that Turkey's elected rulers wore unlikely to ignore the General's pronouncement because of the Turkish military's time tested dominance over the country's civilian administration.

According to a Libyan Commentator, Turkeys highly secular military has been the bulwark of preserving U.S. and western geopolitical interests since the days of the U.S. President, Harry S. Truman. Turkey under the Truman doctrine became the frontline state to check what was seen as the communist threat from the former Soviet Union after the Second World War.

Gen. Ozkok's statement had been hinting that a motion allowing for U.S. deployment in northern Iraq from Turkish soil which the parliament had rejected recently would be once again put forward before law makers soon.

Turkey was under the pressure of a by-election that could elect Erdogan into Parliament and pave the way for him to become the country's Prime Minister.

March 7, 2003 the day of real test for the long wait that every member of the Security Council was waiting and waiting for the report. The United Nations, Chief Weapons Inspector, Hans Blix in his report to the Security Council had stated that "Several inspections have taken place in relation to mobile production facilities. No evidence of prescribed activities had so for been found".

Intelligence authorities had claimed that weapons of mass destruction are moved around Iraq by trucks, in particular that there wore mobile production units for biological weapons. Blix said his inspectors had looked into several mobile facilities as well as "large containers with seed processing equipment".

In a 173 page dossier on Iraq's weapons of mass destruction, the Chef U.N. Weapons Inspector, Hans Blix had said Baghdad, may possess about 10,000 liters of anthrax, Scud missile warheads filled with deadly biological and chemical agents, and drones that far exceed the 150 km limit.

With the announcement of Hans Blick's statement at the Security Council the United States was so much alert that the President Bush had put the U.N. on notice saying that if it comes to showdown then the U.S. will drive the Iraqi President, Saddam Hussein, out of power with or without the backing of the U.N. Security Council.

'I will not leave the American people at the mercy of the Iraqi dictator and his weapons. When it come to our security, if we need to act we will act. And we really don't need the United Nations approval to do so. When it comes to our security we really don't need any body's permission. It is time for people to show their cards and let the people know where they stand in relation to Saddam. If we have to use our troops, we will. Saddam and his group are killers. I hear a lot of talk from different nations around we here Saddam Hussein might be exiled. That would be fine with me. Saddam Hussein is not disarming. This is a fact. If the world fails to confront the threat posed by the Iraqi regime, refusing to use force even as a last resort, free nations would assume immense and unacceptable risks".

Now it was very clear that the debate at the U.N. could be the last phase of diplomacy. But he stressed that inaction was a risk that he would not take for the American people.

Bush finally made his point and commitment to the people of America that "The risk of doing nothing, the risk of hoping Saddam Hussein, changes his mind and becoming a gentle soul, the risk that somehow inaction will make the world safer, is a risk I am not willing to take for the American people".

With this statement it was more than clear that President, Bush was hungry of war than continuing any further diplomacy with Iraq.

For the sake of political diplomacy and to take time for the preparation for a war against Iraq the U.S. and Britain pretended to give the Iraqi leader, Saddam Hussein a short deadline to comply with U.N. inspections or face war.

In Moscow the Russian, President, Vladimir Putin, said that he would not support a compromise resolution moved by Britain if it were just a tactics to win approval for war against Iraq. "We believe the military operation would be a tragic mistake, and we are against it".

The Russian Deputy Foreign Minister, Georgy Mamedov, told at a press conference in Moscow that Russia was ready to discuss the British proposal if it is aimed at finding a political solution".

On the other hand U.S. diplomats wore threatening Russia if it vetoed the U.S. backed resolution, there would be inevitable costs attached to a veto. U.S. could block

Russia's accession to the World Trade Organization, retain cold war trade restrictions against Russia and lock it out of post war Iraq.

The U.S. President Bush had a telephonic call with Putin to try and softer Russia's rejection of the war option hours ahead of a U.N. debate on Iraq. But Bush failed to change Putin's attitude.

The Russian President, Putin, reaffirmed his consistent position in favor of a peaceful solution. It was stressed that all means exist for such a solution and those can be strengthened and augmented if U.N. inspectors require it".

The call between Bush and Putin coincided with U.S. Senate ratification of a treaty intended to reduce the nuclear arsenals of the two countries.

However Russia called the treaty as a "landmark agreement in terms of real and radical nuclear disarmament". It also said that once it was ratified by Russia's parliament, the treaty would become "an important factor of strategic stability and global security".

The British, Foreign Secretary, Jack Straw, said in New York, "We are ready to discuss the wording of that resolution and take on board any constructive suggestions of how the process on that draft resolution can be improved. There is certainly the possibility of an amendment and that's what we are looking at. We do not want military conflict even now. We will strain every nerve to disarm Saddam. U.N. resolution 1441 that called for full active and immediate compliance had not bee completed, Iraq had been destroying some weapons reluctantly, but not all.

There is certainly the possibility of an amendment and that's what we are looking at".

The U.N., Chief Weapons Inspector, Hans Blix, in the last two occasions in January and February had stayed clear of giving any recommendations to the Council. His reports had been a matter of fact presentations. As many as 11 Foreign Ministers had assembled in New York in what appears to the beginning of the endgame. Much of the attention was paid not to what Ministers and their envoys wore saying at press conferences and to the media elsewhere, but in the intense behind the senses talks and negotiations.

The U.N., Secretary General, Kofi Annan, was urging Foreign Ministers, and others to debate the crisis calmly "The positions are very hard now. I am encouraging people to strive for a compromise to seek common ground".

The Ukraine, State Secretary of the Ministry of Defence, Oleksandr Oleinik, announced that Kuwait officially requested that Ukraine dispatch its 500 man special military unit to help mitigate the effects of chemical, biological or nuclear weapons that Baghdad might use in a potential war.

The opinion in Blair's own party was overwhelmingly against any action without a fresh U.N. mandate and there was talk of ministerial resignations in case he plunges Britain into a war which was not seen to have the support of the international community. But even as his supporters warned that he would be risking his political carrier if he ignored the voices around him, Blair appeared to have made up mind to go down the U.S. route regardless of the political consequences for him at home.

Blair made it clear that "I if there was a veto applied by one of the countries with a veto or by countries that I thought were applying the veto unreasonably, in those circumstances we would go ahead."

In a joint letter to the Prime Minister's office a group of prominent legal fighters who said there was no such thing as unreasonable veto under the international law. The Prime Minister's assertion that in certain circumstances a veto becomes unreasonable and may be disregarded has no basis in international law.

The legal fighters reminded that the U.K. had use its Security Council veto on 32 occasions since 1945 and if there had been any attempt to disregard these vetoes on the ground that they were unreasonable they would have been deplored as an unacceptable infringement of the U.K's right to exercise a veto under the U.N. charter article 27. The letter was signed by 16 scholars of international law, from the university of Oxford and Cambridge, the London School of Economics, the School of Oriental and African Studies, the University College, London, and the University of Paris.

Pakistan, President, Pervez Musharraf, told CNN in an interview that Pakistani intelligence agencies were active all over the country tracking down any leads they could get, including in border areas with Afghanistan. "He wouldn't be hiding alone or with one person he seems to be alive. He would be moving with a large number of bodyguards. He can't be in Pakistan". Musharraf had said Pakistani security forces had intensified operations in Baluchistan province where several Al Qaeda and Taliban militants hade been arrested in the past. Mohammed had been giving different statement about his contacts with Osama. "But this is preliminary investigation. I think more will follow when a detailed investigation is done".

The critical U.N., Security Council, session after extensive consultations and the U.S. had made it know that a vote on the amended second resolution could come anytime. And with this notice the hectic last minute lobbying had started in several capitals.

The French Foreign Minister, Dominique de Villepin, was likely to rush to Angola, Cameroon and Guinea in the hope of persuading these African countries to look at the amended second resolution from the French point of view. The three countries wore part of the swinging six countries which wore also actively sought by the U.S. and Britain.

France at the meeting of the Security Council suggested a summit of Heads of State to discuss this Iraqi crisis this was immediately brushed aside by the United Starts.

The Bush administration was simply not willing to let the fence sitters have it both ways. The definite impression was that the U.S. did not have nine votes in the Security Council, forgetting for a minute about vetoes.

Gen. Powell in the Security Council, disputed the optimistic assessments of the top weapons inspectors even while being careful not to question the quality or professionalism of the inspections process.

Gen. Powell was of the view that the Iraqi leader had not voluntarily taken a decision to disarm. Iraq had come in a grudging manner; he maintained "now is the time for the Council to tell Saddam Hussein that the clock has not been stopped by his stratagems and machinations. There wore members who do not want to sand up to the requirements of that resolution and take action that was clearly intended in the absence of Iraqi compliance.

The amended draft introduced by Britain said "Iraq will have failed to take the final opportunity unless on or before March 17, 2003, the Council concludes that Iraq has demonstrated full, unconditional, immediate and active cooperation with its disarmament obligations".

The French Foreign Minister, Dominique de Villepin said "We cannot accept an ultimatum as long as inspectors are reporting cooperation. France will not allow a resolution to pass that authorizes the automatic use of force.

At one point during his presentation the Foreign Minister, Jack Straw, Britain, came strongly in support of the United States looking at the French, Foreign Minister, and said "Dominique said the choice before us was disarmament by peace or disarmament by war that is a false choice".

The voters in the Security Council for the Bush administration in terms of support for its position on Iraq only Britain, Spain and Bulgaria wore on its side.

In London the nervous Downing Street rushed to defend the British and U.S. ultimatum to Iraq, even as anti war MP's reacted with fury saying that it amounted to pulling the trigger without giving the U.N. weapons inspectors enough time to complete their work. "We need some statesman ship from our Prime Minister to make sure President, Bush, does not go ahead with war on a predetermined timetable".

A former Labour Minister said, "I think the Prime Minister, Toni Blair, understands that his position highly dependent on a success full outcome to the efforts to get a second resolution based on credible evidence".

In Belgium, Brussels, hundreds of Kurdish demonstrators outside the European Union, Headquarters demanded Turkey keep its troops out of Northern Iraq, they said in a statement "we call upon the European Union to support the democratic development in Iraq, Kurdistan".

In Moscow the Russian, Foreign Minister, Igor Ivanov warned that "If the United States launches unilateral military action against Iraq, that would be a breach of the U.N. Charter. When the U.N. Charter is violated the Security Council must meet to discuss the situation and take appropriate decision".

Ivanov described the New Anglo-American Draft Resolution, setting a March 17, deadline for Iraq to disarm as an "unjustified ultimatum, therefore we do not think it necessary to adopt any new resolutions at this point. The possibility of political settlement really exist, it would be wrong and dangerous therefore to ignore this, for the other option, the military one, is fought not only with great human losses, but also with serous international consequences. This evolution of arguments is dangerous because it can destabilize and aggravate the situation, not only in Iraq and around it but throughout the region. Such experiments are dangerous for the situation in the Persian Gulf, the Middle East and the Arab world as a whole is explosive in view of major outstanding problems as well as latent and open conflicts in the region".

Pakistan one of the non permanent members of the U.N. Security Council agonizingly weighs its options with regard to the second resolution on Iraq.

Pakistan's Ambassador to the U.N., Munir Akram, in his presentation said "Pakistan believes that an agreed process must be evolved through consultation among Security Council members and U.N. inspectors. The best assurance in success and security in Iraqi Weapon of Mass Destruction disbarment peacefully is the unity of the Security Council".

The Bangladesh's first biggest anti war rally was organized by country's secular intellectuals, left politicians and cultural organizations. Thousands marched through the streets after a mammoth rally in Dhaka under the aegis of "The National Committee to Resist Aggression". Protesters chanted anti war slogans "Bush will be tried for war crime if he attacks Iraq. "Resist the War Mongers". "Attack on Iraq is attack on all Muslims". "No War, No Bush, No Blood".

Maulana Obaidul Haq of Khatib of National Mosque Baitul Mukarram called upon the countries opposing attack on Iraq to boycott U.S. goods if it attacks Iraq.

Israeli attack helicopters fired missiles at a passing car killing one of Hamas key leader and three of his body guards in Gaza city. The apparent target was Ibrahim Makadmeh, 51 a key figure in the Islamic group's military and political wing accused of engineering several terror attacks that killed 28 Israelis, the last being a tank attack that killed four solders in Gaza in last February.

The strike that came a day after the militant Islamic group claimed responsibility for two deadly attacks that killed 16 Israelis.

The Palestinian leader Yasser Arafat, said at the opening of he PLO's Central Council meeting "I want the international community to know that the Israeli occupation is the biggest obstacle standing in front of our reform process".

Hamas spokesman, Ismail Hanyyia said "we know how to deal with this".

The Israeli army did not comment but said it would continue to fight back against Islamic militants.

The President, George W. Bush, who generally spends the weekends at Camp David, stayed back at the White House to attend the Gridiron dinner, a journalist event that happens on Saturday evening. But the environment was totally of political strategy and the votes needed at the Security Council. Bush was in no mood to delay his war strategy and handling of the Security Council with or without the vote.

The U.N., spokesman, for the United Nations Iraq Kuwait Observers Mission, (UNIKOM) had said that reducing down operations had been made after approval from New York. "This move began after it was approved by the Secretary General. The slimming down process was still on the preparatory measure in case there wore diplomats in the situation. It was said that nearly 230 staff wore asked to leave their residential quarters in the de militarized zone. But 195 UNIKOM observers and its 775 military support unit from Bangladesh would remain. The decision of he U.N. was that to evacuate its civilians staff and cut down its patrolling activities came after the observers had noticed the cutting of the border fence in several areas some large enough to be able to pass military convoys".

In London, Andy Reed, MP announced his resignation through a statement on his website and said he would give his full reasons the next day. Earlier he had told news men that he would quit if the second resolution was moved. There wore other members who posed similar threats and among them wore two Cabinet Ministers, Robin Cook and Clare Short, who wore also moving to resign. The increasing dissidence in the Blair government went so high that nearly 200 MPs wore expected to join the anti Blair revolt if there was no U.N. authorization for military action.

The Next day Cabinet Minister for the International Development Secretary, Claire Short, threatened to resign if Blair went to war without a second U.N. resolution. She called Blair's stand as reckless and in breach of international law.

Prime Minister, Tony Blair, was surprised over the latest development in his government. The issue was discussed at a meeting with the Deputy Prime Minister, John Prescott, and the Labour Party, Chairman, John Reid.

The Indian Prime Minister, Atal Behari Vajpayee, said the government preferred a peaceful resolution of the conflict through the United Nations and was against any military conflict.

The External Affairs Minister, Yashwant Sinha, later told media men that while the government did not visualize the need to evacuate on a large scale from the region; the 50 people residing in Iraq had been advised to leave the area.

The Russian Foreign Minister, Igor Ivanov, said "Russia has openly declared that if the draft that has been submitted for consideration and which contains impossible ultimatum type demands, will be put to vote, Russia will vote against this resolution".

In view of the crucial vote in the United Nations Security Council, France was making a final offensive to convince non permanent African members of the Council, to join forces with those opposing a second resolution on Iraq that would gave the Iraqi leader, Saddam Hussein until March 17 to disarm.

De Villepin told news men after his discussion with the Angola Cameroon and Guinea that the use of force against Iraq would be paradoxical and contradictory in the present context of successful ongoing inspections.

The Angolan Foreign Minister, Joao Bernando de Miranda, declared. "War is inevitable. What the international community needs to do now is prepare for what comes after the war".

Angola which was under the pressure of a civil war for over 27 years was slowly coming out of the United States backed rebels. The country's oil wells and infrastructure were completely destroyed in the conflict. The U.S. had promised help to rebuild Angola's destroyed economy, reenergize its oil industry and write of a large percentage of its $10 billion foreign debt.

Guinea and Cameroon wore likely to prove more supportive to France persuasion. Cameroon's President, Paul Biya, had close links with Paris and the French President, Jacques Chirac, that go back many years.

France was likely to get the Cameroon vote with an acceptable aid package. After several differences of opinion for several years Guinea was willing to support France because more than ninety percent of its populations were Muslim.

Guinea depended on Washington for debt relief and it was expected that France would offer whatever Washington had offered to pay.

In New York Gen. Powell had ruled out any extension beyond March 17 for Saddam Hussein. But the administration had not said much on if it would be possible for further modifications in the draft now pending before the Security Council.

Gen. Powell was of the view " if Saddam Hussein was serious, he would not be placing demands on the U.N. he would be saying: Here are all the people you want to interview, here are all the facilities that I have, here are all the weapons that I have, here are all the documents that I have"

The Bush administration was also being reminded of the economic cost of waging a war the military conflict alone was estimated to cost $80 billions, and with this, the constant reminder that unlike the 1991 Persian Gulf War, the U.S. will have to pay the entire cost.

Pakistan denied that Osama bin Laden on its soil and also rejected joint operation by the Pakistani and U.S. forces in search of Al Qaeda members.

The Pakistani, Foreign office spokesman, Aziz Ahmed Khan, said "There has never been a joint search". The Pakistani forces alone were carrying out operations inside Pakistan. Since October 2001 the U.S. led military operations in Afghanistan was going on however since then Pakistan had been maintained that it had not provided any military bases to the U.S. inside Pakistan to search for the Al Qaeda members.

The next day Pakistan's Inter Service Intelligence, (ISI) in a briefing to the media had said the clues given by Khalid Sheik Mohammed, suspected third commander in Al Qaeda, following his arrest from a post locally in Rawalpindi on March 1.

Mohammed had met Osama in December 2002, the officer said; the Al Qaeda operative however did not disclose where he met Osama. The American agents wore present at the time of interrogation.

The reports appearing the Pakistan's English daily had said Mohammed had met Osama in February however the statement by the ISI officer was conflicting.

Mohammed had letters in his possession which he had confirmed written by Osama. The situation of Mohammed's arrest was videotaped and was played.

In view of the U.S. President, George W. Bush, had said the Palestinians had to choose new leaders as a precondition for state hood. Yasser Arafat agreed to name a PM. regarding the Power sharing agreement, by Arafat and his appointee for Prime Minister, Mahmoud Abbas, falls short of demands that a new Prime Minister effectively replace Arafat as the Chief Peace Negotiator.

The diplomats attending The U.N. Security Council, session had opted several ideas to resolve the stalemate were explored and were under active consideration. At the closed door session the sponsors of the second resolution which set deadline for March 17, for Iraq found the going quite tough resulting in Britain and the U.S. forced not only to abandon the early vote sought by them but to look at alternatives.

British envoy to U.N. Jeremy Greenstock, had said" we are busting a gut to see if we can get greater consensus in the Council. We are examining whether a list of tests of Iraqi compliance would be a useful thing for the Council. It doesn't' mean there are any conclusions".

Britain had proposed a two phase approach to a new draft resolution. "One is to be convinced that Iraq is cooperating. The other is to disarm Iraq completely". The Iraqi leader was given 10 days to show that he had taken a strategic decision to fully disarm with a set of bench marks.

France had said that any resolution irrespective of the phases and time lines, that had automatically for use of force would be voted.

The Secretary General of U.N., Kofi Annan, said "if action is taken without the authority of the Security Council the legitimacy and support for any such action would be seriously impaired".

France, President, Jacques Chirac, for the first time addressed to his country men regarding the Iraq crisis, in a live televised interview he said "Whether the present circumstances France would vote no, because there is no need for war to disarm Iraq. I am convinced at this point in time, that this resolution containing an ultimatum that gives the green light to war does not have the support of nine members or the Security Council.

He said Paris would not participate in any military action against Iraq. "We live in a global world", He brushed aside suggestions that Washington could impose sanctions on France and boycott French exports.

With regard to the Iraq issue the polls survey indicated that 59% of the population wore in favor of France using its veto and the French media gave overwhelming praise to Chirac.

The Russian President, Vladimir Putin, in a message had promised Saddam Hussein that Russia would reject any Security Council resolution that will authorize the use of force against Iraq. The message was carried by the Speaker of the Russian Parliament, Lower House, Gennady Seleznyov. He had a three hour meeting with Saddam Hussein, described his one day visit as very successful.

The United States which came under heavy diplomatic setback continuously was restless and the other factor was it was sure that it would not get the required nine votes. The attack with its own strength on Iraq was the only possible way that U.S. could avoid a face off.

There wore two crucial developments that had taken place recently that could support U.S. that it should decide attacking Iraq at the earliest. Even without the authorization of U.N. for the use of force.

The first one was here wore very clear signs that France and Russia would not hesitate to veto a fresh resolution on Iraq. And the second one was that Britain the only supporter of U.S. was singing a different song suggesting that more time to be given for Saddam Hussein in the modified resolution.

There was a possibility of a sand storm in the Arabian desert by the end of March which could continue till the end of the year and that could become a set back for any military operations for U.S.

Apart from the large deployment that U.S. military strategists hand planned to work on contingency of going to war in case the Britain's government controlled by the Labour party leaders avoiding to contribute military support to the U.S. war game.

The charismatic leader of Turkey, Erdogan, who won a parliamentary seat in the by election was expected to take over as the new Prime Minister of Turkey and the current Turkish Prime Minister, Abdulla Gul, resigned so that the change in leadership had been widely expected.

For various political reasons Erdogan could not contest the general election succeeded in winning the by election and was sworn as Member of Parliament as a first step in becoming the Prime Minister.

The U.N., Chief Weapon Inspector, Hans Blix, charged Iraq for not disclosing of possessing the unmanned Drone the pilot less spy aircraft. He told reporters that he was not at that stage yet establish the legality of whether this Drone confined to the stipulations of he U.N. resolution. He said "Iraq should have declared this vehicle and they did not".

Blix informed that his team had discovered the Drone with a wing span of about 25 feet that immediately suggested to some of an illegal range which would not only threaten Iraq's neighbors but also with a capability of carrying banned weapons.

The maximum range allowed under the U.N. permitted range is 150 km. these wore the vehicles that cross the prescribed range and could use this aircraft to attack American and allied troops in the event of a military show down possibly even use a nerve gas or anthrax through this vehicle.

The new discovery was the cluster bombs that could be used for chemical and biological weapons attack. Even Blix had not informed about this bomb in his 170 page report. Blix came under heavy criticism for not been tough on Iraq. "Every one tries to get mileage out of us and they can", said one of the top officials of UNMOVIC.

At the U.N., Executive Chairman Dr. Hans Blix, Briefing of the Security Council on 7 March 2003: Oral introduction of the 12th quarterly report of UNMOVIC.

Dr. Hans Blix, said.

Mr. President,

For nearly three years, I have been coming to the Security Council presenting the quarterly reports of UNMOVIC. They have described our many preparations for the resumption of inspections in Iraq. The 12th quarterly report is the first that describes three months of inspections. They come after four years without inspections. The report was finalized ten days ago and a number of relevant events have taken place since then. Today's statement will supplement the circulated report on these points to bring the Council up-to-date.

Inspection process

Inspections in Iraq resumed on 27 November 2002. In matters relating to process, notably prompt access to sites, we have faced relatively few difficulties and certainly much less than those that were faced by UNSCOM in the period 1991 to 1998. This may well be due to the strong outside pressure.

Some practical matters, which were not settled by the talks, Dr. ElBaradei and I had with the Iraqi side in Vienna prior to inspections or in resolution 1441 (2002), have been resolved at meetings, which we have had in Baghdad. Initial difficulties raised by the Iraqi side about helicopters and aerial surveillance planes operating in the no-fly zones were overcome. This is not to say that the operation of inspections is free from frictions, but at this juncture we are able to perform professional no-notice inspections all over Iraq and to increase aerial surveillance.

American U-2 and French Mirage surveillance aircraft already give us valuable imagery, supplementing satellite pictures and we would expect soon to be able to add night vision capability through an aircraft offered to us by the Russian Federation. We also expect to add low-level, close area surveillance through drones provided by Germany. We are grateful not only to the countries, which place these valuable tools at our disposal, but also to the States, most recently Cyprus, which has agreed to the stationing of aircraft on their territory.

Documents and interviews

Iraq, with a highly developed administrative system, should be able to provide more documentary evidence about its proscribed weapons programmes. Only a few new such documents have come to light so far and been handed over since we began inspections. It was a disappointment that Iraq's Declaration of 7 December did not bring new documentary evidence. I hope that efforts in this respect, including the appointment of a governmental commission, will give significant results. When proscribed items are deemed unaccounted for it is above all credible accounts that is needed - or the proscribed items, if they exist.

Where authentic documents do not become available, interviews with persons, who may have relevant knowledge and experience, may be another way of obtaining evidence. UNMOVIC has names of such persons in its records and they are among the people whom we seek to interview. In the last month, Iraq has provided us with the names of many persons, who may be relevant sources of information, in particular, persons who took part in various phases of the unilateral destruction of biological and chemical weapons, and proscribed missiles in 1991. The provision of names prompts two reflections:

The first is that with such detailed information existing regarding those who took part in the unilateral destruction, surely there must also remain records regarding the quantities and other data concerning the various items destroyed.

The second reflection is that with relevant witnesses available it becomes even more important to be able to conduct interviews in modes and locations, which allow us to be confident that the testimony is given without outside influence. While the Iraqi side seems to have encouraged interviewees not to request the presence of Iraqi officials (so-called minders) or the taping of the interviews, conditions ensuring the absence of undue influences are difficult to attain inside Iraq. Interviews outside the country might provide such assurance. It is our intention to request such interviews shortly. Nevertheless, despite remaining shortcomings, interviews are useful. Since we started requesting interviews, 38 individuals were asked for private interviews, of which 10 accepted under our terms, 7 of these during the last week.

As I noted on 14 February, intelligence authorities have claimed that weapons of mass destruction are moved around Iraq by trucks and, in particular, that there are mobile production units for biological weapons. The Iraqi side states that such activities do not exist. Several inspections have taken place at declared and undeclared sites in relation to mobile production facilities. Food testing mobile laboratories and mobile workshops have been seen, as well as large containers with seed processing equipment. No evidence of proscribed activities have so far been found. Iraq is expected to assist in the development of credible ways to conduct random checks of ground transportation.

Inspectors are also engaged in examining Iraq's programme for Remotely Piloted Vehicles (RPVs). A number of sites have been inspected with data being collected to assess the range and other capabilities of the various models found. Inspections are continuing in this area.

There have been reports, denied from the Iraqi side, that proscribed activities are conducted underground. Iraq should provide information on any underground structure suitable for the production or storage of WMD. During inspections of declared or undeclared facilities, inspection teams have examined building structures for any possible underground facilities. In addition, ground penetrating radar equipment was used in several specific locations. No underground facilities for chemical or biological production or storage were found so far.

I should add that, both for the monitoring of ground transportation and for the inspection of underground facilities, we would need to increase our staff in Iraq. I am not talking about a doubling of the staff. I would rather have twice the amount of high quality information about sites to inspect than twice the number of expert inspectors to send.

Recent developments

On 14 February, I reported to the Council that the Iraqi side had become more active in taking and proposing steps, which potentially might shed new light on unresolved disarmament issues. Even a week ago, when the current quarterly report was finalized, there was still relatively little tangible progress to note. Hence, the cautious formulations in the report before you.

As of today, there is more. While during our meetings in Baghdad, the Iraqi side tried to persuade us that the Al Samoud 2 missiles they have declared fall within the permissible range set by the Security Council, the calculations of an international panel of experts led us to the opposite conclusion. Iraq has since accepted that these missiles and associated items be destroyed and has started the process of destruction under our supervision. The destruction undertaken constitutes a substantial measure of disarmament - indeed, the first since the middle of the 1990s. We are not watching the breaking of toothpicks. Lethal weapons are being destroyed. However, I must add that no destruction has happened today. I hope it's a temporary break.

To date, 34 Al Samoud 2 missiles, including 4 training missiles, 2 combat warheads, 1 launcher and 5 engines have been destroyed under UNMOVIC supervision. Work is continuing to identify and inventory the parts and equipment associated with the Al Samoud 2 programme.

Two 'reconstituted' casting chambers used in the production of solid propellant missiles have been destroyed and the remnants melted or encased in concrete.

The legality of the Al Fatah missile is still under review, pending further investigation and measurement of various parameters of that missile.

More papers on anthrax, VX and missiles have recently been provided. Many have been found to restate what Iraq had already declared, some will require further study and discussion.

There is a significant Iraqi effort underway to clarify a major source of uncertainty as to the quantities of biological and chemical weapons, which were unilaterally destroyed in 1991. A part of this effort concerns a disposal site, which was deemed too dangerous for full investigation in the past. It is now being re-excavated. To date, Iraq has unearthed eight complete bombs comprising two liquid-filled intact R-400 bombs and six other complete bombs. Bomb fragments were also found. Samples have been taken. The investigation of the destruction site could, in the best case, allow the determination of the number of bombs destroyed at that site. It should be followed by a serious and credible effort to determine the separate issue of how many R-400 type bombs were produced. In this, as in other matters, inspection work is moving on and may yield results.

Iraq proposed an investigation using advanced technology to quantify the amount of unilaterally destroyed anthrax dumped at a site. However, even if the use of advanced technology could quantify the amount of anthrax, said to be dumped at the site, the results would still be open to interpretation. Defining the quantity of anthrax destroyed must, of course, be followed by efforts to establish what quantity was actually produced.

With respect to VX, Iraq has recently suggested a similar method to quantify a VX precursor stated to have been unilaterally destroyed in the summer of 1991.

Iraq has also recently informed us that, following the adoption of the presidential decree prohibiting private individuals and mixed companies from engaging in work related to WMD, further legislation on the subject is to be enacted. This appears to be in response to a letter from UNMOVIC requesting clarification of the issue.

What are we to make of these activities? One can hardly avoid the impression that, after a period of somewhat reluctant cooperation, there has been an acceleration of initiatives from the Iraqi side since the end of January.

This is welcome, but the value of these measures must be soberly judged by how many question marks they actually succeed in straightening out. This is not yet clear.

Against this background, the question is now asked whether Iraq has cooperated "immediately, unconditionally and actively" with UNMOVIC, as required under paragraph 9 of resolution 1441 (2002). The answers can be seen from the factual descriptions I have provided. However, if more direct answers are desired, I would say the following:

The Iraqi side has tried on occasion to attach conditions, as it did regarding helicopters and U-2 planes. Iraq has not, however, so far persisted in these or other conditions for the exercise of any of our inspection rights. If it did, we would report it.

It is obvious that, while the numerous initiatives, which are now taken by the Iraqi side with a view to resolving some long-standing open disarmament issues, can be seen as "active", or even "proactive", these initiatives 3-4 months into the new resolution cannot be said to constitute "immediate" cooperation. Nor do they necessarily cover all areas of relevance. They are nevertheless welcome and UNMOVIC is responding to them in the hope of solving presently unresolved disarmament issues.

Members of the Council may relate most of what I have said to resolution 1441 (2002), but UNMOVIC is performing work under several resolutions of the Security Council. The quarterly report before you is submitted in accordance with resolution 1284 (1999), which not only created UNMOVIC but also continues to guide much of our work. Under the time lines set by the resolution, the results of some of this work is to be reported to the Council before the end of this month. Let me be more specific.

Resolution 1284 (1999) instructs UNMOVIC to "address unresolved disarmament issues" and to identify "key remaining disarmament tasks" and the latter are to be submitted for approval by the Council in the context of a work programme. UNMOVIC will be ready to submit a draft work programme this month as required.

UNSCOM and the Amorim Panel did valuable work to identify the disarmament issues, which were still open at the end of 1998. UNMOVIC has used this material as starting points but analysed the data behind it and data and documents post 1998 up to the present time to compile its own list of "unresolved disarmament issues" or, rather, clustered issues. It is the answers to these issues which we seek through our inspection activities.

It is from the list of these clustered issues that UNMOVIC will identify the "key remaining disarmament tasks". As noted in the report before you, this list of clustered issues is ready.

UNMOVIC is only required to submit the work programme with the "key remaining disarmament tasks" to the Council. As I understand that several Council members are interested in the working document with the complete clusters of disarmament issues, we have declassified it and are ready to make it available to members of the Council on request. In this working document, which may still be adjusted in the light of new information, members will get a more up-to-date review of the outstanding issues than in the documents of 1999, which members usually refer to. Each cluster in the working document ends with a number of points indicating what Iraq could do to solve the issue. Hence, Iraq's cooperation could be measured against the successful resolution of issues.

I should note that the working document contains much information and discussion about the issues which existed at the end of 1998 - including information which has come to light after 1998. It contains much less information and discussion about the period after 1998, primarily because of paucity of information. Nevertheless, intelligence agencies have expressed the view that proscribed programmes have continued or restarted in this period. It is further contended that proscribed programmes and items are located in underground facilities, as I mentioned, and that proscribed items are being moved around Iraq. The working document contains some suggestions on how these concerns may be tackled.

Mr. President,

Let me conclude by telling you that UNMOVIC is currently drafting the work programme, which resolution 1284 (1999) requires us to submit this month. It will obviously contain our proposed list of key remaining disarmament tasks; it will describe the reinforced system of ongoing monitoring and verification that the Council has asked us to implement; it will also describe the various subsystems which constitute the programme, e.g. for aerial surveillance, for information from governments and suppliers, for sampling, for the checking of road traffic, etc.

How much time would it take to resolve the key remaining disarmament tasks? While cooperation can and is to be immediate, disarmament and at any rate the verification of it cannot be instant. Even with a proactive Iraqi attitude, induced by continued outside pressure, it would still take some time to verify sites and items, analyse documents, interview relevant persons, and draw conclusions. It would not take years, nor weeks, but months. Neither governments nor inspectors would want disarmament inspection to go on forever. However, it must be remembered that in accordance with the governing resolutions, a sustained inspection and monitoring system is to remain in place after verified disarmament to give confidence and to strike an alarm, if signs were seen of the revival of any proscribed weapons programmes.

The Bush administration came heavily on the Drone and cluster bomb findings to further strengthen its case at the Security Council and in the international community for its support on the resolution.

The U.S. Secretary of State, Gen. Collin Powell said "Iraq continues to demonstrate that it had not really changed its strategic intent which is the case we have been making all along".

In Vienna the United States, Energy Secretary, Spencer Abraham, announced that it would help developing countries track down loose radioactive materials on their soil, the kind of step the Chief U.N., Nuclear Officials said was urgently needed to foil terrorists working on building "dirty bombs". He said "the threat requires a determined and comprehensive international response", and for this U.S. would spend $3 million in the year 2004 to help poorer governments secure high risk radiation sources that could be used for terror weapons.

CHAPTER - 11

The Prime Minister, Atal Behari Vajpayee, responding to the clarifications sought by members on his statement in the Parliament had said "if a change had to come about it should be done by the people of that country. No outside power has the right to do that. I believe it will not happen because if it does, it will undermine the U.N. and also create a grave crisis. I believe there will not be a war. Hence I cannot answer what stand we will take if there is a war. We believe that Iraq must cooperate actively with the inspection process and comply fully with all relevant Security Council resolutions. If the pace of this cooperation had been quicker, it may have enabled UNMOVIC and IAEA to certify to the U.N. Security Council that Iraq was in full compliance of Resolution 1441.The international community must take a very careful look both at the objective of achieving Iraq's full compliance with U.N. resolutions and at the means to be adopted to reach the goal. If permitting more time and formulation of clearer criteria can facilitate a decision within the U.N. framework, we believe this option should be given a chance. We hope that the members of he Security Council will harmonize their position to ensure that its final decision enhances the legitimacy and credibility of the U.N. If unilateralism prevails, the U.N. would be deeply scarred, with disastrous consequences for world order. The Government of India would strongly urge that no military action be taken which does not have the collective concurrence of the international community".

To a question raised by other members of the house to disclose his telephonic discussion with the U.S., President, George W. Bush. Prime Minister, Vajpayee, said he preferred not to disclose what Bush shared with him.

The U.S. military officials said that two American U-2 spy planes were threatened by Iraqi jets and the mission had to be aborted in the interest of safety. Baghdad objected when the second plane undertook the mission. However later it was said the incident occurred due to misunderstanding and the issue being sorted out.

The U.S., Defence Secretary, Donald Rumsfeld, said it was yet to be identified where exactly the mistake took place about the second flight of U-2 aircraft.

At the Security Council Chambers new proposal brought by Canada had caught the attention of at least one fence sitter, Chile. The new plan had three weeks deadline for Iraq to show the Security Council that it is disarming and on a framework set by the weapons inspectors and not on the Anglo-American formula.

The new alternative proposal brought by Canada was only bringing on board the undecided at the same time softening the position of France and hoping with the intention that France might abstain instead of using Veto.

The Bush administration was insisting that it had no intention of dragging the issue but asking to push with the formal veto but to postpone that as it is bound to be defeated or vetoed.

Pakistan which had formally said that it will not back the resolution, had been concluded as being supportive but by one estimate the U.S. had six on its side Britain, Spain Bulgaria, Mexico, Cameroon and Pakistan.

The Iraqi Ambassador to U.N. Mohammad al Douri, charged that the main intention of U.S. and Britain was "to keep their hands on our oil and to control the region, to redraw its borders". He said in fact Iraq had decided to disarm.

France and Russia wore reluctant that they would veto any resolution that's linked to an authorization to the use of force.

The Bush administration had also out rightly rejected for the new proposal brought by the non permanent member Canada.

The United States, Air Force tested its MOAB at a base in Florida and its impact was said to have been felt several km away. This largest conventional bomb which weighs 21,000 pounds shaped like missile and detonates above the ground that flattens almost anything and very thing on the ground.

The conventional bomb known as, Massive Ordinance Air Blast (MOAB).This huge satellite guided bomb dropped from a cargo plane is also called as the mother of all bombs in fact it is the advanced version of the Daisy Cutters which was massively used in the Vietnam War to clear vegetation.

The pentagon wanted to send a message to Iraq indeed to further pressurize psychologically and campaign what was in store that in the event of a military show down could happen.

While all Arab nations oppose a war on Iraq, they were deeply divided on the way to achieve this goal. Syria and

Lebanon are close to the Europeans especially France and wore asking the United States to allow the U.N. inspections to run their course, before considering war as an option. Egypt was arguably Washington's chief ally in West Asia outside the Persian Gulf zone while most of the six countries belonging to the Gulf Cooperation Council (GCC) host major U.S. military bases on their soil which would be used for a possible war against Iraq.

The United Arab Emirates (UAE) on the other hand had opposed that Saddam Hussein should be asked to go to exile on his own in order to avoid war during the course of the Sharm-el-Sheikh Summit.

The idea that regime change in Baghdad can be accomplished peacefully through Saddam Hussein's voluntary exile had found considerable support among the Persian Gulf countries.

Saudi Arabia was also reportedly proposing that Iraq could unilaterally declare a timetable for disarmament ahead of a U.N. Security Council debate on a British resolution. Apart from differences on the matter of opinion the Arab nations wore also debating the possible date of the visit.

The U.S. which badly needed a political decision maker in Turkey by and large was backing on Recep Tayyip Erdogan. The new Prime Minister Erdogan, had to contend with time consuming procedures before reintroducing a resolution in the Turkish Parliament that could allow the U.S. to station and transit its forces into northern Iraq.

Erdogan first step would have to submit a list of Cabinet Ministers for the new government to the President. The second step which involves the presentation and approval of a government programme, was expected to take around a week's time that was the government resolution on Iraq, which also includes the approval for the Turkish forces to enter Iraq territory along with the U.S. forces would get delayed.

Erdogan was willing to give all possible support to the United States and at the same time Erodgan was unlikely to confront the Chef of staff of the Turkish military, Gen Hilmi Ozkok. Who had already announced to the media that the U.S. forces must be allowed to open and send front in northern Iraq?

The Turkish forces in large numbers was likely to face resistance from ethnic Kurds who had already declared they would confront with turkey military so the unilateral move was dangerous for Turkey. As Kurds wore along with the U.S. troops Turkey feared that in the heat of battle talk Kurds may take physical control over the oil cities of Mosul and Kirkuk.

As Turkey went through its motion in the Parliament the United States which was enormously intolerant to open a war with Iraq had to wait for some time before making a two front attack against Iraq which would avoid casualties on its side.

In Hague, Netherlands, with the backing of 89 nations but facing a boycott by the United States the International Criminal Court was formally launched in a borrowed 13th century grand hall in the presence of Queen Beatrix.

The U.N. Secretary General, Kofi Annan, in his remark which could be directed against precipitous U.S. military action on Iraq said "the implications such a court might have for the delicate process of dismantling tyrannies and replacing them with more democratic regimes committed to uphold human rights. He said the world had tried for 50 years to create such a court. He appealed to the eleven men and seven women to act without fear or favor and to demonstrate unimpeachable integrity and impartially in their decisions.

The Iraqi Foreign Minister, Naji Sabri, told media persons in Baghdad that Iraq had rejected the compromise proposal by Britain in the United Nations and named it as "Polish" an attempt to beautify a rejected aggressive project that the majority of the Security Council members had already rejected.

Sabri was of the view that the U.S. was persisting with seeking the Security Council resolution on Iraq as it wanted an international cover for its war.

The French Foreign Minister, Dominique de Villepin, in his statement had sad "it is not a question of giving Iraq a few more days before resorting to force, but of going forward resolutely along the path of peaceful disarmament laid down by the inspections, which are a credible alternative to war. France supports the efforts of those Security Council members who in the spirit of resolution 1441, want to give Iraq a specific time frame in which to disarm effectively. The success of this disarmament demands the full and complete cooperation of the Iraqi authorities. We support the efforts of those calling for a work program and timetable, while rejecting an ultimatum. This is the essence of the proposals France had made to the Security Council". Villepin also had a telephonic conversation with Kasuri, in which they had come to a conclusion to keep their position that the problem of Iraq should be resolved peacefully in accordance with United Nations Security Council resolutions.

British Foreign Minister, Jack Straw, had said "I find it extraordinary that without even proper consideration; the French government had decided they will reject the proposal".

The Russian Ambassador to the United Nations, Sergei Laurov, said "It is still about war and peace. We are not convinced that this proposal takes care of our concerns. We will study it, but we see automation still there.

The Chief Weapons Inspector, Hans Blix, was questioned in the Security Council's meeting if 10 days would be sufficient to report on Iraq's compliance with the Benchmarks. Blix reportedly had told the Council "We could give a report after 10 days, but certainly not in two days".

The White House spokesman, Ari Fleischer said "The President Bush is gong the last mile for diplomacy. We shall see if the other nations in the Security Council are willing to entertain that last mile".

Mikhail Gorbachev, the former Soviet Union President, in a press conference at Moscow had said "There is only one way to avoid war; Saddam Hussein should relinquish his post". He even gave the two best examples of Russian leaders resigning to prevent the country from sinking into armed conflict: The abdication of Nikolai, the Second in 1917 and his own resignation in 1991. After the leaders of three constituent republics, Russia, Ukraine, and Belarus decided to disband the Soviet Union,

Gorbachev, in 1991 was largely believed to have saved the country from civil strife.

Gorbachev in his conclusion said there is no other way to stop the United States from going to war against Iraq. "Saddam Hussein's departure will open the way to changes, to a new political leadership in Iraq and will thereby cancel out military action".

In Bushehr, the Chief of Iranian Atomic Energy Organization, Assadollah Sabori, said "There is nothing secret about our nuclear programme. We want to produce 6,000 megawatts of power through nuclear energy by 2020, and we are intent on accomplishing it. We keep all our nuclear facilities open to IAEA inspection. The United States has more oil, and Russia has more gas, then Iran. Yet, the United States has 104 and Russia 30 operating nuclear plants respectively. So, why they operate nuclear plants despite rich energy resources".

Sobori had said it was not fair to put Iran, under pressure for trying to acquire nuclear technology. He said when the pro U.S., Shah Mohammad Reza Pahlavi, ruled Iran before the 1979 Islamic Revolution, Iran had plans for 23 nuclear plants even though the country's average annual power consumption was less than 3,000 megawatts.

The White House spokesman, Ari Fleischer said the White House had completely rejected Iran's contention that its nuclear programme is for energy and has pointed to the Countries possessing some of the largest reserves of oil and natural gas in the world.

The State Duma Defence Committee, gave green signal to the treaty's ratification after the President, Vladimir Putin, agreed to set conditions for the treaty's implementation as proposed by legislators. Under the reworked ratification act Russia may withdraw from the treaty if the U.S. or any other state builds up a missile defence or offensive nuclear forces that could checkmate Russia's nuclear deterrent.

The Russian Parliament, had moved to ratify a nuclear arm's treaty signed by the Russian and U.S. presidents, but would attach strings in the pact to maintain strong nuclear deterrence. The Defence Committee of the State Duma, Lower House, recommended speedy ratification of the treaty on the Reduction of Strategic Nuclear Arsenals, which calls on both nations to cut their strategic nuclear arsenals from about 6,000 to 1700 to 2,200 deployed warheads by 2012. The treaty was unanimously approved by the U.S Senate and Russia was anxious to reciprocate the move as proof that bilateral relations with the U.S. had not suffered despite differences over Iraq.

In London the British, Prime Ministers, spokesman was saying that Tony Blair was willing to travel to any place for a meeting. It was said the summit might be held in a fourth country ahead of a possible vote on a second resolution in the U.N. Security Council.

Tony Blair had a good natured telephone conversation with the French President, Jacques Chirac, and through both apparently reiterated their firmly held views the fact that the two spoke to each other was seen as a sign of a thaw.

The French Foreign Minister Dominique de Villepin, spoke to British Foreign Minister, Jack Straw, in what was interpreted as a bid to contain the diplomatic row between the two countries after Britain accused France of positioning the atmosphere by threatening to veto a second resolution in the Security Council.

Jack Straw insisted that a compromise over Iraq war still possible even as prospects of Britain and the U.S. being able to get enough support for a second resolution looked increasingly bleach.

In London, Senior Cabinet Minister, Robin Cook, and International Development Secretary, Clare Short, cautioned Tony Blair that they would quit if Britain backed a unilateral U.S. military intervention in Iraq.

They wore of the opinion that if Tony Blair wants to war without the U.N.'s support then that would lead to more dissident voices in the government to speak up. It was reported that in the cabinet meeting Robin Cook raised some sharp questions on Iraq.

The French Foreign Minister, Dominique de Villepin described the six conditions for Iraqi disarmament laid down in the British proposal as a Herculean, superhuman task and said it would be impossible for Iraq to comply with a March 17 deadline.

France proposed that the Council abandon the term ultimatum in favor of a simple timetable fixed by the U.N. for Iraq to follow for total disarmament. Even though the idea had a less chance of being seriously considered, let along adopted, France was pinning all it's hoped on its new initiative to preserve the unity of the U.N. body.

France had pressed on London and Washington to look for what one diplomat described as a genuine solution for a peaceful disarming of Iraq, for this France had stressed on two conditions, firstly that the use of force should not be automatic and that there be no ultimatum and secondly that U.N; weapons inspectors should be allowed to continued with their work so long as there was a chance of progressing towards total disarmament.

France had suggested that its original suggestion of a four month timeframe could be curtailed to half that, Mexico and Chile had suggested a delay of 45 days and was likely that the French could agree to those terms.

Ten Central European leaders including those of Bulgaria, Poland, Romania, Hungary and the Czech Republic and the Baltic countries signed a letter siding with the U.S. against Iraq.

France indicated that it could envisage reprisals against these states by blocking their entry in to E.U.

China continued to tread a fine line across the shifting stands of war and peace diplomacy over the Iraqi crisis at the United Nations.

China had maintained a studied disinclination to disclose whether it would veto or merely abstain from voting on a new war mandate, being sought by the U.S. in the Security Council. This tactical silence by China is directly linked to its strategic calculations of sustaining the positive momentum in Sino-American relations.

China felt compelled to oppose Washington's new military exchanges with Taiwan. In addition, China refuted the claims in some American quarters that it promised its current strides in space exploration to its alleged acquisition of certain aspects of the know how from the U.S. on a clandestine manner.

The U.S. was reckoned to be keen on cooperating not only Taiwan but also Japan for the purposes of the anti missile system. It is in this context that Japan and South Korea raised their diplomatic pressure on North Korea in concerted efforts to prevent it from testing new ballistic missiles. The security interests of Japan and South Korea wore said to be behind their latest concerns about the possibility of new missile maneuvers by North Korea.

The Russian authorities admitted that they received a request from Washington to declare a number of Iraqi diplomats working in Russia as "person non grata' on the grounds that they could allegedly pose a terrorist threat to Americans in this country. The Russian Foreign Ministry believes the request is unacceptable and of course the Russian side will not take such a step the inter fax news agency quoted a spokesman for the Foreign Ministry.

Mean while a senior Russian parliamentary leader ruled out chances that Moscow could soften its rejection of the military option for Iraq. "We will use our right of veto in the Security Council if it comes to that" the Speaker of Parliament's lower house, Gennady Seleznuov, said "all talk that Moscow may change its stand under American pressure is nothing but media speculation. France, China and Russia are against any new resolution".

Turkey continued to go through its mandatory motions before formally considering the U.S. requests to open a second front.

Turkey's leader, Recep Erdogan, who was formally appointed Prime Minister, was unlikely to reintroduce a motion in Parliament that would consider Washington's request before a week.

Meanwhile U.S. continued its air campaign in Iraq under the cover of protecting the no fly zones. Heavy bombing in the Iraqi southern oil rich area could be prelude to a ground offensive in that zone.

British forces wore reportedly been entrusted with the task of taking early control over the oil bearing areas around Basra 32 km from the Kuwaiti border. Specifically the British troops would be looking at establishing rapid control over the Rumaila oil complex west of Basra, it was said the speed of this operations would be vital as the U.S. and British forces wore working on plans to deny the Iraqi forces sufficient time to possibly blow up the key oil fields in southern and northern Iraq.

Repairing damage that happened during the bombing continued to a large number of oil outlet and pumping stations at the Al Faw peninsula at the southern tip of Iraq, which was adjacent to the narrow waterway access to the Persian Gulf.

The U.S. had moved some of is warships into the Red Sea from the Mediterranean. The move is seen as a response to the delay by Turkey to permit the U.S. forces to station and transit through its territory to open a second front against Iraq. Apart from a positive Turkish decision would be necessary for the U.S. warships to launch Tomahawk missiles through Turkey air space before they reach their targets in Iraq.

It was said that the U.S. was expected to launch a full scale air and ground offensive against Iraq only after obtaining Turkey's clearance for opening a northern front.

With the war clouds on Iraq thickening there wore reports that the U.N. Secretary General, Kofi Annan, was preparing to pull out U.N. inspectors from Iraq.

At the United Nations Security Council in New York, the U.S., Britain and Spain had not made much move at the Council in the face of hardening positions by France and Russia. The feeling in the official circles was that this was perhaps the last ditch effort on the part of the U.S., President, George W. Bush and his ally.

Meanwhile, all indications wore that the Bush administration had given up on Turkey for its permission of the use of its territory including airspace in the event of a military show down.

The Foreign diplomat's in the West Asia region indicated that they wore surprised that Washington was calling for more consultations on the plan formulated by the Quartet of West Asia mediators the U.S., the European Union, Russia and the United Nations. The three phase plan envisions a provisional Palestinian state by the end of the year and full independence by 2005.

It was said that President, Bush, appeared to be suggesting that the road map needed more work. He said that after a Palestinian, Prime Minister, had been confirmed in office a move expected shortly, the road map for peace was to be given to the Palestinians and Israelis. The Palestinians and Israelis were given drafts of the plan earlier and had already held initial consultations.

The diplomats wore of the opinion "We feel it is complete and ready to go. The important things is to move forward with out further prevarication"

President, Bush, had said, once this road map is delivered, we will expect and welcome contributions from Israel and the Palestinians to this document that will advance true peace. We will urge them to discuss the road map with one another.

As the Bush announcement came, the Israeli forces in the West Bank Killed 10 Islamic militants in two gun battles including one in Jenin refugee camp.

The United States, President, George W. Bush, and his allies Britain and Spain, had in mind that the island summit at Azores would turn up the heat on the Iraqi President, Saddam Hussein. This summit was considered as the final push for a diplomatic solution to disarming Saddam Hussein.

At the same time the United Nations withdrew five helicopters used by the disarmament inspectors after insurers refused to cover the aircraft. The U.S. made Bell 212 helicopters wore withdrawn from Baghdad.

The Iraqi, President, Saddam Hussein, had divided four divisions for the military to face a possible U.S. and British assault, the Iraqi News Agency (INA) reported. The youngest son Qusay had been entrusted with the defence of Baghdad.

President, Saddam Hussein, had assumed sole authority to use aircraft and surface to surface missiles against the invaders. "Take the necessary steps to repulse and destroy any foreign aggression".

As Iraq had denied possession of unconventional weapons its adversaries point out that Baghdad could use unmanned drones, the French F-1 and the Russian MIG-21 planes as well as the Al Samoud-2 and Al Hussein missiles to deliver weapons.

Hussein as usual during the Gulf War with the U.S. in 1991 was consolidating his forces around his strongholds of Baghdad and Tikrit rather than stretching them out towards the border areas.

Meanwhile, Iraq is continuing with the destruction of its Al Samoud-2 missiles under the supervision of the U.N. weapons inspectors. Two missile teams wore involved in the destruction of Al Samoud-2 missiles continued.

Iraq also invited Chief Weapons Inspectors, Mohmmad El Baradei and Hans Blix to visit Baghdad for further weapons inspections.

In New York, Hans Blix, said that he would discuss the Baghdad invitation in the Security Council.

In the related development France continued its peace negotiations with the Persian Gulf countries.

With a pre emptive military action looking increasingly likely that anti war Labour MP's insisted that they be given details of the Attorney General's advice which according to the government, was in line with its own view that legally a second resolution was not necessary to launch an attack.

Amid the legal battle the Liberal Democratic leader, Charles Kennedy, warned that any military intervention in Iraq without the U.N. backing would undermine its authority and set a bad precedent.

With the crisis in Iraq seemingly in the last stages of diplomacy Russia, France and Germany had called for the meeting and there was no formal word from the Bush administration.

It was business as usual for the two missile teams wore busy and conducted destruction of Al Samoud-2 missiles. Iraq had so far destroyed 68 out of around 120 Al Samoud-2 missiles.

In an unexpected development at the United Nations the United States, Britain and Spain withdrew their resolution from the Secretary Council.

The British, Ambassador, Jeremy Greenstick, said "we have had to conclude that Council consensus will not be possible. He announced the withdrawal of the resolution on behalf of the sponsors".

The American Ambassador, John Negroponte, said "we regret that in the face of an explicit veto threat to veto the veto counting becomes a secondary consideration".

In yet another surprise the White House announced that the President, George W. Bush, will address the nation later.

At the State Department the Secretary of State, Collin Powell, maintained that a judgment had been made that "no further purpose would be served" by continuing with the tabled resolution, noting in the process that Iraq was in clear material breach even as early as late last year when it turned in a false declaration.

General Powell, was of the view that there may have been some improvements in process or perhaps even some grudging moment by Iraq but that this was not the kind of compliance that resolution 1441 required.

Even before the final day of diplomatic consultations completed its session the Bush administration had asked the U.N. to pull its weapons inspectors out of Iraq in what indicates to be the green signal and the war could begin any moment.

At the U.N., Executive Chairman, Dr. Hans Blix, at the Security Council, while Introduction of the draft UNMOVIC Work Programme on 19 March 2003

Dr. Hans Blix revealing his findings, said.

Mr. President

UNMOVIC was established by the Security Council resolution 1284 (1999) and was enabled to enter Iraq and carry out its inspection work almost three years later.

It might seem strange that we are presenting a draft work programme only after having already performed inspections for three and a half months. However, there were good reasons why the Council wanted to give us some time after the start of inspections to prepare this programme. During the months of the buildup of our resources in Iraq, Larnaca and New York and of inspections in Iraq we have - as was indeed the purpose - learnt a great deal that has been useful to know for the drafting of our work programme and for the selection of key remaining disarmament tasks. It would have been difficult to draft it without this knowledge and this practical experience.

The time lines established in resolution 1284 (1999) have been understood to mean that the work programme was to be presented for the approval of the Council at the latest on 27 March. In order to meet the wishes of members of the Council we made the Draft Work Programme available already on Monday this week. I note that on the very same day we were constrained together with other UN units to order the withdrawal of all our inspectors and other international staff from Iraq.

I naturally feel sadness that three and a half months of work carried out in Iraq have not brought the assurances needed about the absence of weapons of mass destruction or other proscribed items in Iraq, that no more time is available for our inspections and that armed action now seems imminent.

At the same time I feel a sense of relief that it was possible to withdraw yesterday all UN international staff, including that of UNMOVIC and the IAEA. I note that the Iraqi authorities gave full cooperation to achieve this and that our withdrawal to Larnaca took place in a safe and orderly manner. Some sensitive equipment was also taken to Larnaca, while other equipment was left and our offices in Baghdad have been sealed. Some inspection staff will remain for a short time in Larnaca to prepare inspection reports. Others who have come from our roster of trained staff, will go home to their previous positions and could be available again, if the need arises.

Mr. President,

I would like further to make some specific comments that relate to the Draft Programme. I am aware of ideas which have been advanced that specific group of disarmament issues could be tackled and solved within specific time lines. The programme does not propose such an approach, in which, say, we would aim at addressing and resolving the issues of anthrax and VX in March and Unmanned Aerial Vehicles (UAVs) and Remotely Piloted Vehicles (RPVs) in April. In the work we pursued until now we worked broadly and did not neglect any identified disarmament issues. However, it is evidently possible for the

Council to single out a few issues for resolution within a specific time, just as the draft programme before you selects twelve key tasks progress on which could have an impact on the Council's assessment of cooperation of Iraq under resolution 1284 (1999). Whatever approach is followed, results will depend on Iraq's active cooperation on substance.

May I add that in my last report I commented on information provided by Iraq on a number of unresolved issues. Since then, Iraq has sent several more letters on such issues. These efforts by Iraq should be acknowledged, but, as I noted in this Council on 7 March the value of the information thus provided must be soberly judged. Our experts have found so far that in substance only limited new information has been provided that will help to resolve remaining questions.

Mr. President,

Under resolution 1284 (1999) UNMOVIC's work programme is to be submitted to the Council for approval. I note, however, that what was drafted and prepared for implementation by a large staff of UNMOVIC inspectors and other resources deployed in Iraq, would seem to have only limited practical relevance in the current situation.

UNMOVIC is a subsidiary organ of the Security Council. Until the Council takes a new decision regarding the role and functions of the Commission, the previous resolutions remain valid to the extent this is practicable. It is evidently for the Council to consider the next steps.

In its further deliberations I hope the Council will be aware that it has in UNMOVIC staff a unique body of international experts who owe their allegiance to the United Nations, and who are trained as inspectors in the field of weapons of mass destruction. While the International Atomic Energy Agency (IAEA) has a large department of skilled nuclear inspectors and the Organization for the Prohibition of Chemical Weapons (OPCW) has a large staff of skilled chemical weapons inspectors, no other international organizations have trained inspectors in the field of biological weapons and missiles. There is also in the secretariat of UNMOVIC staff familiar with and trained in the analysis, both of discipline specific issues and in the broad questions of proliferation of weapons of mass destruction. With increasing attention being devoted to the proliferation of these weapons this capability may be valuable to the Council.

According to a report there wore at least 135 weapons inspectors in Iraq.

The first team of inspectors wore in search of chemical and biological weapons and the second team of inspectors wore in search of the nuclear weapon. Now that the indications for the inspectors was to pack up and leave Baghdad if possible by air or by road journey which was going to take a long time. Even the Chief of UNMOVIC Mohammad El Baradei had given the same advice to pull out his inspectors.

In yet another development the U.N. decide to pull out all its observers UNIKOM stationed along the Iraqi Kuwaiti border, the mission which had already suspended its operation along the 200 km border which was set up in 1991.

The total withdrawal would include a 775 member's infantry unit from Baghdad and an addition of 195 observers wore ready to leave Iraq.

The United Nations was taking all precautions and the situation in Iraq and had made the point that it would ask the U.S. for some time to make the evacuation of staffers and humanitarian workers to come to safer zones from Iraq as many of them had to leave by road to cross the border.

The White House spokesman Ari Fleischer said to avoid a military conflict Saddam Hussein must leave Iraq. The diplomatic window has closed as a result of the U.N.'s failure to enforce its own resolution for Saddam Hussein to disarm".

The Bush allies announced that they would give the U.N. one day to resolve the diplomatic dispute.

Speaking at the Spanish, American, British summit in the Azores the U.S. President, George W. Bush had said, "France showed their cards. They said they would veto anything that would hold Saddam Hussein to account. So, cards have been played and we have to make an assessment after tomorrow to determine what those cards have meant".

President, Bush, had planned to address the nation on Monday 17, night and give the Iraqi President, Saddam Hussein, a final deadline.

Amid fears that war was imminent, U.N. weapons inspectors flew most of their helicopters out of Iraq. While Germany advised its citizens to leave the country immediately and said it would shut down its embassy in Baghdad.

People in Iraq lined up for gasoline and wore buying canned food and bottled water. All the pharmacies wore crowded with people buying medicines particularly antibiotics and tranquillizers. Many fighting positions wore sand bagged across the government buildings.

In a meeting with military commanders the Iraqi leader Saddam Hussein threatened a broader war if the U.S. invades Iraq. "When the enemy starts a large scale battle he must realize that the battle between us will be open wherever there is sky, land and water in the entire world".

The Foreign Minister, Naji Sabri, speaking to the Arabic satellite channel Al Arabiya said "Iraq had long been preparing as if war is happening in an hour. We have been preparing our people for this for more than a year".

Reacting on the Emergency Azores, Island summit, in which U.S., Britain, and Spain participated; Sabri said "there is a big impasse in which the Bush Blair policies of war have fallen. This impasse is causing embarrassment day after day through widespread rejection of this policy". Sabri also complained about the breaches in the fence, along the Iraqi-Kuwait border, which was already reported by the U.N. military observers. The U.S. British military buildup was also a major concern for the border fence breaching problem. In light of these flagrant threats and violations of the U.N. resolutions, the Iraqi authorities wanted to take the necessary measures to exercise the legitimate right of self defence"

With nearly 3,00,000 U.S. and British troops in the Persian Gulf ready to invade Iraq was just waiting for orders from their commanders.

In Baghdad the Iraqi President, Saddam Hussein, admitted that long before Iraq was in possession of weapons of mass destruction but he was very clear that his country doesn't posses such weapon now.

Hussein said "we have a real intent to eliminate weapon of mass destruction in our region and everywhere in the world. We had such weapons to defend ourselves when we were at war for eight years with Iran and the Zionist entity 1980-1988 that threatened us as it continues to do, the necessity of those weapons wore then needed to avoid casualties in during that time nearly one million lost their lives on both the sides".

In Beijing both Russia and China insisted on a political solution to the issue within the framework of the U.N.

The Newly appointed Chinese foreign Minister, Li Zhaoxing, said "the Iraq issue was at the most crucial juncture of war or peace and China will spare no efforts to avoid war together with the international community".

The two ministers also talked about bilateral ties. Ivanov briefed Li on Russia's view on the current situation, saying relevant parties should make the utmost effort to solve the problem through political means.

In Islamabad the German Foreign Minister, Joschka Fischer, called the Pakistan Foreign Minister, Kasuri, and they had discussed the latest developments regarding Iraq.

The Russian Foreign minister Igor Ivanov also telephoned Kasuri and discussed with him about the latest development regarding Iraq.

The Pakistan office spokesman Aziz Ahmed Khan, addressing the media said that Pakistan was playing its role both at leadership and diplomatic level to give peace a chance. He had said Pakistan would not allow its military bases to be used against Iraq.

The French Foreign Minster, Dominique de Villepin, said "France cannot accept this ultimatum. I cannot see how this resolution can be envisaged. I would like to tell our American Spanish and British friends that the Iraqi crisis is not a problem between the United States and France but between those who want to move forward in the logic of War and between the intentional community".

The French officials had their opinion that France is not opposed to war as a last recourse if the inspectors say Iraq is no longer cooperating. That stage has not yet arrived.

Under the World Food Programme (WFP) U.N. food aid for North Korea in months had arrived that could feed two million people for over two months. The arrival of food worth $10 million from the European Union coincided with an increase in donor pledges that diplomatic sources said which could be aimed at calming Pyongyang in its tense nuclear standoff with Washington.

In what was called as the first significant shipment to arrive in months to North Korea under the WFP about 39,500 tonnes of wheat was unloaded at Nampo on North Korea's west cost and another 8,000 tonnes had arrived at Hungnam in the east.

The U.S. President, George W. Bush, issued an ultimatum to the Iraqi President Saddam Hussein, giving him and his sons 48 hours to get out of Iraq or face war. He said "instead of drifting along towards tragedy, we will set a course towards safety".

Bush also issued ultimatum to foreign nationals, journalists and U.N. officials to leave Iraq immediately for their safety. He said "for the last four and a half months the United States and its allies have worked with the Security Council to enforce the Council's long standing demands. Yet some permanent members of the Security Council had publicly announced that they will veto a resolution that compels the disarmament of Iraq. These Governments share our assessment of the danger, but not our resolve to meet it. The U.N. Security Council had not lived up to its responsibilities, so we will rise to ours. If we must bring a military campaign it will be directed against the lawless men who rule Iraq and not against Iraqi people. In a free Iraq there will be no more wars of aggression against your neighbors, no more poison factories no more executions of dissidents, no more torture chambers and rape rooms. The tyrant will soon be gone. The day of your liberation is near. If war comes do not fight for a dying regime which is not worth your own life. In any conflict your fate will depend on your actions. Do not destroy oil wells, a source of wealth that belongs to the Iraqi people. Do not obey any command to use weapons of mass destruction against anyone, including Iraqis. War crimes attract prosecution. War criminals will be punished. And it would be no defence to say I was just following orders. We will not be intimidated by thugs and killers.

If our enemies dare to strike us, they and all who have aided them will face fearful consequences. I am saddened - saddened that this President failed so miserably at diplomacy that we re now forced to war".

CHAPTER - 12

The Iraqi President, Saddam Hussein rejected the U.S. ultimatum to go in exile or face war. He said Iraq does not choose its path on the orders of a foreigner and does not choose its leaders according to decrees from Washington, London or Tel Aviv but through the will of the great Iraqi people. Iraq and all its sons were fully ready to confront the invading aggressors and repel them".

Husein's eldest son Uday and Qusay rejected the ultimatum and said "The proposal comes from a person who is not completely capable or fit. The proposal should be that Bush leaves office in America, he and his family. The wives and mothers of those Americans who will fight us will weep blood, not tears. They should not imagine that they will have a safe spot inside the land of Iraq or outside it".

In Britain the political crisis deepened after two more Ministers resigned protesting their decision to support an invasion of Iraq without a fresh U.N. mandate. The home office Minister and the Junior Health Minister, Lord Hunt, quit even as the government was still smarting from the resignation of the leader of the commons, Robin Cook.

The resignations came ahead of a crucial vote in Parliament over Iraq amid threats of a massive revolt by Labour MPs who planned to defy the party whip and oppose the official motion.

Blair amidst interruption from his own MPs told the Commons that there was no question of a retreat and claimed that it was in the interest of Britain's national security to disarm Iraq. He was of the view that the division in Europe over the Iraq issue misguided the dangerous.

The Indian government expressed its deep disappointment at the United Nations Security Council's inability to act collectively and the permanent members to harmonies their positions on the Iraq issue.

New Delhi said "as long as the peaceful disarmament of Iraq has the slightest chance, India would continue to urge cautions, self restraint and high sense of responsibility on the part of concerned parties. India's counsel has been against war and in favor of peace. We have emphasized that all decisions on Iraq must be taken under the authority of the U.N. We have stated that any move for change in regime in Iraq should come from within and not be imposed from outside. We have also been drawing attention to the precarious humanitarian situation of the Iraqi people which war would only aggravate".

In Karachi, Prime Minister, Mir Zafarullah Khan Jamali, Foreign Minister, Khurshid Mehmud Kusuri, President, Parvez Musharraf expressed that "Pakistan believes that time and space for diplomacy never ends".

The Russian Foreign Ministry spokesman Alaxander Yakovenko said "Moscow believes there are no grounds for stating that a political diplomatic solution to the situation in Iraq has no chances and that the time for diplomacy is over. It is clear from the UNVOVIC head, Hans Blix's report that much had been done in this area and it is important to reaffirm the key role of the United Nations in resolving the Iraq problem".

The French President, Jacques Chirac, said "jeopardizes future methods of peaceful disarmament in crises linked to the proliferation of weapons of mass destruction. Inspections showed that they are a credible alternative for disarming. To act without the legitimacy of the United Nations, to favor the use of force over law is taking a serious responsibility. Iraq does not represent today an immediate threat that would justify an immediate war".

In Berlin, the German Chancellor, Gerhard Schroeder, said "The world stand on the eve of war. My question remains: Does the level of threat posed by the Iraqi dictator justify war, which will result in the death of thousands of innocent men, women and children? My answer remains. No".

As Iraq was preparing to defend the U.S. invasion the fear among the Children, aged persons and pregnant women increased regarding the existence of the new born child and their safety over the impact of the explosion that might occur during the war.

As the seconds started tickling on the clock the war in Iraq was certain closer to a showdown.

The unleashing of the American military might was not the only thing meriting attention. On Capital Hill and elsewhere, lawmakers wore asking not early the cost of military operations but also in what the whole thing would entail, for American tax payers in a post invasion and reconstruction of Iraq. Estimates differ, but when the first bombs or missiles are dropped on Iraq the administration is expected to go to Congress for a budget of about $90 billions. That too many is the price of a go it alone foreign policy. In the 1991 Persian Gulf War, America's allies picked up much of the tab. This time around, it seems that America is paying allies to be in the war.

Bush in his address to the nation warned the people of terrorist attacks but said the Federal Government was taking every possible measure.

As Pentagon had declared that the U.S. forces were ready for invasion and were awaiting a final order from the U.S. President, George W. Bush, the actual timing of the invasion was likely to depend on military considerations on the ground. A severe sandstorm, which had hit Kuwait-Iraq borders area, was likely to be one such consideration on which the U.S. decision was based. Though the visibility was likely to improve high surface winds wore expected to engulf the battle zone and that could hamper military action. Besides the land invasion of Iraq was likely to be synchronized with a high profile air campaign.

Mean while the Iraqi Deputy Prime Minister, Tariq Aziz, fleeing to Kurdistan and similar root was followed by the Iraqi Vie President, Taha Yassin Ramadan, who wore not to be seen in public for more than three days.

The information Minister, Muhammed Said Kazim al Sahhaf, told media persons that the U.S. troops were fooling themselves if they thought invading Iraq would be like a picnic. "Any aggression against our country or our people will be met with resistance. Stay away from Iraq if he wanted to save his skin".

The leaders of Jordan, Iran, and Pakistan wore making a last ditch effort to discuss the possibility of a peaceful settlement to resolve the Iraqi crisis.

Hosni Mubarak, President of Egypt, expressed "My hope is that the Iraqi government will realize the seriousness of the situation in which it put itself in and us in and that the different international forces will relies the dangerous repercussion of an military action on the safety and stability of the middle east region as well as on the safety and stability of the work as a whole. Protecting our internal front we will work together to maintain our national security.

King Fahd's statement was red by Prince Abdullah on Saudi Television that "We reject outright any infringement on Iraq's unity, independence, resources and internal security as well as a military occupation, and we have informed the United States of America of our position".

In London The British Prime Minister, won Parliament's backing for a preemptive military attack on Iraq even without an explicit United Nations mandate, but with as many as 139 of his own MP's voting against the government with this Blair's political authority was seen to have been greatly damaging.

The countdown for a possible war led by the United States against Iraq approached its end. The allied forces wore ready to take an early hold over two out of Iraq's four zones strategy, but Iraq's oil fields wore the targets that U.S. forces wore concentrating.

After the expiry of a U.S. ultimatum to Iraq the U.S. President, George W. Bush, announced the start of a war to oust Saddam Hussein and disarm Iraq. Bush said selected targets were hit. But U.S. officials said an all out air and ground offensive might be delayed. "These are the opening stages of what will be a broad and concerted campaign".

Bush said in his two hour long television address, the U.S. military would seek a swift victory while trying to avoid civilian casualties. But he warned that the conflict could be longer and tougher than any one could expect.

The Iraqi Information Minister, Mohammed Saeed al Shaf, said the U.S. strikes hit mainly empty media and customs buildings and civilian districts. One civilian was killed and several were wounded.

An Iraqi Minister said a U.S. bid to assassinate Saddam Hussein, had failed. The raid was ordered after the CIA had located where Saddam Hussein, and two close associates wore holding a discussion.

Hours after the raid the Iraqi leader appeared on the Television in military uniform, and thick framed glasses, urging Iraqis to defend their country. "The Criminal little Bush has committed a crime against humanity"

The first U.S. missile hit Baghdad 90 minutes after the ultimatum given to Saddam Hussein. The fighter jets roared over the capital apart from anti aircraft guns and signaling sirens. Deafening sound and thick smoke frightened the civilians.

Though there wore no orders for the ground army to precede both the U.S. and Britain military force wore anxiously waiting to cross the fence. However there wore reports exchange of artillery firing.

The U.S. military appeared and took over the main frequency of Iraqi radio announcing that Saddam Hussein's rule was under attack. "This is the day we had been waiting for" the radio voice said.

The Iraqi Kurds who wore least bothered by the government tried to move to safer places particularly to mountain regions where they wore said to be safe in caves as they had no money or cars to flee to far of pleases or other countries.

Condemning the U.S, action Russia said the military campaign that has started all that one could do was regret and hope that the number of casualties and wounded would be minimized.

The Russian President, Vladimir Putin, condemned the U.S. action. He said "Military action has been launched contrary to world public opinion and contrary to the principles and norms of international law and the U.N. Charter. There is no justification to this military action. If we allow international law to be replaced by the right of might this would jeopardize the principle of the sovereignty of states. No country would feel safe and a big hotbed of instability that has emerged today will grow and cause negative consequences in other regions of the world. It is for these reasons that Russia is insisting on an early end to military action. We remain convinced that the pivotal role in defusing crises in the world, including in Iraq, must belong to the U.N. Security Council".

French President, Jacques Chirac, in an address to the nation said "regrets this action undertaken without the approval of the United Nations. Whatever the duration of this conflict it will be heavy with consequences for the future". Chirac expressed the war should be made short and blood less as possible. He stressed the need for collective action within the frame work of the United Nations for building peace in Iraq and elsewhere.

China accused the U.S. of violating the norms of international behavior.

Germany said the U.N. and the Security Council must play a roll to re establishing peace in Iraq. "The goal is to maintain Iraq's territorial integrity and put the Iraqi people in a position to form a united Iraq and getting out of weapon of mass destruction as a recognized and prosperous member of the international community".

The Indian foreign office spokesman said "it is with the deepest anguish that we have seen reports of the commencement of military action in Iraq it is unjustified".

In London the BBC was reported to have said that Tony Blair was woken up just two hour notice after midnight and given him the timing of the first military strike

The Foreign Secretary, Jack Straw, told journalist's that he was informed in the early hours though he did not remember the time.

The Defence Secretary, Geff Hiin, said he was well aware of when and where the strike was going to take place.

The real fact is that President Bush announced declaration of war against Iraq at midnight without informing about it to his close allay Britain's PM Toni Blaire, however Jack Straw who headed the Foreign Affairs in Blairs Government knew about the war secret he also did not inform about it to Blair as he was more sincere to President Bush instead of PM Tony Blair.

The next morning the media knocked on the door at 10 Downing Street only then Blair came to know about the war. When the media asked Jack Straw, he said he knew very well about the Declaration of War.

It was very clear that Jack Straw not only lied to PM Blair but also to the people of Britain.

Jack Straw had several rounds of discussion with President Bush much before the Declaration of War was announced, he was more aggressive than Bush to go for war against Iraq because the White House radicals had threatened Jack Straw that he would lose his job if he did not support Bush.

In Jerusalem, The Israeli spokesman confirmed reports that U.S. President, George W. Bush, informed Sharon about the intended attack on Monday and that final continuation had come in the Powell-Sharon conversation about an hour and a half before the offensive started.

Meanwhile in an important decision the Turkish Parliament voted to allow the U.S. military to use Turkish airspace for the war against Iraq. The Government baked proposal was passed by a majority of 332 to 202 with one abstention.

The U.S. President, George W. Bush, while addressing the nation from the White House said that the military campaign would not be one of half decisions and that the U.S. would accept anything less than a full victory. "I want Americans and the entire world to know that coalition forces will make every effort to spare innocent civilians from harm. A campaign on the harsh terrain of a nation as large as California could be longer and more difficult than some predict. And helping Iraqis achieve a united, stable and free country will require our sustained commitment. Our nation enters this conflict reluctantly, yet our purpose is sure. The people of the U.S. and our friends and allies will not live at the mercy of an outlaw regime that threatens the people with weapons of mass murder. On my orders, coalition forces have begun staking selected targets of military importance to undermine Saddam Hussein's ability to wage war. There are opening strategies of what will be a broad and concerted campaign".

In Baghdad the Iraqi President, Saddam Hussein, appearing in full military dress, accused the United States and Britain of committing shameful crimes and referred to the American President as 'Little evil Bush'. They will face a battle of defeat. God willing He said. "You will be able to achieve glory and your despicable infidel enemies will be defeated".

Nearly 63% of Americans and 81% of Britain's wore against war in Iraq. People in France, Britain, Germany and India wore the most disappointed humans as they fought and protested in large numbers to avoid a conflict in Iraq but in vain. It was unfortunate that despite long political and crucial diplomatic consultations the world leaders failed to make a head way in resolving the crisis.

The U.S. was rigid in its stands and behaved nothing less than a dictator despite the world having U.N. and international court.

The concern of the civilized population is that "there will be thousands of deaths in this kind of war, is this international law? Tomorrow they could turn around and say to President of Zimbabwe, Emmerson Mnangagwa, to President of Palestine, Mahmoud Abbas, to President of Brazil, Jair Bolsonaro, to President of Cuba, Miguel Diaz-Canel.

We don't like your ideology, you are a tyrant and we are going to bring about regime change".

Abbreviation

IAEA	(International Atomic Energy Agency)
U.N.	(United Nations)
U.S.	(United States)
U.K.	(United Kingdom)
WMD	(Weapon of Mass Destruction)
VX	(is a lethal chemical weapon in the V-series of nerve agents. Although commonly referred to as nerve gases, the chemicals are usually liquids at room temperature. ... Like all nerve agents, the V-series block the biological action of the enzyme acetylcholinesterase (AChE))
CIA	(Central Intelligence Agency)
WU	(Western Union)
UNMOVIC	(United Nations Monitoring Verification and Inspection Commission)
DPRK	(Democratic People's Republic of Korea)
NATO	(North Atlantic Treaty Organisation)
E.U.	(European Union)
NPT	(Nuclear non Proliferation Treaty)
ASEAN	(Association of South East Association Nation)
ARF	(ASEAN Regional Forum)
KEDO	(Korean peninsula Energy Development Organisation)

MIAI	(Moderately Intelligent Artificial Intelligence)
UNSC	(United Nations Security Council)
IREA	(International Renewable Energy Alliance)
UNMV	(United Nations Monitoring Verification)
WHO	(World Health Organisation)
GCC	(Gulf Cooperation Council)
TUC	(Trades Union Congress)
UNHRC	(United Nations Human Rights Council)
PUK	(Patriotic Union of Kurdistan)
KDP	(Kurdistan Democratic Party)
NSPD	(National Security Presidential Directive)
UAE	(United Arab Emirates)
NAM	(Non-Aligned Moment)
PKK	(Kurdistan Workers' Party)
AWACS	(Airborne Warning and Control System)
AKP	(AK Party of Turkish President Tayyip Erdogan)
DST	(Disarmament and International Security Committee)
OPEC	(Organization of the Petroleum Exporting Countries)
OIC	(Organisation of Islamic Conference)
FBI	(Federal Bureau of Investigation)
UADA	(United Africa Development Aid)
PLO	(Palestinian Liberation Organisation)
UNIKOM	(United Nations Iraq Kuwait Observers Mission)
ISI	(Inter Service Intelligence)
UNSCOM	(United Nations Special Commission for the Elimination of Iraq's Weapon of Mass Destruction)

RPVS	(Remotely Piloted Vehicles)
MOAB	(Massive Ordinance Air Blast)
	(Mother Of All Bombs)
INA	(Iraqi News Agency)
UAVs	(Unmanned Aerial Vehicle)
OPCW	(Organisation for the Prohibition of Chemical Weapon)
WFP	(World Food Programme)
UNVOIC	(United Nations Volunteer Network)

Please Note :

Reffer Oxford New Word English Dictonary for Reference.

www.ingramcontent.com/pod-product-compliance
Lightning Source LLC
LaVergne TN
LVHW091253150826
845673LV00006B/1402
9789360391669